D1523948

Death Education in the Writing Classroom

Jeffrey Berman

Death, Value, and Meaning Series
Series Editor: Dale A. Lund

Baywood Publishing Company, Inc.
AMITYVILLE, NEW YORK

Baywood Publishing Company, Inc.
26 Austin Avenue
P.O. Box 337
Amityville, NY 11701
(800) 638-7819
E-mail: baywood@baywood.com
Web site: baywood.com

Library of Congress Catalog Number: 2010051920

ISBN: 978-0-89503-403-8 (cloth : alk. paper)
ISBN: 978-0-89503-428-1 (pbk. : alk. paper)
ISBN: 978-0-89503-464-9 (epub)
ISBN: 978-0-89503-465-6 (epdf)
http://dx.doi.org/10.2190/DEI

Library of Congress Cataloging-in-Publication Data

Berman, Jeffrey, 1945-
    Death education in the writing classroom / Jeffrey Berman.
        p. cm. -- (Death, value, and meaning series)
    Includes bibliographical references and index.
    ISBN 978-0-89503-403-8 (cloth : alk. paper) -- ISBN 978-0-89503-428-1 (pbk. : alk. paper) -- ISBN 978-0-89503-464-9 (epub) -- ISBN 978-0-89503-465-6 (epdf) 1. Death--Psychological aspects--Study and teaching. 2. Death in literature--Study and Teaching 3. English language--Rhetoric--Study and teaching--Psychological aspects. I. Title.
    BF789.D4B465 2011
    155.9'37071--dc22
                                                    2010051920

Cover photo by Julie Nark.

Dedication

For Julie

By the Same Author

Joseph Conrad: Writing as Rescue
The Talking Cure: Literary Representations of Psychoanalysis
Narcissism and the Novel
Diaries to an English Professor: Pain and Growth in the Classroom
Surviving Literary Suicide
Risky Writing: Self-Disclosure and Self-Transformation in the Classroom
Empathic Teaching: Education for Life
Dying to Teach: A Memoir of Love, Loss, and Learning
Cutting and the Pedagogy of Self-Disclosure (with Patricia Hatch Wallace)
Death in the Classroom: Writing about Love and Loss
Companionship in Grief: Love and Loss in the Memoirs of C. S. Lewis,
    John Bayley, Donald Hall, Joan Didion, and Calvin Trillin

Table of Contents

PART 2: Breakthroughs

Acknowledgments

"It is students, not teachers, who make any class memorable," Donald Hall (2008) observes in *Unpacking the Boxes* (p. 54), and I wish to thank the following people who made my 2008 Love and Loss class (English 450) so memorable: Alexa, Alexandra, Amanda, Anna, Ashley, Candice, Christina, Claudia, Diana, Ivana, Jackie, Jamie, Jessicca, Juno, Kara, Kareema, Katie, the three Laurens, Rashaun, Richard, Roel, and Scott. A statement from the *Talmud* reflects my feelings toward everyone in the class: "Much have I learned from my teachers, more from my colleagues, but most from my students."

Love and Loss would not have been as successful without the help of my superb teaching assistant, Nico Suarez, who offered his own unique perspective throughout the semester in his weekly diary, from which I quote often.

I'm grateful to Dale Lund, Professor & Chair of the Department of Sociology at California State University for including my book in his series on *Death, Value and Meaning*. I'm also grateful to everyone at Baywood Publishing Company, especially Julie Krempa and Bobbi Olszewski. Thanks also to the two anonymous readers for their helpful suggestions to improve the manuscript. A special thanks to David E. Balk, Professor of Health and Nutrition Sciences at Brooklyn College and the Editor-in-Chief of the *Handbook of Thanatology*, for inviting me to participate in the 32nd Annual Conference of ADEC, the Association for Death Education and Counseling, held in Kansas City, Missouri, in April 2010.

I want to thank Julie Nark not only for her many insights into love and loss and her careful reading of the manuscript but also for the joy she has brought into my life.

Introduction: "Life Lessons"

Dear Professor Berman,

I hope this email finds you well. As you might recall, I was a former student of yours and took several of your courses throughout 2004 and 2005.

While I regret to say that many of your valuable lessons around grammar and punctuation may not have stuck with me as I would have liked, the life lessons I learned in your writing and literature courses have stayed near to my heart since graduating three years ago.

You will remember that I was a student in your Expository Writing course during the time in which you were losing your wife to cancer. I never forgot the beautiful eulogy you shared with us and the raw emotion and harsh realities that lay between the words.

This summer, I lost my father to cancer and as he slipped away from us in the hospital room I began to think of you. I wrote his eulogy in my head as I drove to and from our apartment to the hospital—half asleep, rushing to return to him. While he was still alive I began to etch the sentences on a yellow notepad outside the hospital during the times when I was asked to leave the room. It was both painful and therapeutic. I stopped when he took a turn for the worse and finished after his death. I wrote the last few sentences as I stared at the bay (by which he had raised me) the evening before his wake.

I wanted to share the attached eulogy with you because I don't believe I would have had the courage to write it had I not taken your class. I have been meaning to write you and thank you for the life lesson you taught me some years ago about courage and truth in writing; I never realized it would make such an impact on my personal life. It has been quite a difficult summer and so I have only now been able to gather myself to send this to you.

Again, I hope you are doing well and inspiring students as I know you do.

Best,

Catherine Lennon

Catherine was a member of an Expository Writing course I taught at the University at Albany in the spring of 2004, the semester when my beloved wife lay gravely ill from pancreatic cancer. In early March, when the doctors told us Barbara was close to death, I informed my students about her condition. The news stunned everyone, for I had not shared this information with them earlier in the semester. Nor could they have known from my demeanor—I am usually playful and exuberant in the classroom—that Barbara was dying. She did not want to read the eulogy—she said it would make her too sad—but she allowed me to read it to the class. Before beginning, I announced that it would take me about 20 minutes to read the eulogy and that class would end when I finished. Anyone who wished to leave early, I added, could do so. Finally, in a quiet, measured voice, I began the reading. I struggled to maintain my composure, and when I finished, everyone filed slowly out of the room, shaken by my words.

Barbara died on April 5, and I immediately began writing a book about our life together after her diagnosis on August 12, 2002, one day after our thirty-fourth wedding anniversary. I wanted the book to have a pedagogical focus—a writing teacher sharing the most harrowing experience of his life with his under-graduates, many of whom were sharing painful experiences with him. How did my students feel about hearing me read the eulogy? Was it an appropriate "teachable moment?" Should teachers use the classroom to discuss their own experiences of love and loss? I couldn't answer these questions unless I found a way for my students to tell me. And so during the next class I asked them to describe, in an anonymous in-class assignment, how they felt about hearing my eulogy of Barbara. Their responses, which I then photocopied and shared with them, became a chapter in the book. Before the semester ended, I told my students that I would send each of them a copy of the manuscript as soon as I completed it. I invited them to share their impressions of reading the entire work and promised to include their letters in the appendix of the book.

The Appendix of *Dying to Teach* (Berman, 2007) contains letters from 16 of the 24 students who were in the class, including Catherine, who spoke about reading the book on the way to work each morning. "On the Long Island Railroad, miles away from Albany and you, Barbara came alive to this 22-year-old post-graduate. Upon arriving at Penn Station, I would stuff the draft back into my bag and wonder if you knew how your words, your life were floating around in my mind. Looking back, I guess I felt such relief because you had managed to keep a part of your beloved wife alive to others" (p. 252).

After completing *Dying to Teach*, I created a new undergraduate course, "Love and Loss in Literature and Life," which I taught in the spring of 2006. Within a few days the course closed at its maximum, 60 students. We read several eulogies, elegies, poems, and novels that focused on the literature of bereavement. There were seven writing assignments, each exploring a different aspect of death. In one assignment, I paired each person with a classmate, and each wrote the other's obituary; in another, students wrote a eulogy about a person living or deceased; in another, students wrote about how their attitudes toward religion affected their views of death. I graded these essays not on content or degree of self-disclosure but on the quality of their writing. (I graded each essay with a plus, check, or minus.) It would be inappropriate for me to grade them on their feelings, beliefs, or values. After teaching Love and Loss, I then wrote a book about the course—*Death in the Classroom* (Berman, 2009; see Vance [2007] for a discussion of the course, the students' reactions, and the syllabus).

Most of the students concluded in their anonymous evaluations at the end of the semester that Love and Loss was one of the most powerful educational experiences of their lives. It certainly was for me. The students knew that I was teaching the course because I had recently lost the most important person in my life, and they also knew that the theme of love and loss would inevitably apply to them too. Many of the classes were emotionally charged. The course affected not only my students but also their families: Several students told me that they telephoned or emailed their parents after a writing assignment to express love and gratitude. Students emailed me after the semester ended, telling me, as Catherine did, that the course helped them write eulogies for loved ones who had died recently.

And yet despite the success of the course, we could not overcome problems caused by the class size. The large number of students and lecture format made class discussions difficult. Few people were willing to speak in class even when I encouraged them to do so. There were too many students to sit in a semicircle, as they do in my smaller courses, and the poor acoustics of the classroom posed another challenge. I couldn't remember the names of all my students, as I can in smaller classes. Before returning essays, I read a few of them aloud, always anonymously and always with the permission of the authors, but the anonymity prevented students from getting to know each other.

There was also a problem unrelated to class size. I was so interested in my students' writings on love and loss that I found myself in an unusual pedagogical conflict of interest: There was never enough time to discuss the canonical literature we read and the riveting personal essays my students wrote. The personal writing took on a life of its own, and within a few weeks the students' loves and losses became our main object of interest.

And so I decided to teach Love and Loss again, in the spring of 2008, not as a large literature course but as a writing course with 25 students. The only book I asked my students to read was *Dying to Teach*. I wanted to share my story with students so that they would be willing to share their own stories with their classmates and me. Instead of speaking abstractly about death education, I wanted students to read about our family's experience with dying and death: how Barbara reacted to the shock of her diagnosis; how she responded, physically and psychologically, to the relentless onslaught of cancer; how she used daily diary entries and letters to reflect on her life and impending death; how she held onto life and then slowly let go. I also wanted students to know how I struggled with the daunting challenges of caregiving; how our attitude toward death dramatically changed during her nearly 20-month ordeal, from that of a feared adversary to that of a welcome ally; how I sought to keep her memory alive through writing; and how our family has reacted to her death. *Dying to Teach* focuses on the many complex aspects of death education, including dying, death, and bereavement, and it takes a multidisciplinary approach, touching upon medicine, psychology, philosophy, sociology, cultural studies, religion, education, literature, and writing. The book explores such topics as palliative care and pain management, hospice, physician-assisted suicide, the stage theory of dying, anticipatory grief, traumatic forgetting, mourning rituals, and the taboos surrounding death, especially in death-denying cultures such as ours. By writing about my own experience, my *lived* experience of Barbara's dying and death, I take a personal approach to death education. Here is my story, I tell my readers; yours may be similar or different. You can learn from my experience, and I can learn from yours.

There were several major differences between the 2006 and 2008 Love and Loss courses. First, the students now read their essays aloud, and they began to feel a close connection with each other. (They had the option of allowing me to read aloud their essays anonymously, but this occurred only a few times during the semester.) This connection was based on trust, empathy, and shared vulnerability. Second, reading *Dying to Teach* strengthened their connection with me. Many students said that they felt they knew my family and me after finishing the book. Third, I chose different writing assignments for the new Love and Loss course, assignments that encouraged students to focus on the ways in which loss shattered their assumptions about life and created new assumptions. Finally, I asked students in the second Love and Loss course to keep a weekly diary in which they recorded how their own and their classmates' writings affected them.

The diaries turned out to be one of the most noteworthy elements of the course, revealing students' emotional and cognitive changes throughout the semester. Each week I would read aloud a few entries anonymously before returning them to the students. The diaries demonstrated the students' growing connection to their classmates and teacher. The students came to view me as an attachment figure, a person to whom they confided their deepest feelings about love and loss. Unlike large lecture courses in which a single person speaks, the diaries reflected a different model of teaching, one based on intersubjectivity and multi-vocality, in which each person's life story became a part of his or her classmates' life stories.

The second Love and Loss course was even more intense than the first one, mainly because students wrote essays *every* week, which they read aloud. Many wrote for the first time about the death of a parent, grandparent, sibling, cousin, niece, or best friend. Three students wrote about having an abortion, an experience that filled them with ongoing grief, guilt, and sadness. One student's grandfather died during the semester, and his classmates wrote heartfelt comments on a condolence card that we presented to him when he returned to class. Many students stated in their anonymous evaluations at the end of the semester that Love and Loss was the most life-changing course they had taken. Like Catherine, *all* the students concluded that their writings were painful yet therapeutic.

How can writing be painful *and* therapeutic? Beginning with James Pennebaker's (1990/1997) classic book *Opening Up*, researchers have confirmed the many striking health benefits of self-disclosure, especially the benefits of *painful* self-disclosures. In *Emotion, Disclosure, & Health*, Pennebaker (1995) uses research on thought suppression to explain why self-disclosure leads to both physical and psychological health: "The reason that we ruminate about events is because we are trying not to ruminate about them. . . . The mere act of thought suppression—whether about distressing traumas or titillating secrets—makes the thoughts more accessible and difficult to dislodge from our minds" (p. 5). Because self-disclosure facilitates emotional processing and problem-solving, it has profound clinical and social implications, as Pennebaker (1995) points out. "Disclosure of one's deepest thoughts and feelings is a powerful social phenomenon, whether in a therapeutic setting or in daily life" (p. 7).

Self-disclosure also has important pedagogical implications. My books on teaching affirm the pedagogy of self-disclosure, a model that I now use in *all* of my literature and writing courses. The model has support from the growing body of research that demonstrates the many benefits of teacher and student self-disclosure. Jourard (1964) shows convincingly in his groundbreaking book *The Transparent Self* that self-disclosure begets self-disclosure: "participants disclose their thoughts, feelings, and actions to others and receive disclosure in return"(p. 66). Goldstein and Benassi (1994) confirm that this phenomenon, called the dyadic or reciprocity effect, is one of the most consistent findings in the self-disclosure literature (p. 210). The two researchers also confirm that "teacher self-disclosure is positively associated with student participation, thereby documenting the reciprocity effect in classroom settings. Specifically, students' perceptions of teacher self-disclosure were significantly correlated with students' perceptions of the amount of class participation and with students' willingness to participate in class" (p. 215).

Some of the research on self-disclosure reaches puzzling or ambiguous conclusions, such as McCarthy and Schmeck's (1982) finding that a male teacher's self-disclosure raises the recall of male students but lowers the recall of female students—perhaps because "self-disclosure between same-sex individuals is maximally effective because the recipients can more readily identify with the self-disclosure" (p. 48). I'm not aware of this phenomenon occurring in my own classes—my self-disclosures seem to raise the recall of both male and female students. Pennebaker (1995) suggests that "the degree to which one discloses personal experiences may have profound positive or negative effects on the relationship. Whereas talking about a trauma may make the discloser feel better, it can make the listener feel worse" (p. 7). This phenomenon has occurred in my classes; students become sad when they hear their classmates' wrenching stories, though the sadness is only temporary. There are sometimes ethical dilemmas associated with self-disclosure in student writing, as Haney (2004) cautions, particularly the "inherent imbalance in the power structure" (p. 167). In both *Risky Writing* (Berman, 2001) and *Empathic Teaching* (Berman, 2004) I discuss the protocols I put into place to minimize the possibility that students who write on traumatic topics are retraumatized. These protocols include empathizing, avoiding critique, observing professional boundaries, allowing students not to write on topics that are too personal, grading pass/fail whenever possible, permitting anonymity, prescreening essays, protecting self-disclosures, balancing risky and nonrisky assignments, having conferences, and knowing how to make appropriate referrals.

Teachers are probably as wary of self-disclosure as therapists, and my own experience parallels that of the existential psychiatrist Irvin D. Yalom (2008), who admits in *Staring at the Sun* that therapist self-disclosure "is a complex and contested area. Few suggestions I make to therapists are as unsettling as my urging them to reveal more of themselves. It sets their teeth on edge" (p. 241). Yalom offers several reasons why self-disclosure is important to the therapist and, by implication, to the teacher. "In close relationships, the more one reveals of one's inner feelings and thoughts, the easier it is for others to reveal themselves. Self-disclosure plays a crucial role in the development of intimacy. Generally, relationships build by a process of reciprocal self-revelations" (p. 131). Neither teachers nor students should be required to be self-disclosing, but there is a place for careful and appropriate self-disclosures in the classroom, especially for those who believe, as I do, in an intersubjective model of education, in which teachers and students learn from each other.

Why do I continue to write books about death education? For many reasons. First, writing is a way to bear witness, to observe and record solemn and sacred experiences that must be told. As Dori Laub (1992) observes about those who have endured traumatic experiences such as the Holocaust, "The survivors did not only need to survive so that they could tell their stories; they also needed to tell their stories in order to survive. There is, in each survivor, an imperative need to tell and thus to come to know one's story, unimpeded by ghosts from the past against which one has to protect oneself" (p. 78). I honor and celebrate Barbara's memory by writing books about her, which enables students like Catherine to learn about her life and reflect upon her courage, determination, and strength.

Second, writing about death helps me understand and cope with the feelings of sorrow, loss, and existential guilt that are implicit in bereavement. Writing about Barbara became the major element in my process of mourning, a way to work through dark feelings. I am one of a countless number of writers who continues to write about death. As Nicholas Delbanco (2005) remarks, writers have "an oxymoronic compulsion to write in lively fashion about the lack of life" (pp. 36–37)—a compulsion that certainly applies to me. Writing is a counter-phobic activity, helping one to master fears and losses. Paradoxically, I was so absorbed while writing *Dying to Teach* that I often forgot about my grief, a phenomenon the psychologist Mihaly Csikszentmihalyi (1990) would call a "flow" experience.

Third, writing about death keeps me securely attached to Barbara, making her a part of my everyday life. Contrary to Freud's (1917/1957) influential theory of bereavement in "Mourning and Melancholia"—"Reality-testing has shown that the loved object no longer exists, and it proceeds to demand that all libido shall be withdrawn from its attachments to that object" (p. 244)—I believe, along with a growing number of contemporary psychoanalysts, that the mourner needs to maintain a relational bond with the deceased. Many therapists are now adopting a new paradigm of mourning, one that recognizes, as Marilyn McCabe (2003) explains in *The Paradox of Loss*, "both that the lost other is an ongoing part of our existence, and that the *processes* of relationship continue to be reintegrated, transferred, rejuvenated, and transformed" [italics in original] (p. 13). Silverman and Nickman (1996) observe that the deceased "are both present and not present at the same time. It is possible to be bereft and not bereft simultaneously, to have a sense of continuity and yet to know that nothing will ever be the same" (p. 351).

Finally, I write books about death and teach courses on love and loss so that students like Catherine can write about their own losses—past, present, and future. I'm grateful that students find these courses helpful, and their enthusiasm validates my own belief in the importance of death education in a college-level English course.

Grief changes over time. I no longer feel the horror and shock of loss that I experienced immediately after Barbara's death, the desperate feeling of the newly bereft, the "raw emotion and harsh realities" to which Catherine refers, but these emotions abound in *Dying to Teach*. I'm glad I wrote the book when I did because it captures the intensity of grief I felt at the time. Now, six years after my wife's death, I am more accepting of loss than I was then, more in control of my emotions. One's relationship to the dead changes. "Companionship in grief—"to use a term from Donald Hall's (2005) memoir *The Best Day the Worst Day* (p. 118)—often turns into companionship in joy. To my great surprise and delight, I've learned to love romantically and intensely again.

Those who are interested in death education must be prepared to acknowledge the power of emotions. It is not intellectual but emotional knowledge that proves to be the more daunting challenge when talking about death. Academics are famously suspicious of anything that smacks of the emotional. Nearly everyday I hear colleagues praise someone's "intellectual" brilliance, but emotional sensitivity, empathy, and compassion are lesser-praised qualities, at least in academia.

The philosopher Martha C. Nussbaum (2001) characterizes emotions as "geo-logical upheavals," and she points out that we "experience emotions in ways that are shaped both by individual history and by social norms" (p. 140). In her magisterial study *Upheavals of Thought*, she analyzes her own emotional landscape following the death of her mother. Rather than viewing emotions as antithetical to reason, a binary that does justice neither to emotion nor reason, she sees emotions as a source of deep wisdom. Nussbaum's belief that emotions are also cognitions is supported by Antonio Damasio's (1994/2005) neuro-psychiatric research. "It does not seem sensible to leave emotions and feelings out of my overall concept of mind," he writes in *Descartes' Error*. "Yet respectable scientific accounts of cognition do precisely that, by failing to include emotions and feelings in their treatment of cognitive systems" (p. 158). Damasio argues that *"feelings are just as cognitive as any other perceptual image*, and just as dependent on cerebral-cortex processing as any other image" [italics in original] (p. 159).

Like Nussbaum and Damasio, the philosopher Robert C. Solomon has long asserted that emotions are more complex than most scholars have implied. He argues in *True to Our Feelings* (2007) that emotions are "not only intelligent but also purposive in a surprisingly robust sense." Emotions are also strategies: "They are a means of motivating our own actions and attitudes as well as influencing and manipulating the actions and attitudes of others" (p. 3). Solomon does not write about death education, but he makes an observation that my Love and Loss students and I confirmed in every class: "grief, laughter, and happiness are all emotions that are most meaningful when they are shared" (pp. 72–73). This is not the accepted view, he concedes. It is certainly not the view that is expressed by many writing teachers, who are generally wary of allowing emotions into their classrooms. In *Spirituality for the Skeptic*, Solomon (2002) notes that "Socrates, the great champion of reason, took as his motto the slogan at Delphi, 'know thyself,' and the rather extreme injunction that the unexamined life isn't worth living. The most important part of self-knowledge, surely, is our understanding and appreciation of our emotions, which are, after all, what makes life worth living" (p. 58).

Nothing arouses our emotions more quickly or violently than the idea of death. "Die at the right time," quipped Nietzsche, who, as Solomon (2002) wryly informs us, died 10 years too late. Those who die too soon or too late awaken our deepest grief. Many of my students write about untimely deaths, cousins who die in their teens and grandparents who die after suffering for years from Alzheimer's disease. Barbara was far too young to die at age 57.

Death seldom comes at the right time, and many deaths occur accidentally, without a moment's notice. Hence the value of death education. "Hanging on the edge of a precipice, engulfed by terror, is not the time or place to learn about emergency rock-climbing procedures," Virginia Morris (2001) remarks in *Talking about Death Won't Kill You*; "you have to learn them before you start the expedition. Likewise, we have to start learning about death now, while we are still healthy" (p. 3). Death education focuses on both the cognitive and affective implications of human mortality, and it emphasizes the continuity between life and death. A Google search of "death education" turned up nearly sixty-two million results, but educators have not rushed to include death education in their courses, partly because of personal and cultural resistance to talking about death; partly because of teachers' lack of training or interest; partly because of the opposition of conservatives such as Phyllis Schlafy, who maintain that death education should be taught not by teachers but by parents; and partly because of the controversies arising over different religious and spiritual attitudes toward death—some people fear that death education will focus more on "subjective values" than on "objective knowledge."

Most death education training takes place not in undergraduate humanities or social science courses but in medical and nursing schools, social work and professional development programs, and religious schools. Much of the research on death education appears not in academic humanities or social science journals but in the specialized "thanatology" publications, such as *Omega: The Journal of Death and Dying, Death Studies*, and *The Forum: Newsletter of the Association for Death Education and Counseling*. The *Handbook of Thanatology* (David E. Balk, Editor-in-Chief, 2007) offers an encyclopedic overview of death education, including a chapter on "Historical and Contemporary Perspectives on Death Education," in which Illene C. Noppe discusses the cognitive and affective components of death education:

> One of the unique features of death education is the inescapable fact that it offers students opportunities to explore the subject both on intellectual and affective planes. The two major teaching methodologies are didactic, involving the dissemination of knowledge, and experiential, providing a focus on affective factors. While the didactic method, emphasizing lecture, reading, and discussion of context-driven material promotes increased cognitive awareness, . . . [a] metaanalysis of death anxiety indicated that it is the experiential method, with a focus on personal reflection, or a combination of didactic and experiential methods, that aids in reduction of death anxiety. Students' knowledge, behavioral, and affective changes with respect to death-related issues is tied to the type of education received. (pp. 332–333)

Geoffrey Gorer (1965) has observed that just as sex was the great taboo in the nineteenth century, so is death the great taboo in the twentieth—and now the twenty-first century. Other researchers, such as Howard Spiro (1996), have reached similar conclusions. "Once, when grandparents, parents, and sometimes children—too often children—died at home, everyone knew death first hand. Death is as common as birth, but it went into hiding in our twentieth-century" (p. xv). Gabriel Moran, who teaches a course at New York University called "The Meaning of Death," argues that what is taboo is not the media's portrayal of death but the lack of reflection of one's personal mortality. Death education is particularly appropriate in a college curriculum because many students lose beloved relatives during this time. "The myth of the carefree college student permeates our culture," declares Kirsten Tyson-Rawson (1996). "In contrast, recent surveys of college campuses indicate that from 40 to 70% . . . of traditionally aged students will experience the death of an important person during their college years." She adds that the "combination of geographical separation, the possibility of a lack of support in the immediate environment, and the interaction of bereavement and psychosocial tasks can increase the intensity of the crisis experienced because of the death of someone important" (p. 28). Neimeyer, Laurie, Mehta, Hardison, and Currier (2008) suggest that bereavement may be a "silent epidemic" on campuses and cite studies indicating that "25 percent of college students have lost a significant family member or friend in the past year and nearly 50 percent have suffered a loss in the past two years" (p. 28). Ellen S. Zinner (2002), who has been teaching death education courses for nearly 30 years, reports that "No issue is more applicable to the lives of death education students than that of the grief process" (p. 389).

Many losses involve what Kenneth J. Doka (1989) calls "disenfranchised grief." Grief is disenfranchised, he writes, if a person "experiences a sense of loss but does not have a socially recognized right, role, or capacity to grieve" (p. 1). Examples of disenfranchised grief include perinatal death and abortion, the death of someone in a nontraditional relationship (such as in an extramarital relationship), or the death of a pet. Even the death of an elderly grandparent may produce disenfranchised grief because such losses are "natural" and "expected." Robak and Weitzman (1995) cite research indicating that the two most frequently occurring losses reported by young people are the breakup of a romantic relationship and the death of a loved one, events that produce depression in nearly three-quarters of those surveyed (p. 270). Many of these losses involve disenfranchised grief. Grieving, both "enfranchised" and "disenfranchised," involves, in the words of Thomas Attig (1996), a "process of relearning the world" (p. 11), and I believe that the classroom is an appropriate place to study the grief process in all its cognitive and affective dynamics.

Death is often encountered in English courses—Hamlet's death, celebrity death, death from the terrorist attacks during 9/11—but students rarely have the opportunity to write about their own experiences with death. I provide that opportunity by creating a safe, empathic classroom where students have the freedom to write about their experiences without the fear of being criticized by their classmates or teacher. Their essays are often emotionally intense because they write about the most important people in their lives. Sometimes they cry when they read an essay aloud, and sometimes their classmates and teacher cry, but there are many more smiles than tears in my classrooms. Students know that only their grammar and punctuation will be discussed in class, not their emotions. They also have the freedom *not* to write about anything that is too personal.

Just as teachers inspire students, so do students inspire teachers. The courage and truth of students' personal essays are striking. Many students have suffered earlier and more frequent traumatic losses than I have. Some have lost a parent at an early age, and a few have lost both parents. Many have suffered a loss that I have not experienced, the breakup of their family through divorce. Losing parents through divorce can be more shattering than losing them through death. If children engage in "magical thinking" after the death of a parent, hoping that their mother or father will magically return to life, the illusory hope that their divorced parents will be reconciled can awaken greater pain. "The greater the ambiguity surrounding one's loss," Pauline Boss (1999) writes, "the more difficult it is to master it and the greater one's depression, anxiety, and family conflict" (p. 7). Students write about this and other types of loss. As Catherine implies in her letter, teachers can have a therapeutic impact on their students without pretending to be therapists. Students learn the art of "critique" in their other courses; they learn the art of empathy in mine. They learn to listen carefully and respectfully to each other, gaining knowledge that helps them understand the other. My students see me as both a teacher and a "real person." They know that I struggle with many of the same life issues as they do. They hear the sadness in my voice when I talk about Barbara, but they also hear my love for her along with my undying gratitude for having known her. Equally important, they can see that I have survived a devastating loss, which gives them the hope that they, too, will be able to survive the loss of a loved one.

Death Education in the Writing Classroom focuses on my 2008 Love and Loss course. Like my other books about teaching, I have received written permission from all the students whose essays and diaries appear in this book. I have also received permission from my university's Institutional Review Board (IRB), which must approve all human research. I have followed the *Code of Ethics* of the Association of Death Education and Counseling (2004), particularly the statement that "Good education and counseling are based upon an understanding of, and a respect for, the students' or clients' cultural background, developmental status, perceptions, and other individual difference and need" (p. 1). After I receive permission to use my students" writings, I show them precisely how I intend to use and contextualize their words. I do this for their protection and for my own. They have chosen pseudonyms for this book, and many of them read the entire manuscript before I submitted it for publication in the fall of 2009. I have not edited their writings. My students know that I am an English professor, not a therapist or a counselor, and they neither ask me for nor do I offer clinical advice. This is important to remember because, as Brabant and Kalich (2008) point out, "there is a strong possibility of at-risk students in death education classes" (p. 6). Those who teach death education courses need to know how to make appropriate referrals to their university counseling centers. As with my other personal writing courses, I do not interpret or psychoanalyze my students' writings. Such interpretation is appropriate when we discuss fictional characters, but it is not appropriate when we discuss real people. Fictional characters cannot be traumatized by a careless or cruel interpretation; real people can. Students may be ready to write self-disclosing personal essays on wrenching topics, such as dying, death, or bereavement, but they may not be ready to hear their classmates or teacher "critique" the content of their essays. When writing a book about my students' writings, I permit myself to comment on—not judge—their lives, but I always show them my commentary before I submit a manuscript for publication. I never pretend to know more about their lives than they know themselves.

To author a book about a writing course is a formidable challenge, for each student turned in a minimum of 40 pages, typed, double-spaced, and another 25 pages of diary entries. I thus received over 1600 pages of writing—and that doesn't include several in-class writing assignments in which students commented anonymously on specific pedagogical questions that arose during the semester. While teaching the course, I couldn't always see how each student's writing changed week-by-week. Inundated by these writings, I struggled to comment on each essay and keep up with my other teaching and departmental responsibilities. I sensed some of the major changes in my students' writings but not the subtle changes that I discerned only after the course ended, when I had the time to read and study each student's work from beginning to end.

Part I, "Diaries," is organized around the diary entries I wrote immediately after each class. These entries provide a week-by-week glimpse of our class discussions, highlighting the essays we heard and the students' developing bond with their classmates and teacher. The diary entries, my own and my students', are a vital source of information about how everyone responded to the course. I was what sociologists call a participant-observer, that is, both a member of the course who participated in every discussion and who affected and was being affected by the others in the class, and also an observer who tried to understand the larger story of love and loss as studied in an undergraduate course. My diary entries give a chronological view of the course, which began in late January, 2008 and ended the first week of May. We met two days a week, on Mondays and Wednesdays, from 5:45–7:05 pm. Students turned in a diary every Wednesday, and I returned them the following Monday after reading a few aloud anonymously. To make the book more reader-friendly, I discuss the diaries during the week in which they were written.

I was fortunate to have Nico Suarez, a doctoral student in the English Department, serving as my teaching assistant. He attended every Wednesday class, helped me read a set of student essays, and taught a class during my absence. Nico is smart, funny, and irrepressible, a jokester with a rapier wit. The students adored Nico, and I rely extensively upon his diaries, which are insightful and witty.

Part 2, "Breakthroughs," focuses on several students who made important educational and personal breakthroughs in their understanding of love and loss: Chipo, who wrote several essays about his mother's death when he was 14 years old and his grandfather's death a few weeks before our course began; Lia, who wrote about how her parents' divorce and her grandfather's death led to clinical depression; Shannon, who feared that she could not express her feelings about death; Faith, who wrote a graphic essay about her experience with cutting and a close call with suicide; and three anonymous students who wrote about abortion. Their writings touch on many different aspects of death education, including disenfranchised grief. These students came to feel a close connection with their classmates and teacher, as we can see from their diary entries. It is unlikely that any of these students would have written about these topics in a conventional writing course. My aim throughout the book is to contextualize their writings, comment on the classroom dynamics that made possible their emotional and cognitive growth, and record how they felt about having their writings published. I conclude with a discussion of what my students learned from reading *Dying to Teach*. The Appendix contains the course syllabus, the 13 writing assignments, and a copy of the IRB consent form that each student signed.

Throughout this book I explore how students write about not only dying, death, and bereavement but also about depression, cutting, and abortion, topics that occupy the ambiguous border of death-in-life. "Death is not the ultimate tragedy of life," Norman Cousins (1979) states in his justly famous book, *Anatomy of an Illness as Perceived by the Patient*. "The ultimate tragedy is depersonalization" (p. 133). Students seek to make these issues of depersonalization come alive through their writings. In writing about love and loss, they create verbal portraits, or at least snapshots, of deceased relatives and friends. We first become aware of death through the deaths of others, and my students show us how they struggle with the everyday reality of these losses. Writing is a self-preservative act, one that is, by its nature, on the side of life and thus opposed to death.

Death Education in the Writing Classroom is the first book to show how love and loss can be taught in a college writing class—and the first to explore the week-by-week changes in students' cognitive and affective responses to death. We spoke about death from many points of view and subject positions, and though some students had not yet lost a beloved relative or friend, they all knew that sooner or later death would enter their lives. Robert Kastenbaum (1992) observes in *The Psychology of Death* that although there are many ways to describe a person's attitude toward death, probably the best distinction is that between the touched and the untouched. "This is the most basic and natural distinction that I have observed, whether in a hospital, a classroom, or a community setting. There are people who convey a sense of having been touched by death, and others who behave as though untouched. Becoming aware that the next person we interact with is likely to represent one or the other type of orientation can help us to be more perceptive and helpful, and reduce the probabilities of miscommunication" (p. 233). Death education can be valuable for students in both categories, those who have been touched by death and those who haven't. In a course in which students' personal writings are the primary focus, those who have been touched by death can teach those who haven't.

Death education raises intriguing pedagogical questions. What motivates students to take a course on love and loss? Will they find such a course engaging or disengaging? Will students drop the course when they discover its emotional challenges? Will students become "infected" by their classmates' dark writings? How do students respond to their teacher's painful self-disclosures? What are the benefits—and risks—of empathy? Will writing about traumatic events lead to retraumatization? How will students who have not been "touched" by death respond to their classmates who have been "touched" by death?

Those who have been touched by death are not "experts" on the subject. No one, teacher or student alike, is an authority, as Oliver Leaman (1995) points out in an early book on death education. "When it comes to attitudes to death, to risk and to loss there are no experts, only a variety of views. It is up to teachers to encourage pupils to reflect on their experiences, and this has to be done in a subtle and non-judgmental way" (p. 83). Jonathan Silin (1995), an educator who has written about being touched by death, observes that the "introduction of a discrete death curriculum allows us momentarily to hold mortality at bay, finally dismissing it to the edges of classroom life" (p. 40).

Wendy Bishop (1997) states, wishfully, that composition teachers "should be paying attention to issues of affect and providing teachers and program administrators with a course of study that includes introductions to personality theory, gender studies, psychoanalytic concepts, and basic counseling, even if such study mainly confirms that there are large differences between a teacher/ administrator's and therapist's roles" (p. 143). I would add death education to this wish list. Many students would be interested in taking such a course, though few educators might be willing to teach it. An undergraduate who took my 2006 Love and Loss course told me that when she expressed the desire to teach a similar course at the university where she is now enrolled as a doctoral student, she was dubbed the "touchy-feely" instructor and told by a colleague, "I don't mind my students having emotions. I just don't want to know about them."

Regardless of whether we embrace or deny our emotions, all of us confront love and loss, and all of us struggle with age-old questions about death. Although death education is relatively new—some educators trace its origins to Herman Feifel's 1959 edited book, *The Meaning of Death*—Plato argued more than 2000 years ago that philosophy is a "meditation upon death." Other philosophers such as Montaigne (1946) have asserted that preparing for death will help us live a better life. "If I were a maker of books I should compile a register, with comments, of different deaths. He who should teach men to die, would teach them to live" (p. 84). One need not be as obsessed with death as Montaigne was—he admitted he was always thinking and speaking about death—to believe in the importance of death education. As Simon Critchley (2009) contends, not only about Montaigne but about philosophers in general, "the premeditation of death is nothing less than the foretelling of freedom" (p. xvi). I believe that teachers will be more willing to allow personal discussions about death in the classroom when they realize that death education is mainly about life education. David Wendell Moller (1996) makes a similar observation at the conclusion of his book *Confronting Death*: "thanatology itself stems not from a morbid preoccupation with mortality, but from a concern for and love of life" (p. 246). What better place to talk and write about death and life than the college classroom, where education can become transformative? Educators have long known about the power of teaching. "Education is not a preparation for life, education *is* life," John Dewey affirmed. Henry Adams also knew this: "A teacher affects eternity; he can never tell where his influence stops." Students remember those courses in which they have learned, in Catherine's words, life lessons. These life lessons help all of us, teachers and students alike, when we confront the loss of our loved ones.

PART 1
Diaries

"Nervous Undergraduates Avoiding Eye Contact"

All writing courses in the English Department are capped at 25 students, and Love and Loss closed quickly. I'm reluctant to add students to a closed writing workshop because the more students, the less time we have to discuss each student's writing. Twenty-five students is a large writing class—most advanced writing courses are smaller and do not fill up. As soon as Love and Loss closed, I began receiving emails from students asking—in some cases, imploring—me to allow them in. It was not easy to refuse their compelling requests. "I am interested in your course for many reasons," a woman wrote, "mainly because a few years ago, during my college application process, I wrote my application essay to this university on a topic that indeed involved love and loss, the loss of my baby brother when I was a child. I learned a lot from writing this piece, and I also feel I can learn a lot from this course." Another person wanted to take the course because of the recent loss of her aunt. Another mentioned the deaths of two family members in the last year. "I have had trouble coping with these losses since they are the first ones I have experienced in my life, but it has been worse for my mother. I was hoping to learn and progress in this course and convey what I have learned to the rest of my family." I emailed them and more than two dozen others, telling them, regretfully, that I wasn't able to honor their requests. Kamilluh had taken my Expository Writing course last semester and sent me the following handwritten note:

Dear Mr. Berman,
    My cousin died this past March at my age, 19. She was my first and best friend, and the closest person to me besides maybe my mother. I've watched you openly talk about your wife to the class, and I admire you for it. Excuse me if I am wrong, but I think a lot of the reason why you are so open and accepting about her death is through your books, your writing.
    Writing is my way of expressing my feelings too, Mr. Berman. It has been since I began at the age of six. I have tried poetry, and it works to a certain extent, but after hearing about a course on love and loss, I thought maybe this is what I needed.

> I think I have come to some type of understanding of her death through my belief in God, but I do not think I have *faced* it. To my observation, you have. When you said in the class what we would write on, I thought, "I couldn't handle it." At the same time, I realized I needed something like this to release and come to grips with internal feelings I have put aside for some time.

After reading Kamilluh's letter, I decided to allow her into Love and Loss— it's always hard for me to turn down a student who has done well in one of my courses. I accepted two other students who had taken my Expository Writing course the previous semester, Chipo and Javarro. During the first assignment in Expository Writing, Chipo had mentioned the death of his mother, but he rarely returned to this subject in his later essays. When I asked him this week whether he wanted to take Love and Loss because of his mother's death, he replied "yes"—and also because of his grandfather's death last month. Four other students from Chipo's class—Cecilia, Cath, Scout, and Scotty—had registered for Love and Loss as soon as the course opened, so nearly a quarter of the present class were members of last semester's Expository Writing course. In addition, two other students, Shannon and Lucy, had taken literature courses with me.

Wednesday, January 23

Today was the first day of class, and I began as I always do by taking attendance. Three students who had registered for the course dropped it before the first class; with the addition of Kamilluh, Javarro, and Chipo, the enrollment is back to 25. Four students who were not registered for the course left after I told them that I wouldn't be able to allow them in. After taking attendance, I commented on the fact that only five of the twenty-five students are male—and I wondered aloud why there were so many more women. "Men are afraid of emotion," Nico exclaimed, provocatively. After I gave out the syllabus, I discussed why I was teaching the course and how it would differ from the Love and Loss course that I taught two years earlier.

This semester's course, I explained, is a writing class, not a literature class, and students will be writing weekly essays on different aspects of love and loss. In the first Love and Loss course, I read aloud only a few of the essays, always anonymously; in this course, students will read aloud their own essays, and we'll be able to observe how these essays impact everyone in the classroom. Most of the writing topics for this course will be different from those in the first course: now, for example, I'm interested in seeing how loss has affected students' assumptions about the future. I'm also interested in seeing whether students will be able to translate intellectual knowledge of loss and death into deeper emotional understanding, thus increasing what Daniel Goleman (1995) calls "emotional intelligence." Will they be able to learn from their classmates' experiences of love and loss and, if so, use narratives to facilitate, in the words of Robert

A. Neimeyer (2001), the "re-authoring of the self in the wake of loss" (p. 180)? Will they be able to reinterpret their experiences of love and loss, recognizing, as White and Epston contend (1990) in *Narrative Means to Therapeutic Ends*, that "every telling or retelling of a story, through its performance, is a new telling that encapsulates, and expands upon the previous telling" (p. 13)? Will they be able to discover that although we cannot change the past, we can change our understanding of the past, learning to see healthier ways to reframe experience? Will they be able to see how they are not the only ones struggling with loss, and that we can learn from others' experiences? I'm not a "narrative therapist," that is, a therapist who helps clients discover richer or thicker narratives that emerge from their life stories, but I can help students see, from my own experience, how someone can survive a crushing loss.

One of the writing assignments I'll give in a few weeks is on posttraumatic growth. Two writing assignments will involve each student working with a classmate. Students will share with each other not only their writings but also their emotions about love and loss. I anticipate that a strong bond will form among the students—they will learn a great deal about their classmates' lives. They will also discover how their classmates have reacted to death. I've never taught a writing course before in which students turned in a weekly diary (though students in my literature courses write reader-response diaries), so this will give me a new source of information about how they are doing, emotionally and cognitively, in the course. The diaries will be especially valuable for those students who write on traumatic topics. Will they be retraumatized as a result of writing? The diaries will also demonstrate the extent to which students feel connected with each other and their teacher. Unlike lecture courses in which a single person speaks, this course will highlight many voices and points of view. I expect there will be emotional as well as intellectual and cognitive growth.

The course will focus as much on love as on loss; I hope to maintain a balance between the two in the writing assignments. I believe, with Freud (1914/1957), that "in the last resort we must begin to love in order not to fall ill, and we are bound to fall ill if, in consequence of frustration, we are unable to love" (p. 85). We may also fall ill if a loved one dies—bereavement can throw us into the deepest depression, as Freud (1917/1957) suggests in "Mourning and Melancholia." I am reminded of Bruno Bettelheim's (1977) comment in *The Uses of Enchantment*: "There is no greater threat in life than that we will be deserted, left alone. Psychoanalysis has named this—man's greatest fear—separation anxiety; and the younger we are, the more excruciating is our anxiety when we feel deserted, for the young child actually perishes when not adequately protected and taken care of. Therefore, the ultimate consolation is that we shall never be deserted" (p. 145).

Love and Loss will be an emotionally fraught course, I told my students, but I will do my best to prevent it from becoming depressing or morbid. I then gave out copies of the following statement by Alfred North Whitehead (1954): "Ninety per cent of our lives . . . is governed by emotion. Our brains merely register and act upon what is telegraphed to them by our bodily experience. Intellect is to emotion as our clothes are to our bodies: we could not very well have civilized life without clothes, but we would be in a poor way if we had only clothes without bodies" (p. 188). What makes this observation more remarkable, I added, is that Whitehead was one of the twentieth century's greatest mathematicians and philosophers. We'll have much more to say about emotion throughout the course, and I plan to discuss the theory of emotional contagion during next Monday's class. The diaries will help me understand my students' emotional responses throughout the course, particularly if they find themselves becoming at risk. I then reported on the chilling statistics of the types of losses experienced by American children:

By high school's end

Around 50 percent of students experience divorce

About 20 percent experience the death of a parent

One out of three girls will be in some way sexually abused

One out of seven boys will be in some way sexually abused

By age fourteen, children have witnessed eighteen thousand deaths on TV, usually violent

About 3.3 million children in America witness domestic violence each year

An estimated forty-one million children globally will be orphaned by one or both parents from the AIDS virus by the year 2010

About 160,000 children in the United States stay home from school daily for fear of bullying

One out of six children between the ages of ten and sixteen report they have seen someone or know someone who has been shot

In 1992, 632 children under the age of five were murdered—two-thirds of these children were murdered by one or both parents

Suicide has become the second leading cause of death for our young people today, with one young person completing suicide every ninety seconds

Ten percent of the teenagers polled in Washington, D.C., stated they had attempted suicide in the past year. (Goldman, 2002, p. 194)

Throughout the semester we'll have much to say about grief, but one observation I made at the beginning of the course is that "grieving never ends," a statement that appears in a slim book called *Helping the Grieving Student* (Heilman, 2006) published by the Dougy Center, a national center for grieving children and their families:

> This is perhaps one of the least understood aspects of grief in our society. It seems that most people are anxious for us to put the loss behind us, to go on, to get over it. When a person dies, the death leaves a vacuum in the lives of those left behind. Life is never the same again. This doesn't mean that life can never again be joyful, or that the experience of loss cannot be transformed into something positive. But grief does not have a magical ending time. People comment on the pangs of grief 40, 50, or 60 years after a death. For the student, the grieving process will be re-experienced in some new way at each developmental level or experience of personal accomplishment. (p. 6)

In every writing course I have taught, the two most wrenching topics are the impact of parental divorce—many students have no contact with one of their parents, usually the father—and depression or suicide. I expect that many of my Love and Loss students will also write on these topics. One of the main losses is a grandparent's death. Every semester one or more students tell me that a grandparent is gravely ill or has just died. I never doubt the veracity of these statements, though I know some of my colleagues do. A graduate student showed me the syllabus from his undergraduate Shakespeare course at another university in which the instructor stated his attendance policy in the following words: "Participation accounts for 10% of the course [grade]. If you are not in class, I fail to see how you can participate. I realize that this may well be the semester one or more of your grandparents may choose to shuffle off this mortal coil." The professor was no doubt trying to be witty, but many students are devastated by grandparents' deaths. I've never heard anyone comment on this, but many grandparents die when their grandchildren are in high school or college. For some grandchildren, the death of a grandparent also involves the death of a parent surrogate, resulting in a double loss. I then asked each student to write a brief paragraph on the following questions:

Why I'm Taking This Course

Please discuss in a paragraph or two why you are taking this course. What would you like to learn from Love and Loss? How can I help you achieve your educational goals? Do you have any anxieties or concerns about the course and, if so, how can I help you overcome them? Please sign this sheet so that I can be as sensitive as possible to your situation. What if anything should I know about your life at the beginning of the course? I'll read some of these paragraphs *anonymously* in class next week.

At the end of class, I gave the first two writing assignments. Assignment 1, due next Monday, asks students to write about four loves and four losses in their lives, devoting a paragraph to each one and ranking each in importance. Assignment 2, due next Wednesday, is a collaborative effort. During the second half of Monday's class, I'll pair each student with a classmate, and each will interview the other and then write an essay on one of the classmate's loves or losses. We'll then read these essays aloud.

I spent nearly the entire first class talking about the course, and I didn't have an opportunity to notice the students' reactions, apart from extensive note-taking. Nico's diary entry, I suspect, conveys their edginess:

> The usual sort of introduction, a collection of nervous undergraduates avoiding eye contact. I arrived three minutes late, riding my skateboard in the cold, wondering where on earth the Earth Sciences building was. The students faced forward, and Jeff stood there and talked to them for the better part of an hour and twenty minutes.
>
> Looking around the classroom as Jeff laid out the emotionally charged course plan, it seemed to me that the students were even more fidgety and nervous than is typical of undergraduates. One young woman picked at her nails, another chewed her nails, and another kept bridging her fingers under her chin. Almost everyone in the room exhibited a highly visible nervous tick. (I wonder if I was exempt? I think I was; God bless getting older.)
>
> What was it that the students were feeling? I tried to get inside the mind of the average student by putting myself in her position. How would I feel if I were about to write about my fear of my father's death? About the difficulty I've had dealing with his illness in the past few years? About the decline and ultimate dissolution of my relationship of six years with Nina, a woman to whom I often imagined I would one day be married? I suspect that as I considered this, I began to chew my nails, or flick my pen about.
>
> A few nice quotes from Jeff:
>
> Listen with empathy.
>
> Tears are as appropriate in the classroom as are smiles.

CHAPTER 2—WEEK TWO
"Hearing It Made His Death More Real"

Monday, January 28 and Wednesday, January 30

I began class on Monday by reading aloud several students' paragraphs about why they are taking Love and Loss. Many want the course to help them understand and cope with losses, most of which involved, not surprisingly, grandparents' deaths. Bianca's response is representative:

> I like writing, and love and loss are not topics I have ever written about. I tend to be an emotional person and cry very often, so that is something I might be slightly embarrassed about. My grandmother passed away a year ago next week, and we were very close. It might be challenging for me to write about her, but at the same time I hope it is also a good experience.

Daphne wrote about a double loss, her grandmother's death followed by her father's decision to leave his family.

> On October 2, 2005, my grandmother died. She was diagnosed earlier that year, January, to be precise, with pancreatic cancer. Two weeks after my grandmother's diagnosis, my father left a note on the kitchen table. It was midnight when I got home from a friend's house, and I opened the door to face my youngest brother and my mother, drowning in tears around my father's letter. He had left us, and said he couldn't take much more. Since then many things have changed; I have changed. And now I would like to write about them.

Maggie mentioned a grandparent's recent death.

> My grandfather died a year ago this past October, and I've still not gotten over it. It seems that I can write about anything, but when it comes to him, even though I want desperately to put him in words, I cannot. I can't even go through the produce section of a grocery store sometimes without smelling fresh green beans and tearing up. My grandpa was a farmer and shared that love with my sister and me. I guess what I hope to gain from this class is the ability to write about that loss and also other loves and losses in my life without the fear of judgment.

Addison is taking Love and Loss to help her come to terms with her brother's suicide.

> I think what I really want from this course is to learn more about myself—how I love and how I grieve. I am a bit anxious about "spilling my guts" to strangers, but I believe once I see others doing it I can feel more comfortable. My brother committed suicide when I was young, and very often people are shocked and upset by it. I feel comfortable talking about it, but I do get upset when I think about how hard it was (and still is) for my mom to deal with it. However, I am looking forward to sharing.

About a third of the students wrote about experiencing anxiety over the course. Their reasons ranged from the "fear of judgment" to the fear of disclosing their work to classmates. "I don't have any concerns," Ayla wrote, "although I am extremely emotional. However, I know that it will be difficult to read my work aloud because I have written journals since I was nine years old, and I have never shared their contents with anyone." A few people expressed the fear of crying in class, including one man, Saverio: "My main concern for this class is that I will cry because I dislike crying." Shannon expressed the opposite fear, that of emotional inhibition: "My biggest concern is that I not hold myself back and just write, just let it go." Nicholette expressed a different fear, though she remained vague about it, perhaps deliberately: "I have one anxiety—that a certain topic might trigger some emotions that I don't want to feel again." Cath pointed out a fascinating contradiction in her friends' reactions to the course: "I wanted to let you know, Jeff, that everyone I tell about this class says they really want to take it. They say it sounds great. Then I tell them they would have to share their stories. Most people are no longer interested."

During the last 20 minutes, I paired each student with a classmate, and each then interviewed the other about one love or loss. They seemed to enjoy the opportunity to interview each other, for when I left the room, a few minutes before the end of class, their chatter animated the classroom.

On Wednesday I handed out a statement I had written on emotional contagion, a phenomenon I have noticed in my other writing courses:

Emotional Contagion
One of the most curious of all psychosocial phenomena is the contagion effect, in which a person can become "infected" by another's emotions. This "infection" can lead to anxiety, depression, anger, and even suicide. Hatfield, Cacioppo, and Rapson (1994) assert in their book *Emotional Contagion* that people are more likely to catch others' emotions "if their attention is riveted on the others than if they are oblivious to others' emotions"; "if they construe themselves in terms of their interrelatedness to the others rather than in terms of their independence and uniqueness"; "if they are able to read others' emotional expressions, voices, gestures, and postures"; if they tend to "mimic facial, vocal, and postural expressions"; if they are "aware of their own emotional responses"; and if they are "emotionally reactive people" (p. 148).

Females are more susceptible to emotional contagion than are men, mainly because they are freer in expressing their emotions and because they are more empathic. "Awareness of others' feelings," Hatfield, Cacioppo, and Rapson suggest, "is a predictor of sharing those feelings even if it is not a necessary condition for contagion" (p. 154). Negative emotions, such as anger, depression, or fear, are generally more contagious than positive emotions. There are sometimes advantages to being able to infect others with one's emotions. "When we try to distract an irritable child, when we go to the hospital to 'cheer up' a friend, when we try to liven up a dull party, we are trying to dominate an interpersonal encounter" (p. 202).

It has long been known that humor is infectious, and recent medical studies have confirmed the striking medical benefits of humor, including heightening the body's immune system, lowering blood sugar among diabetics, reducing heart attacks, and alleviating pain. Just as crying spreads sorrow, so does laughing spread hope. Norman Cousins (1979) trained himself to laugh, in the process repairing his damaged heart. "I made the joyous discovery that ten minutes of genuine belly laugh had an anesthetic effect and would give me at least two hours of pain-free sleep."

There are many striking examples of the contagion phenomenon, beginning with the Werther effect, in which scores of young men committed suicide after reading Johann Wolfgang von Goethe's highly autobiographical novel, *The Sorrows of Young Werther*, which ends with the hero shooting himself. (Goethe, by contrast, seems to have exorcized his demons by writing the novel.) Other documented examples include hysterical illness mysteriously sweeping over communities. Many people learn to cut themselves through the contagion effect.

If you find yourself becoming "infected" by reading *Dying to Teach* or your classmates' writings, please indicate so in your weekly diaries. Tell me when the infection begins and when it ends. What were the symptoms? Have you been susceptible to emotional contagion before taking this course? If you find yourself becoming infected by the dark emotions of a book or essay, try to think what, if anything, we could have done differently to prevent this from happening.

As early as 1897 the great French sociologist Emile Durkheim wrote that suicide was "very contagious," relating the "well-known story of the fifteen patients who hung themselves in swift succession in 1772 from the same hook in a dark passage of the hospital. Once the hook was removed there was an end of the epidemic. Likewise, at the camp of Boulogne, a soldier blew out his brains in a sentry-box; in a few days others imitated him in the same place; but as soon as this was burned, the contagion stopped" (p. 97). Albert Camus (1955) asserts in the opening sentence of *The Myth of Sisyphus* that "There is but one truly serious philosophical problem, and that is suicide. Judging whether life is or is not worth living amounts to answering the fundamental question of philosophy" (p. 3). William Styron (1990) suggests in *Darkness Visible* that Camus's death in an automobile accident in 1960 at the age of 46 may not have been entirely accidental.

"Although Camus had not been driving he supposedly knew the driver, who was the son of his publisher, to be a speed demon; so there was an element of recklessness in the accident that bore overtones of the near-suicidal, at least of a death flirtation, and it was inevitable that conjectures concerning the event should revert back to the theme of suicide in the writer's work"(pp. 22–23).

My first classroom encounter with emotional contagion occurred in 1994, when I taught a graduate course on Literary Suicide. As I report (Berman, 1999) in *Surviving Literary Suicide*, one student, Mary, sent me a disturbing letter several weeks after the semester ended. She told me that the recent breakup of a relationship triggered a depression and a deliberate drug overdose, during which she kept thinking about a statement made by Edwin Shneidman, a leading suicidologist whose writings we had discussed in class: "*Suicide is characterized by ambivalence*" (Berman, 1999, p. 260). Mary knew that she was ambivalent about suicide, and she immediately called her therapist and then rushed to a hospital where her stomach was pumped. She wrote in a subsequent letter that, with the help of an antidepressant, she was no longer depressed. Her letters raise two crucial questions that she could not resolve: first, whether Literary Suicide planted a "seed" of suicide that had not existed before the course, and, second, whether the knowledge she gleaned from the course, including her awareness of the ambivalence most people feel when they attempt suicide, helped to insure her survival.

Mary's classmate Ultra found himself becoming anxious at the end of the semester when he read *Darkness Visible*, William Styron's memoir of his psychological breakdown and near-suicide attempt. What was puzzling to Ultra was that he became infected by a story with an affirmative ending by an author who did not take his own life. Oddly enough, none of the other stories and poems about suicide written by authors who later committed suicide—Virginia Woolf, Ernest Hemingway, Sylvia Plath, and Anne Sexton—had infected Ultra the way *Darkness Visible* did. His anxiety lasted only a few weeks, after which he began to feel better.

The word *contagion*, Priscilla Wald (2008) points out in a book about the "outbreak narrative," means literally "to touch together" (p. 12), but few literary or composition scholars have studied emotional contagion despite the fact that many social scientists have documented the phenomenon. I suspect that a personal writing course on Love and Loss will be a "breeding ground" for emotional contagion, both positive and negative, and I want to do everything possible to avoid infecting my students with the dark emotions associated with loss.

Hatfield, Cacioppo, and Rapson write about the spreading of dark emotions, but my experience with the self-disclosing classroom is that hope is more contagious than despair. Students reveal in their personal essays serious problems in their lives—to cite only one example, about half of them come from divorced families, a situation which often creates ongoing conflicts. And yet students also display courage, strength, and resiliency when writing about problematic issues. Their willingness to write about their lives, opening up to a group of strangers, is a sign of their trust in the good will of their classmates. I have never seen this trust betrayed in any of my writing courses: Students respond empathically, not judgmentally, to their classmates' writings. One of the paradoxes we'll explore is that we become *less* vulnerable when we acknowledge our vulnerability. This paradox remains true, however, only in an empathic classroom, where students remain supportive and nonjudgmental of each other. Another paradox is that to write effectively about love and loss, one must reproduce the dark emotions of anxiety, fear, and sadness within the reader. A third paradox is that although dying is, as Irvin Yalom (2008) suggests, the "loneliest event of life" (p. 119), a process in which we are separated not only from others and ourselves but from the entire world, talking and writing about death help to offset some of that loneliness. We feel less lonely, less scared, when we share our emotions with others. And a fourth paradox is expressed by E.M. Forster in *Howards End* (1910/1985): "Death destroys a man: the idea of Death saves him" (p. 239). We'll comment on these paradoxes throughout the semester.

After talking about emotional contagion, I read aloud part of my eulogy for Barbara in *Dying to Teach*. I read it without difficulty, and afterwards I told my students that until the moment I began the eulogy during the memorial service, I wasn't sure whether I had the emotional control to read it without breaking down. What helped me remain composed was that I read the eulogy aloud so many times before the funeral that I had it memorized. "If it's important for you to eulogize a loved one in the future," I told my students, "then I suggest that you write it down and practice reading it before the funeral."

On Monday students began reading aloud their biographies of each other's loves and losses (Assignment 2). Five students read their essays in class. For each essay we commented on the best sentences and identified other sentences that contained grammatical or stylistic errors. We then revised the faulty sentences. It was a good class. I spent several minutes explaining misplaced and dangling modifiers and comma splices, errors which appear on many of their essays. I'm certain that I'll have to discuss these common errors during nearly every class. I also spoke about the need to use more pronouns.

At the end of Monday's class, students turned in their first set of diaries, and I read several of them aloud at the beginning of Wednesday's class. They were fascinating. Maggie remarked that hearing me read her diary aloud about her grandfather's death was more upsetting than when she wrote the diary a few days earlier.

> When you read the first line of my response, my throat closed up, and I desperately tried to remain calm so that no one would realize that hearing my own words about my grandpa was killing me inside. Not because I didn't write them, but because hearing it made his death more real. Even though I miss him more than anything, I think my reaction is because I don't want his death to be real, and because I know he would want me to concentrate on

being happy and working toward my goals, rather than being sad for him. Maybe that's why I haven't written about him before this class.

Would we interpret Maggie's response as an example of emotional contagion? If so, the irony is that she was infected by grief not when she wrote the essay but when she heard me read her words aloud anonymously. This observation seems counterintuitive, and yet it helps to explain a phenomenon I have noticed in every writing course I have taught: students tell me that it is much harder to read aloud an emotionally charged essay than it is to write it. Students did not cry when they wrote the essays, but they found themselves surprised, even stunned when they burst into tears while reading their writings aloud in the classroom. How do we explain this phenomenon? The answer, I believe, is that reading an essay aloud to classmates makes the experience seem "more real" and therefore more powerful. Classmates bear witness to the event and, in many cases, share the writer's suffering. Writers do not need an audience to experience the therapeutic benefits of self-expression, but there is less at stake when writing remains unread. The writer may decide to tear up the page or bury it in a desk, never to be seen again. This is, in fact, what Pennebaker (1990/1997) urges his undergraduate research subjects to do after they have written about a painful experience; he fears that the writers may be hurt or betrayed by an unscrupulous reader. Pennebaker's fear is understandable, but private writing does not have the same impact of writing that is read or heard aloud by other people. Unlike private writing, writing that is read aloud to a group of classmates cannot be easily denied, ignored, or forgotten. There is something irrevocable about reading one's writing to a classroom of people, something that can never be erased or denied. There are greater risks but also greater benefits when one discloses a secret to another person. It is for this reason that one of the events in twelve-step programs is sharing one's secret with other people. It is painful to reveal a secret, but afterwards we usually feel better, released from its terrible power over us.

Two students wrote diaries about non-classmates' reactions to Love and Loss. Both diaries reveal how the students are sharing the contents of the course with those outside the classroom. Ayla asked her mother why she was never permitted to attend a funeral or a wake as a child. "She told me she doesn't think funerals and wakes are places for children to go because the memories of the events will always be very vivid and traumatizing in their minds. So I guess I appreciate not being allowed to go in that sense; but I do wish that I was allowed to support my parents through their grieving moments." Lucy told both her parents about the course. "While writing the first two assignments, I would say that there were more tears than smiles. However, when I was in the middle of writing my first assignment, I called my parents to talk to them; for some reason writing about why I love them and the effect they have had on my life made me want to talk to them. During my phone call I was smiling."

Several students commented on their reactions to hearing me read my eulogy for Barbara. "As I listened to you talk so fondly about her," Gloria wrote, "I found myself at many passages smiling and even laughing. I did not laugh because I thought it was funny that you wrote Barbara's eulogy, but I smiled and laughed because I thought it was beautiful. We are all human and share such similar feelings and experience common situations, therefore making it easy for us to connect." Scout observed, "I held back from fully crying at your eulogy for your wife, because I was—and still am—scared that it is too early to trust everyone with my emotions."

After I read aloud several diary entries, we continued hearing the Assignment 2 essays. Nico's diary entry captures the mood of the second week of the course:

> The second week has taken students further into the process of coming to terms with tough subjects. I'm beginning to discern to what extent Jeff has implemented measures to make students less anxious, and to make the process of writing about emotion and sharing that writing with others less jarring. Students were matched in pairs and instructed to interview one another about love and loss. The results of these interviews were typed up and distributed to the entire class, and the authors of these reports read them aloud. This procedural decision on Jeff's part has a dual effect: (1) Students had a chance to start hearing about emotionally charged subjects; (2) Students whose personal stories were read aloud were spared the potentially difficult and anxiety-producing task of having to read their own accounts to the class. (Their project partners acted as surrogates and buffers.) This transitioning into the process seems prudent. I'm sure that in future assignments students will be required to read their own work aloud and to confront the difficulties produced by so doing, but doubtless there is yet time in the semester for that painful step toward raw emotionality. Hmm—it's never occurred to me before, but watching the reading of essays, I now see Jeff's obsession with grammatical and stylistic concerns as one that serves a purpose beyond the purely pedagogical.
>
> The scene is as follows: Gloria reads aloud the result of her interview with Chipo, a young man whose mother's life ended tragically and prematurely in a car accident. During and after the reading a pin drop can be heard clearly. It's like all the air has been sucked out of the room. No one wants to say jack. And then Jeff says, "Tell me about a favorite sentence from the essay." And people take a deep breath. And a little later Jeff says, "How can we fix the grammatical error in the first sentence of the second paragraph?" And a few hands go up. Do you see what's happened? We're back on neutral ground, or at least we're navigating the terrain between extreme loss and the commonplace, and in so doing, bringing death into the realm of that which can be discussed among reasonable, empathically-oriented people. Grammar and style are a buffer as much as a writing concern. Might this help students improve as writers? Might they, when writing about painful subjects, come to pay greater attention to grammar and style as a way of lessening the emotional burden of their subject matter?

I've also reread the student submissions entitled "Why I'm Taking This Course." Patterns emerge. Most students report a fear of expressing emotion in front of others, a fear of being taken back to traumatic events, and a hope that writing about difficult or emotional events will help them to cope with pain or heightened emotionality. Several students also report a desire to get more in touch with their emotions. One student reports that she excessively fidgets with her ring out of anxiety about the course material. (Per my first entry, I was right about the fidgeting!)

CHAPTER 3—WEEK THREE
"She Helped Me Say What I Could Not Say Myself"

Monday, February 4 and Wednesday, February 6

Time did not permit us to discuss how biographers transformed their classmates' love or loss paragraphs into an entire essay, but it is instructive to focus on a few students. Here is how Isabella commented in the Assignment 1 essay on the most serious loss in her life:

> The greatest loss in my life is not something which has directly happened to me, but it affects me and my family greatly. My greatest loss is that of my father's health, to be specific, his battle with an unknown, unexpected lung condition, of which there is minimal to no medical history. It is a direct result of his work as a firefighter during the attacks on New York City on September 11. It is a condition which doctors for the past few years have been trying to figure out, of which they have not even derived a name. While we accept that those in the medical field speculate as to the extent of certain conditions, how they will progress, and how they may be treated, my father's is a condition of which the speculation is truly a mystery. He has not lost his life, but he is slowly losing much of his ability to breathe properly and easily. It is a battle my family and I witness on a daily basis as he coughs, struggles to do some physical activities, and can always be heard taking deep breaths while he is sleeping. We do not speak much of his condition because I think our fear of the inevitable forces us all to push this problem aside. When I speak to him about what the doctors have said about the progress of the condition, he is always very honest. He tells me in his most optimistic voice that they think it will not spread any more, that the steroids they give him are working. Every conversation is either interrupted by or followed by a full, deep, heavy cough. It is no surprise that even his optimism does not comfort me. He is a strong man who will do everything that he can to not let us see that he is hurting. However, I know that he has physically changed in these few, short years that have passed since he spent weeks at a time breathing in the poisonous air with his colleagues. I can only hope that he has many years to his life, however, now at the age of 44, I fear that the loss of his lungs will take him from us much sooner. It will always be too soon.

Isabella gives us few specifics in the paragraph about her father's deteriorating health, apart from his increasing difficulty breathing, and she is similarly reluctant to disclose her emotions, apart from her generalized fear. The entire paragraph is emotionally restrained, suggesting her wariness about self-disclosure. The first five sentences remain abstract and general; the writing becomes more animated only in the sixth sentence, when she tells us that "He has not lost his life, but he is slowly losing much of his ability to breathe properly and easily." The family doesn't speak much about his illness, and one infers that this may be the first time she has written about it. The tone of the paragraph is somber, befitting the subject. She tells us that her father is "always very honest" when conveying the "progress of his condition"—notice her euphemistic language—yet in the next sentence she implies that his statements, expressed in his "most optimistic voice," may be motivated by the wish to protect his family from excessive worry. We are left with the contrast between the father's optimism and the daughter's pessimism. She ends on a short, powerful sentence, one that is unambiguous and heartfelt.

Isabella reveals in her diary entry that she was impressed by her classmates' first assignment on Love and Loss, but she was unsure how she felt about her own essay. "My dad's problem is not something I talk about with anyone, and when my partner emailed me her paper I cried before I even read it over. While reading it on the computer screen, it affected me very much." Nicholette expanded Isabella's paragraph into the following essay:

> When someone invites you into their life, it is often difficult to completely grasp the emotions and ideas that they experienced, especially when given such a short period of time to comprehend their personal life. After reading Isabella's short paragraphs on her beloved father who has contracted an unexpected and unknown lung condition, I really got a true understanding of how she feels about her father and family. As I was reading her work, I could hear her voice throughout the whole piece and I felt as if she was speaking directly to me, inviting me into her personal world and sharing her emotions with me about her father. Although I just met Isabella, I know that she is a very caring and loving daughter.
>
> One specific phrase that caught my eye was when Isabella wrote, "The greatest loss in my life is not something which has directly happened to me, but it affects me and my family greatly." I was touched that she brought her family into the equation as well, and that she didn't focus on herself solely. This showed me that she really cares about her family, and being that she comes from a large family shows that they are always there for each other during the good times and bad. While I was interviewing Isabella, I felt as if I were a part of her family for that brief moment because we both shared similarities in terms of religion, faith, hope, and most importantly the bonds between siblings.
>
> The title of my essay, "Isabella's Hero," has such a strong connection to Isabella's story and I felt it was appropriate for many reasons. Isabella's father has done endless amounts of work during the 9/11 attacks in New

York City as a FDNY firefighter. Because of his brave efforts to help the victims of 9/11, he now has to battle an unknown lung illness that causes him and his family great pain. I remember reading about this illness but I never really understood how serious it was or how it can affect a family until I saw it through the eyes of Isabella and her family. Isabella's father cannot breathe properly, and has difficulty with breathing during his sleep. His pride in being Isabella and the rest of her family's father makes him want to be brave and strong for them and himself during his struggle with this illness. Isabella is constantly reminded of her father's illness on a daily basis, even during conversations. She writes, "Every conversation is either interrupted by or followed by a full, deep, heavy cough." For Isabella and her family, they are constantly reminded of her father's illness and are forced to deal with it every day. I don't think that I am strong enough where I could face a loved one's illness all the time without wanting to break down emotionally. This made me realize that it is obvious that her father is the backbone of their family, but it is the family coming together that is supporting the backbone and keeping everyone together.

After talking with Isabella, I felt such strong emotions and wanted to cry, but I didn't. Part of me wanted to cry because such a tragic illness has struck a man who is only 44 years old, and yet a part of me wanted to cry because I never had the brave father that Isabella has. We both share such similarities in that our parents are both young, but the similarities end there in terms of our parents. When Isabella and I were interviewing each other, I told her that the one word that I never use is the word "dad." That's because my father left when I was two, came back when I was 16, then disappeared again. I didn't have the brave FDNY for a father, or the father who never wanted to let his family know he was hurting all the time like Isabella has. I didn't know what my father was. Talking with Isabella, I think we both came to an understanding that she doesn't take her father for granted one bit, and I respect her even more for that. At the end of her piece when she explains how she fears her father will be taken from her sooner than he should be, she writes, "it will always be too soon." I thought about that phrase and was trying to understand what she was feeling when she wrote that line. I felt a strong connection here with her because my mother is only 44 years old as well, and if she were to leave within the next five to ten years, I would feel that it was too soon also. No matter what age, it will always be too soon in my situation because my mother is all I have and Isabella has made me more aware of that.

When a family member has an illness, it can often be difficult to discuss. Isabella told me that she and her family don't really converse about the situation of her father's illness due to fear of the inevitable. I think that Isabella and her family are a close-knit family and can get through this hardship together. I never had to deal with a family member who had an unknown illness, but I hope that if god forbid I had to, I could be strong like Isabella and her family.

Nicholette captures Isabella's love and concern for her father, the family's closeness and "fear of the inevitable." She uses paradox to suggest how Isabella's father strengthens those who strengthen him. She also expresses gratitude to Isabella for inviting her into Isabella's personal world, an invitation that has made Nicholette feel a part of her classmate's family.

Nicholette could have ended her essay after the third paragraph, but she writes two more paragraphs, one of which, the fourth, reveals more about her own life than her classmate's. The fourth paragraph evokes the great loss in her own life, the fear she mentions enigmatically on the first day of the semester: "I have one anxiety—that a certain topic might trigger some emotions that I don't want to feel again." She contrasts Isabella's "heroic" father with her own absent father, the man who has disappeared twice from her life. Despite the many similarities she feels with her classmate, there is one glaring difference, one that she cannot help disclosing in her essay.

Almost anyone in Nicholette's situation would feel jealous of Isabella's close relationship with her heroic father, yet there is no hint of this in the essay. Instead, we see her admiration for her classmate in every sentence, along with her sympathy and empathy. Isabella's sadness has moved Nicholette deeply, even infected her, resulting in what Dominick LaCapra (2001) calls "empathic unsettlement," being "responsive to the traumatic experiences of others, notably of victims, [but without] the appropriation of their experiences" (p. 41). Nicholette's decision not to cry reveals her protectiveness, the wish not to upset her classmate, recalling, perhaps, Isabella's father's decision to remain optimistic to avoid burdening his family with worry. One senses from Isabella's and Nicholette's writings that people need to be "strong" for each other, a strength that arises from close interpersonal connections. The positive side of contagion is inspiration, and we can see how Isabella's courage in the face of adversity inspires her classmate.

Struggling to remain composed when she read her essay aloud, Nicholette became teary-eyed when she heard her classmates' response to it, as Ayla reports in her diary entry.

> Listening to Nicholette read her essay about Isabella's father struck me for many reasons. The first being the fact that I've known Isabella for four years and I had no idea that her father had an unknown illness. The second was the reaction Nicholette had as the class read their favorite sentences; she started to cry. Although her cry was silent, I could see her wiping her tears and using a piece of paper to hide her emotions. Immediately, I wanted to cry. My eyes welled up faster than I could control, and as I looked around the room, I noticed that I was not the only one. I don't know what it is like to not have a father and my heart sincerely goes out to her. She made me feel like it was okay to cry in class.

Sharing a problem with a stranger may prove to be either a burden or a release to both the self-discloser and the recipient of the self-disclosure. Recall Pennebaker's (1995) observation that talking (or writing) about a trauma may make the discloser feel better but the listener (or reader) feel worse. To write about loss is to acknowledge vulnerability, which may lead either to increased or decreased vulnerability in the writer and the reader. There is always a risk in disclosing one's vulnerability, a word that derives from *vuln*, Latin for *wound*. "To become powerfully vulnerable," Ken Macrorie (1974) suggests, "is to expose oneself to possible wounds. One cannot create valuable things without risk" (p. 184).

How did Isabella feel about the first two love and loss assignments? How did Nicholette's essay affect her? Writing teachers cannot answer questions like this unless they provide an opportunity for students to answer these questions themselves, as Isabella does in her next diary entry:

> This is the first journal entry which I have actually written directly after class. If I do not write this now, I feel I may forget what I am feeling at this exact moment; I am confused about my emotions. Nicholette's essay is the first time I have ever heard my own words spoken out loud, and I am unsure how I feel. She wrote a beautiful essay which I read over about fifty times. As I write, I try to grasp what is churning inside my head and my heart, which bring me to the tears that I refused to cry in class. I cannot find the words, yet, in my throat they are pushing to be released. Where should I begin?
>
> My father's illness has brought me to the point of anxiety attacks. I have never considered before a few years ago that I could lose anyone close to me. I never have, only burying older aunts, great grandmothers, and family members whom I was too young to really connect with. I recall the afternoon of September 11, 2001, when the commotion filled my school. I did not leave school that day. I recall walking home after school to my mother at home with the television on, and not once did it occur to me where my father was. He was at work. I would see him later. The whole day passed by without him ever entering my mind throughout the sadness and confusion which filled those initial hours. That evening we would all go to my aunt's house to eat dinner; my father would meet us there. I do not know if I was numb or naive to not think of my father, which is probably because I never considered the fact that I could ever lose him. Somehow I grew up thinking I was immune, and moreover, that he was immune. When I saw my father that evening, covered in dust, filthy with dirt and agony, I knew our lives would never be the same. It did not hit me that my father's work could amount to this. Nicholette's essay has helped me to clear some of the dust.
>
> I am not afraid of death. I often think about how or when I may die, but I always believe that God has a purpose for me. When my time has come, I will die. However, I refuse to believe this for my family. I am emotionally and physically exhausted daily, worrying about my parents, my sisters, and my brother. I cannot sleep at night because anxiety fills my body, and I shake down to my bones. I cried to my mother about a month ago because of the helplessness I feel on a daily basis. I am a controlling person, at least for my own life. I cannot control the well-being of my family; I cannot control when they will die. My mother tells me that I will make myself sick worrying about where everyone is going and if they are safe. She tells me that I am exactly like my father. My father tells me that I should not worry about his lungs, that is why we have doctors. Will I forever toss and turn through sleepless nights,

pondering every possible bad scenario? I am afraid. I cannot turn back the clocks and tell my father to stay home from work, to make sure he wears his mask. If I could give him my lungs I would, although he would probably not take them. He is the most selfless individual I know, which makes me angry with him. He does not want to inconvenience anyone, nor does he want to abandon his optimistic outlook. I think it is natural to worry about the people we love, but for me that is not enough. My hands are tied and I cannot break loose. There is nothing I can do to help my father, I think even if I was a doctor, my efforts would be to little avail. I have watched my friends lose their parents, and I have seen how they hurt to this day. My father appears to be a healthy 44-year-old man, and his illness slowly progresses. But I know better than to believe what you see. I know that parents will do everything in their power to protect their children, especially mine. I know that I am helpless, and all the worrying in the world will change nothing.

I think that there are students in my class who feel the same way; they may feel either helpless about past situations, or be troubled right now. I am comforted listening to everyone's essays in class, not because of their sadness or hardships, but because I feel less alone. We can all relate to each other, and perhaps provide each other with an outlet for our pain. These are not feelings I discuss with anyone, however, knowing that I am not alone gives me hope. I am inspired to see that Professor Berman and so many of my classmates are strong individuals. I think there will be other essays like Nicholette's to help me open up and face talking about the things which I fear the most. I am thankful that she wrote so emotionally about my love and loss; she helped me say what I could not say myself.

What shall we say about this remarkable diary entry? To begin with the obvious, it *is* a remarkable entry, remarkable in the power of its prose, its honesty and openness, and its awareness of what may be called connected knowledge, which Belenky, Clinchy, Goldberger, and Tarule (1986) describe as knowledge based on personal, subjective truth. Gone are the flat, imageless sentences of the first love and loss assignment, replaced by sentences that implicate us in the anxiety she feels over her father's health. Isabella writes with a testimonial fervor that is absent from her earlier writing; her sentences now combine emotional intensity and cognitive insights. She shows us how worry and rumination take their toll on her body. Regardless of whether it was numbness or naivete that prevented her from realizing her firefighter father was at "work" rather than at the scene of the vaporized World Trade Center, she recalls the sleeplessness and worry, the unending helplessness, the feeling that she is literally sick with worry.

Isabella's diary shows us not only how she grieves over her father's health but also how her classmate's words have affected her understanding of her father's situation. She cannot explain why Nicholette's words have affected her so deeply, at least not in the beginning of the diary, but she shows the emotional impact of her classmate's words. Nicholette's essay has allowed Isabella to open up, revealing her anxiety. She doesn't regret disclosing this terror even if it results in exposing her vulnerability to classmates and teacher. Isabella's connection with her classmates is so strong that she is comforted by the knowledge that they can understand how she feels. There is nothing naive or sentimental about Isabella's closeness with her classmates. She affirms not the platitude that "misery loves company" but the insight that we feel less alone when we know others can understand our fears. I cannot imagine a more eloquent ending to an essay or diary entry than Isabella's final sentence, in which she pays tribute to her classmate Nicholette: "she helped me say what I could not say myself."

How did Nicholette feel about her own essay? Why was she willing to disclose the "one anxiety" that she intended to keep hidden? She confronts these questions in her next diary:

> My absent father is a sore subject to discuss. I don't really talk about it to anyone other than my brother or my aunt who I am really close to. My mother and I don't really speak about it because she tried to conceal that part of my life as much as possible throughout my childhood. It is a sort of understanding that we have in which case we just leave it as "I don't have a father" and that's all. I anticipated that I would be nervous reading the essay that I had written out loud because I only like to share my writings with my teachers, not my peers. Towards the end of reading the essay, I started to choke up on some sentences in which I pretended to clear my throat so that I can try and compose myself. The weird part is that I haven't cried about my father in a long time and for some reason I cried during this class. I don't know if it's because I was talking about Isabella's wonderful FDNY father and was wishing that I had her father, but it got to me. After class, Isabella came up to me and gave me a hug and said, "thank you." I think we were both deeply affected by the essay, and I guess hearing someone read it out loud in front of a silent classroom just makes it more effective because more than 20 other people now know our stories.

"There's Too Much Covering Up of Grief in America"

Monday, February 11 and Wednesday, February 13

It took us five full classes, two and one-half weeks, to read aloud the Assignment 2 essays. They were moving in many ways: as a reflection of the students' major loves and losses; as a record of their anticipated fears, as we saw in Nicholette's essay about Isabella's dread of her father's worsening health; and as a snapshot of contemporary American society, where so many grown children continue to grieve over their parents' failed marriages. Some of these students, like Nicholette, grow up without knowing their fathers, and they experience what James Herzog (2001) calls "father hunger," the yearning for a father who is either physically or emotionally absent from his children's lives as a result of divorce.

Apart from the loss of an intact family, the first two writing assignments revealed that the greatest single loss for most students is a grandparent's death. Many students listed these deaths in their Assignment 1 essays, though their biographers did not select them for the Assignment 2 essays. "My grandma died a year ago this month," Bianca states:

> No one close to me had ever died until her. She was such a strong woman, and although she was always in and out of doctors' offices because of health problems, no one really thought she would die. It happened very quickly and it was the worst thing I have ever experienced. It was especially tough on my mother because they were so close. I think about my grandma everyday, and I just hope she knows how grateful that I am to her for having been in my life.

Lucy was similarly devastated when her grandfather died more than a decade ago:

> I still remember the day so vividly, and I still cry when I think about it. This was the hardest day of my life. I was so young and had to deal with such a massive concept that I was not ready to, nor able to, accept it. It was the worst pain I have ever felt and when I think of him that feeling comes back. I barely remember him and I will never really know him, but the worst

41

part is that the day of his death was the day that my family fell apart. Eleven years later, almost to the date, I had to watch my family drift even further [apart] when my uncle (my dad's brother) died from lung cancer.

Maggie's greatest loss was also her grandfather, who died in 2006. She included a paragraph from the obituary she wrote for her local newspaper.

I wrote his obituary because I couldn't stand the thought of someone from a newspaper, who didn't even know him, write the basic information without understanding that he was more than just a father, and a husband, and a grandpa. He was a friend and someone who made you laugh at the dinner table, and someone who cleaned your scrapes and cuts after you had fallen off your bike. The obituary had the usual information in it, but I added touches to it, to make it more personal.

Daphne listed her grandmother as her second greatest love (next to her boyfriend) and her greatest loss:

My grandmother was a huge part of my life before she died. She died on October 2nd, 2005. Things in my life occasionally seem to follow a pattern of uncertainty ever since. My grandmother was terrified of her death. She was diagnosed with pancreatic cancer in early 2005. As the months went by I grew less and less able to come over. Everyone else in my grandmother's family discouraged her from talking about her fears as she went through chemotherapy. At 2:23 AM on October 2nd, I woke up alert from a dream that my grandmother had died. I saw a vision of her in the hospital bed at hospice. My other deceased relatives surrounded her. When I awoke, I first looked at the clock. The minute changed to 2:24, and the phone rang. My life hasn't been the same since.

Daphne's premonition of her grandmother's death, awakening from a dream precisely at the moment of the death, illustrates what Janice Winchester Nadeau (1998) calls "coinci*dancing*," a term that captures "the action of grieving people as they used coincidences to construct meanings. The *dancing* part of the term is intended as a play on the active and interactive nature of using coincidences to make sense of a death" [italics in original] (p. 126).

Many students imply in their essays or diaries that they continue to grieve over loved ones years after their deaths. Rather than detaching themselves from the deceased, withdrawing their "libido," as Freud (1917/1957) recommends in "Mourning and Melancholia," they remain connected to the dead. These students demonstrate what Klass, Silverman, and Nickman (1996) call a "continuing bonds" approach to bereavement. Citing a statement made by the playwright Robert Anderson after the death of his first wife—"Death ends a life, but it does not end a relationship, which struggles on in the survivor's mind toward some resolution which it never finds" (p. 17), Klass, Silverman, and Nickman propose that "it is normative for mourners to maintain a presence and connection with the deceased" (p. 18). Few people consciously seek to hold on to grief, but

I'm reminded of a statement in Philip K. Dick's 1975 novel, *Flow My Tears, the Policeman Said*: "grief is the final outcome of love, because it's lost love" (p. 102). Tolstoy also knew about the redemptive nature of grief; the epigraph to J. William Worden's (2002) *Grief Counseling and Grief Therapy* contains an often-quoted passage by the Russian novelist: "Only people who are capable of loving strongly can also suffer great sorrow, but this same necessity of loving serves to counteract their grief and heals them."

For some students, like Daphne, it was understandably easier to write about love than loss. "I could talk for hours about the things I love, but my losses, well, I've tried to tuck them away." Nicholette felt the same way. "The losses were hard to write about because I didn't want to think about those memories, and it took time to get over the losses, and writing about them just brings up memories that I didn't want to think about." And yet for a surprising number of students, writing about loss proved unexpectedly easier. "When I wrote about the losses," Lucy comments, "all of my feelings seemed to pour out; there was no thinking about why it was hard or how I felt, I just knew." Cath felt that love, unlike loss, is impossible to describe. "I knew the losses would be easier to write about. Losses are more concrete. A loss I can clearly see—I can describe it and what made it so painful." Gloria pointed out that most of the Assignment 2 essays were written on loss. "I first thought that it was going to be easier to write about our greatest loves; however, in my first two writing assignments, I found it was just the opposite. I am finding that when writing about death, you don't have to make it depressing or morbid. A perfect example of this is your 'Eulogy for Barbara'."

A course devoted to love and loss heightens one's awareness of life and death, reminding us to appreciate those who are still with us. "After every class," Addison writes in her first diary entry, "I have spoken to my parents and boyfriend and expressed how much I love and need them. My friends and I discuss how this class is extremely helpful in making me realize just how special the people in my life really are. I have tried to imagine where I would be if (God forbid) any of them were to pass away tomorrow. My first reaction is that I don't think I could continue living. I don't mean that I would want to kill myself. I mean that quite simply, it would be difficult for me to continue living life without them there by my side." Cath expresses a similar fear that she would not survive the death of her mother, though she immediately qualifies herself. "My mom is the most important person [in my life]. Like Jeff said, I always think I would die if something happened to her. But I know she would not want that. She'd be furious. She would want me to live my life; she would want me to make something great of myself." I can't recall whether in *Dying to Teach* I implied that I might not be able to survive my wife's death, but the fact that I have survived—and continue to write about her ongoing importance to my life—reassured my students that they, too, could survive the deaths of their loved ones.

No one regretted a self-disclosure in the first two writing assignments, although Ayla wondered whether she should have revealed that her parents almost divorced. "I wrote about how my parents almost got a divorce, and that's not something that a lot of people know. I wanted to take back what I wrote because I think that when I was writing the assignment, I forgot that I would have to share it with the class. But I'm glad that I got it out there because people have written more personal things than that and what I wrote about was minute compared to things others have experienced."

Many students find the contagion phenomenon intriguing, and they are becoming aware of it in their own lives. "I was happy that you handed out the 'emotional contagion' text at the beginning of Monday's class," Scout writes. "After telling my friends for the last couple of days about the classes I am taking, I have repeatedly heard similar statements about how sad this class must be, and I have had questions about why I would want to learn about death. Although I knew when I was signing up for this class, and even when I was handed the syllabus on the first day, that I want to take this class, as I started telling other people about the class, my confidence seemed to waiver." With each negative response from her friends, she began to fear that she had made a mistake in signing up for the course. When she received the class handout on the contagion theory, however, she decided she was glad she was in the course. "I realized that I did not have to be so sad, and that, moreover, just as sadness is contagious, so is happiness. I think I might like you to reinforce throughout the semester the benefits of this class."

For Assignment 3, a continuation of Assignment 2, I paired each student with a different classmate, and each wrote an essay describing how love or loss has changed the other person's life. This assignment was due on Monday, and I asked students to bring only two copies, one for their partner and the other for me. (We were still discussing the Assignment 2 essays, and we did not have time to discuss the Assignment 3 essays in class.) With a few exceptions, students were reluctant in the early assignments to describe in detail how a relative's or friend's death has changed their lives, a criticism that Nico points out in his diary entry:

> A noted deficiency in most essays: events such as death and loss are outlined, but the effect of these events upon the subject is outside the scope of the argument. What happens when people die? Sure, they decompose at a more or less constant rate. But what happens to the people left behind who have to cope with the life altering changes produced by the death of a loved one? How are daily schedules, the minutiae of life, affected by death? We register death in how it affects the living. Thus far, most essays choose either to talk in general terms about the now deceased, or to give a flattering obit/biography. . . . There's too much covering up of grief in America. I remember a wonderful scene in an early episode of *Six Feet Under*, in which the good looking brother comments on the death ritual in America, how sanitized it is, how the funeral home director will take a crying mourner

into a private room. But he remembers being on a boat off the coast of Sicily, and seeing a funeral procession on the beach, and he remembers how the wife of the dead man and her children threw themselves on the casket and wailed in total despair. Yes, that's what death is like. Let's not rush to what we've learned from it all before we've done a good job of feeling it. The students are not yet really talking about death. Will they?

I suspect that one of the reasons most students are not yet ready to write specifically about death is that they have never done so in another course. Their anxiety is still high. They must be emotionally ready to write about painful topics, a conclusion Mark Bracher (1999) also reaches in his insightful book *The Writing Cure*: "a truly psychoanalytic pedagogy would allow students to confront the contingency of their identity and the ineluctability of their unconscious desires and gratifications at their own pace, taking care that the student's level of anxiety never becomes overwhelming" (p. 6).

Addison and Chipo

Of the Assignment 3 essays turned in this week, Addison's was one of the most moving and memorable. Clinicians tell us that suicide is the most difficult death to work through because relatives and friends are usually overwhelmed by grief, anger, sadness, confusion, and guilt. One of the paradoxes is that the closer one is to the person who commits suicide, the more guilt one feels. Another paradox is that suicide is a symbolic murder of another person, which helps to explain why the legacy—or illegacy—of suicide is a lifetime of anger, guilt and grief. Because of the cultural and religious stigma of suicide, a relative or friend often experiences disenfranchised grief, making it difficult to express sorrow. The first loss Addison cited in Assignment 1 was her brother's suicide. "My brother committed suicide when I was six years old. He was 21. Although his loss did not affect me directly (I was too young to really understand), it has affected me throughout these years through my mom. My mom did not have a chance to grieve." A few days after Addison's brother died, her mother came to her dance recital, and then to her kindergarten graduation. Addison added that as much as her mother wanted to lie in bed and never get up, she knew she had other children who needed her. "This loss is important to me," she concluded, because it has shaped my opinion of my mom. Hearing her tell me about these things makes me hope that someday I can be as strong as she has been for all these years." Addison's first biographer did not focus on this event, but her second biographer, Chipo, did:

> Addison's brother, Mick, committed suicide. She was only six when her family was shocked by the news. Her mother was distraught because she had to bury her son. Saying goodbye is not a memory she wishes to have had, instead she would rather attend Addison's dance recital and graduation. Unfortunately, she attended both. All the while juggling emotions that would make anyone have an anxiety attack.

Addison could not understand death. How could she, when grown-ups don't understand death? But she remembers her mother's pain. Her mother did not have time to grieve. But her character shined like gold for enduring the pain to be present for her remaining children. Addison believes her mother is "admirable" for her strength. She says, "If I lost a child, I would lay in bed and be miserable." She is effected more by suicide because she is older.

Suicide has to be one of the worst experiences a family can be put through. Addison's father was Mick's step-father so he did not take his death as hard. But on birthdays and the anniversary of Mick's death her mom is saddened. She thinks about her son often, but she is more willing to talk about him now.

Growing up, Addison recalls her mom blaming herself for her sons actions. But after going through therapy that is changing. Addison does not mind talking about her brother. She just does not like seeing her mom sad because her emotions affect her. She uses her experience as a tool to prevent further suicides. She would rather talk about her loves, but when she speaks about her losses, she becomes more grateful.

When I read Addison's story about her brother, my mind went blank. I wondered how I would deal with an experience like that. I don't know if I could even though I lost my mom in 2001 and my grandfather in 2007. I still don't know if I can handle life without them. If a relative committed suicide, I would feel like there was more I could have done to prevent the loss of my family member. I would think I was selfish and did not put enough effort towards understanding how this person felt. Addison is courageous for being able to talk about her brother and remain positive. Her courage ignites my desire to be happy and chase my dreams. I do not understand how strong either of us are. When people are forced to be strong, we exceed expectations.

When I spoke to Addison over the phone, I could not stop thinking what a difference communicating our experiences makes. I never knew anyone who committed suicide, and I don't think I took the time to think about how families are affected. Her experience makes me understand that I was not the only one hurt by losing my mom. My sister is forced to grow up without her mother and no longer able to have as intimate a relationship with that side of her family. My sister's father grieves over my mom and how he deals with those emotions effects my sister and I. I can only imagine how my grandfather felt about burying his daughter. Addison's experience brings forth thought about how I can deal with the loss of my grandfather differently. But what remains uncertain is how my family is going to recover from losing him, when the wounds of my mother's death never healed.

I thought it would be important for the entire class to hear this essay, and so I asked Chipo and Addison for permission to read it aloud. They readily agreed. Everyone in the class could hear how the collaborative assignment enabled Chipo to discuss not only Addison's losses but his own as well. He writes about personal knowledge; suicide is not simply a statistic that happens to other families but an event that his classmate and her mother live with everyday. Suicide is so shocking to Chipo that his "mind went blank." And yet he tries to imagine its impact on Addison's family. Despite the comma splice and sentence fragment in the first paragraph, the incorrect conjugation of "lie" in the second paragraph, the failure to include the apostrophe in "son's" in the fourth paragraph, and the confusion of "effect" and "affect" in the second and final paragraphs, the essay is thoughtful, empathic, and respectful. He captures the ways in which a son's suicide affects his mother and sister differently, Addison's sensitivity to her mother's grief, and his classmate's desire to prevent future suicides. In the last two paragraphs he shows how Addison's ability to survive her brother's suicide inspires him to remain hopeful about his own future. His point of view has suddenly expanded: he now thinks about his sister's and grandfather's grief over his mother's death, something he did not write about the previous semester. Feeling kinship with Addison, a fellow sufferer, he concludes the essay by reflecting on how families heal from devastating losses.

By the end of week four, everyone seems comfortable with the format of the course. They indicate in their diaries that they find Love and Loss challenging. No one has expressed any criticisms or problems, and no one has dropped the course. We begin each class in the same way, revising sentences from the preceding week's essays. Each class contains both playful and serious moments, as Nico suggests in this week's diary entry:

> Class began in the usual fashion, with nervous chit-chat dying down as Jeff and I walked in. I've started to pay closer attention to how long we spend on various tasks, and I've realized just how much time Jeff devotes to helping his students become better writers. We spent the first 25 minutes of the class on student-generated sentence corrections. Jeff is *amazing* at this. Who else could make sentence correction so entertaining? He takes what might otherwise be a boring procedural and turns it into a contest of intellect, wills, and cunning between his students and himself. He's willing to bet a dollar when he senses that the answer to a problem might be slightly beyond the class's ability, and this causes excitement and anticipation as students enact a Freudian fantasy of taking down a figure of Authority.
>
> At around 6:15 Jeff read Addison's essay about Chipo, the young man mentioned in previous journal entries who lost his mother due to a car accident at the tender age of 14. Generally, there's a convivial air in the room, with quick, pithy interjections from students breaking up Jeff's flow, but when Jeff read Addison's essay the class was dead silent. Students conspicuously avoided eye contact. Four students covered their mouth with a hand, a sign of a desire not to speak or to be called upon to speak. What, after all, can you say about a mother's death? Fuck! Jeff found ways to lighten the mood, and I wondered if this was intentional, or if he too was reacting to the content of the essay by pulling back, even unconsciously. He made corrections as he read along. He joked about his big ears. The whole thing took only five minutes per my notes, but in my memory, this was a much longer period of time.
>
> At 6:20 we moved from the pain of parental loss to the pain of spotting misplaced and dangling modifiers. At 6:35 we started in on students' essays.

Jeff has a policy of not commenting on the content of student writing and of focusing instead on stylistic and grammatical issues. He does this out of sensitivity to their feelings, especially when the subject matter is touchy. However, my experience as a fiction teacher leads me to believe that there are additional ways that students could grow as writers through writing non-fiction essays of a personal nature, and that a methodology could be implemented that would not harm students. Any piece of writing can be improved through not only fixing style and grammar, but also by finding ways that the author could make a true account more vivid, specific, suspenseful, a reflection of authentic character development. . . . As I tell my students of fiction, "Make your reader suffer!" I also tell them, "Make us *care* about your characters."

CHAPTER 5—WEEK FIVE
"We're Going To Die"

Monday, February 18 No Class—President's Day

Wednesday, February 20

I handed back the Assignment 3 essays, and we began to discuss the Assignment 4 essays, which were due today, on "Shattered Assumptions," a topic I began to research after Barbara's death. As defined by Colin Murray Parkes (1975), an assumptive world is a "strongly held set of assumptions about the world and the self which is confidently maintained and used as a means of recognizing, planning and acting" (p. 132). Before Barbara's diagnosis, we shared the three beliefs that Ronnie Janoff-Bulman (1992) proposes are at the "core" of most people's assumptive worlds: the belief that the world is benevolent, the belief that the world is meaningful, and the belief that the self is worthy (p. 6). *Dying to Teach* opens with the destruction of a major component of my assumptive world, the belief that Barbara, who could have been a poster child for living a healthy life, would reach her nineties, an age attained by all of her relatives, including her parents and grandparents. There was no hint of cancer on either side of her family. Because many of my own relatives have died prematurely of cancer, I had always assumed that I would predecease Barbara by 20 years. I imagined, as I lay dying, that I would tell her she meant the world to me, a statement I expressed nearly every day of our married life. "I never viewed this fantasy as morbid or unrealistic," I wrote in the opening paragraph of *Dying to Teach*, "though it might have been self-centered, as fantasies often are, in that I was not only the center of attention in this dying drama but also spared from the grief of watching a loved one suffer."

Barbara's death shattered my assumptive world, forcing me to develop new assumptions. Like others, I have experienced posttraumatic growth, a heightened ability to empathize and sympathize with other people, especially with those who have endured a devastating loss. Barbara is no longer here, but I continue to write about her, trying to bring her to life for my students and readers. Life is diminished in many ways, but it is still filled with beauty and meaning. Bernard

Malamud's statement that life is a tragedy filled with joy reflects my own experience. I feel joy when I am with my children and grandchildren, when I am in the classroom, when I am with my friends, when I am with Julie, and when I am, paradoxically, writing about lost love. Love is never lost as long as one continues to write about it.

For Assignment 4, I asked my students to write an essay showing how an experience of love or loss has shattered their assumptive world and led to a new assumptive world. Unlike Assignments 2 and 3, this was not a collaborative effort. I asked about a third of the class to volunteer to read their essays aloud.

Kasia and Lucy

Kasia's assumptive world—her innocence—was shattered on September 11, 2001, as she noted in Assignment 1.

> I wouldn't say that this day was the worst of my life even though I was in the World Trade Center that day, but I would definitely say that the effects of that day will keep coming and haunting me for the rest of my life. Before then I never had any real anxiety about anything and I wasn't afraid of so much. I have never been as scared as I was on that day and the only reason I got through it was because my sister was with me. I am not sure what I lost on that day but even though I always knew the world wasn't a safe place, that day I found out that it was a malicious one."

In her diary that week, Kasia noted that she and her partner for Assignment 2 had agreed to focus on love rather than loss, but she did not object when her partner for Assignment 3, Lucy, decided to write about Kasia's experience in the World Trade Center on that fateful day:

> September 11, 2001: a day made infamous to Americans. On that date, I was a sophomore in high school, attending classes in Colonie, N.Y., almost 200 miles from the attacks on the World Trade Center. At this vulnerable age, I could not grasp this concept as suddenly as it happened. It took me a few hours to understand the severity of the situation. Kasia, however, did not have a few hours; she had only seconds to take in what was happening. On the morning of September 11, 2001 Kasia was walking through the towers on her way to school when the attacks occurred.
>
> Kasia was also a sophomore in high school in the fall of 2001, and on that particular day she was running late. She and her sister Katia were cutting through the towers as they normally did on their way to school. The two were in the building during the attacks, but fortunately were able to make their way out safely to the front of the buildings. It was not before long that the true terror of the situation would surface. Kasia wrote, in an email to me, "The most vivid and horrific memory of my life is when I got out of the building and stood across the street with my sister and a crowd of people. Constantly looking up I saw many things falling from the office and when my eyes focused hard on one of the objects I saw legs and arms and realized I

was looking at people falling and not things. That is when I lost my composure and my sister basically had to take care of me."

I cannot begin to imagine the sight that Kasia had described to me, and as a teenager in high school, I cannot imagine what must have been racing through Kasia's mind after seeing what she saw. Luckily for Kasia, she had a loved one with her that day, her sister, her "angel." Katia helped her sister through this traumatic event, even though Katia was only a teenager herself. Kasia was hysterical because she was in this place she had known forever, a place that was part of her home, but she had no idea where to go or what to do. She was amazed at how calm and collected her sister seemed to be during the disaster. Katia, whether she was fearless or full of fear, showed only a mask of bravery to her baby sister that day.

Kasia has since had to deal with a developing anxiety; she is constantly worrying about those with whom she is close, and fears for the lives of her friends and family on a daily basis. Kasia worries about incidents that, prior to September 11, 2001, she probably would have deemed insignificant. She wrote, "if I haven't heard from [my dad and my sister] in three or more days I get worried. . . . If I call and they do not pick up, I really freak."

I felt it best to end with Kasia's words, because I agree completely and I am very sorry that she had to experience at such a young age, or at all, for that matter, how malicious the world can be. She writes, "I know that if I hadn't been there that day, then I would never have been so deeply touched and disturbed by [the attacks]. I never would be able to grasp the idea of [them] no matter how many pictures or news stories I heard about [that day]. You had to be there to truly understand how horrific it really was.

In her diary that week, Lucy wrote about her shock when interviewing Kasia; Lucy feared that she did not do justice to her classmate's horrific experience:

When I read Kasia's paper for Assignment 1, I was surprised. I don't know a better way to describe it. She was in the World Trade Center during the September 11 attacks, and up until now, I have never known anyone who was affected by the terrorist attacks directly. Because of my shock (I had not anticipated questioning anyone about September 11), I ran out of questions for Kasia quickly. We exchanged email addresses and assured each other that we check our accounts regularly, and we would be willing to answer any questions that might arise during the writing process.

I began writing the paper, but was not sure where to go. I emailed Kasia with a few questions I had thought of, and she sent me back beautiful, yet heartwrenching answers to my questions. There were many powerful statements in her response, and I could not help but tear up. She brought me back to that day, and I'm sorry, Jeff, but I don't know that I was able to empathize with her. I tried. But I knew that I would never be able to grasp completely how she felt that day. I have never watched people plunge to their deaths, or been so scared that I could not move, and, as tears stream down my face as I think of it now, I thank God that I have been protected from the malicious world that Kasia spoke of.

I was scared in upstate New York after learning of the attacks; I cannot imagine being right there, being part of the tragedy. I believed her when she wrote, "You had to be there to truly understand how horrific it was." I can only try to understand her feelings that day and the anxiety she has to overcome everyday; I think she is much stronger than she may give herself credit for.

One senses from every paragraph of Lucy's essay and diary how sensitive she is to her classmate's experience. Just as Kasia lost her composure on that fateful fall day, so did Lucy lose her composure when writing about her classmate's experience. Kasia's dark emotions spread to her, evoking shock, sadness, and tears. And also, inexplicably, guilt. Lucy would be less self-blaming if she realized that no one is able to "grasp completely" another person's feelings, especially if that person has experienced a traumatic event. Kasia didn't comment on her reactions to Lucy's essay, but she said that she intended to use Assignment 4 to write about her experience on September 11. "I have been thinking about our next assignment a lot because I know that I have a challenge ahead of me. I have written about 9/11 once before and that was in my journal the week that it happened. One of my former teachers had actually asked me two years ago to write about my experience that day and I told her that I just couldn't. Now it doesn't feel as much of a threat but I would just feel more comfortable if someone else read it aloud." Kasia's statement reminds us that students must be psychologically ready to write about traumatic experiences. They should not be pressured into self-disclosure. She almost certainly would not have agreed to write about her experience if she feared criticism from her classmates or teacher.

Kasia volunteered to bring in copies of Assignment 4 if I agreed to read it aloud in class, a request to which I immediately agreed:

At times I feel guilty saying that September 11th, 2001 may have been the worst day of my life because I didn't lose a loved one as others I know did. But being at the World Trade Center that day shattered the world I knew, or maybe the world I wanted to keep on living.

My sister and I attended the same high school, and we took the E train to school every weekend to its last stop, the World Trade Center. Running late, as we often did, we arrived at the WTC at 8:47 am. When the train doors opened, we stepped out into the platform into chaos. All the people were running around, scattering as fast as they could, and we had no idea why. When we asked someone what was all the commotion about, the lady replied, "there's a fire." Because we didn't see any fire or smoke, we stayed calm and found our nearest exit. Coming out from the tower, we led our way across the street where many people were looking up. So we did the same thinking that anything postponing further going to first period would be fun. Looking up, we saw a lot of smoke but it didn't seem like anything serious. In my mind, everyone had already evacuated the building and the fire would be put out soon.

Staring for a few minutes, we decided it would be best to head to class. "Look, there's another one. Look!" Who could keep from looking when hearing that plea? My eyes searched the sky surrounding the building but I only saw papers and other office supplies falling from the smoke. Once again I heard the plea and I desperately wanted to see what everyone else saw, that is, until I did. I focused on one of the falling pieces and realized that what I was looking at was flailing arms and legs. Instantly I averted my eyes, and they were filled with tears.

I am blessed that I had my sister there with me because at that moment, I would have remained in that place, crippled by death. I never understood how she kept so calm, but I am forever grateful to her. "There's another one. Oh my god, there's another one." I no longer looked up and couldn't believe the people surrounding me acted so jaded. With each of their screams I fell further apart, and my sister kept me breathing.

As my sister held me, the second plane hit, and the ground shook as I had always imagined it would during an earthquake. "We're going to die" was the only thought in my head as my sister grabbed my hand and started running. I have always been terrible with direction but at that moment, you would have never thought that I had been going to a high school a block away for over a year.

I followed my sister while she tried to get her cell phone to work. I desperately wished to be home, but even then I felt that there was nowhere I would be safe. On the way home we saw the towers fall, and my sister kept me from doing the same. She led us to Brooklyn and after four draining hours we were home.

I didn't know what to do or what to think. The images kept replaying on the television for weeks, and I never looked at them again after that day. I never spoke about the events of that day. But I remember them all too well and think of them often. I had always known that the world was a dangerous place, but I had never felt that fear until 9/11. I have never felt such hatred until 9/11. And I had never truly understood the value of life until 9/11.

That day shattered my world. It shattered who I was and made me who I am today. I never valued my former world until it was gone. Even though it took a few years to realize the effect that 9/11 had on me, I now know that it was that day that made me fear life itself.

The destruction of Kasia's assumptive world required, as Samuel Heilman (2005) observes about those who experienced the horror of September 11, a "transformation and 'meaning-making' of prodigious proportions" (p. 11). Robert A. Neimeyer (2001) argues that *"meaning reconstruction in response to a loss is the central process in grieving"* [italics in original] (p. 4). Kasia still ponders the traumatic destruction of her assumptive world. She has not yet emerged from the dark aftermath of loss, including her fear of life; nevertheless, for the first time she is willing to write about the experience so that others can understand how she felt on that fateful day.

"I didn't enjoy writing Assignment 4," Kasia admitted in her diary that week, "but I wanted to do it for myself and I am proud that I did. I thought it was going to be harder than it was, but I think that while I was writing I distanced myself. The hardest part was finding the write way to say what I wanted to say, but no words seemed to be able to fulfill that. But I think that I did the best I could about describing what I felt and feel." Kasia refers to finding the "write" way to express herself when she obviously means the "right" way, but perhaps this error suggests the importance of writing to help her make sense of her shattered assumptions.

It was easier for Kasia to write about her traumatic experience than to speak about it, as she makes clear in a postscript in her next diary:

> Something happened in Monday's class, and when it did I immediately thought that I had to write it in this entry. It's such a silly thing and yet it was important to me. You announced in class that I would be reading my Assignment 4 essay in class, and I immediately froze and thought I would faint. I stopped and thought, "Oh my God, did he forget that I had asked him to read my assignment? Or does he want me to push myself and read it myself?" It was such a silly thing, but I got so scared for some reason, and I felt myself turning very red. I think that you might have forgotten that I had asked you to read my paper or that you meant that it was just going to be read regardless by whom. Clearly from the intense reaction that I experienced, I am not ready or feel the least bit comfortable reading it aloud myself.

I hadn't forgotten. I would never force a student to read aloud a personal essay about a traumatic experience. Nor would I force a student to write about a traumatic experience. Just because students are ready to write about an experience does not mean they are ready to read it aloud. As I suggested earlier, it is often more difficult to read an essay aloud than it is to write it. I don't recall how I managed to maintain my composure while reading Kasia's essay in class, but ironically, I found my body shaking as I typed her words into my word processor for this book. Kasia's courage in writing the essay awed everyone in the class. Opponents of personal writing claim that students who write on traumatic experiences will be retraumatized in the process, but this can be avoided if they have the freedom *not* to write—or speak—on any topic that is too personal or threatening. I agree with Marian Mesrobian MacCurdy's (2007) observation in *The Mind's Eye*: "My first dictum—never mandate a topic—allows students to choose their own and protects both student and teacher. I have never had a student choose to venture into difficult territory who was not ready to make the journey" (p. 87).

However chaotic her experience was in the World Trade Center, Kasia now writes with admirable clarity and control. She begins by expressing guilt that she didn't lose a loved one, existential guilt, which one may feel when losing a relative or friend. She begins the essay slowly, telling us that one of her first thoughts was that she was happy to miss the first period of school. She then points us in the direction of the falling objects from the towers. She masterfully reproduces in us the dilemma between responding to or ignoring the pleas, "Look, there's another one. Look!" She can't help looking—nor can we—until she realizes that the falling objects are the flailing arms and legs of people jumping to their deaths. She then immediately averts her eyes, blocking our own vision of the horrific scene. She shows us only that which is necessary: not for a moment does she sensationalize the event. I can't improve upon the simple power of the words, "We're going to die."

We can understand Kasia's reluctance to speak or write about September 11th, yet we're glad that she was able to break the seven-year silence. If many of us are exhausted by the countless stories we have read about that day, like the people Kasia describes who appeared "so jaded" by the falling bodies, we are nonetheless moved by her account, as Nico reveals in his diary:

> Kasia's essay was a heartfelt account of a subject that, in my mind, always runs the risk of sounding cliched and like a fabrication handed down through so many bits of media: the events of 9/11. Kasia told the story of witnessing the disaster one day while on her way to school with her sister. She described the horrors of realization, as her mind moved from state to state, from the interest that is natural in all human beings when in the presence of the catastrophic, to the moment beyond adrenaline when the mind turns to feelings of panic and revulsion. Through Kasia's eyes we witnessed the transformation of bits of falling debris into human beings plummeting to their death. One line, in particular, demonstrated Kasia's progress as a writer and her development of formidable poetic powers. "On the way home we saw the towers fall and my sister kept me from doing the same." During Jeff's reading of Kasia's essay, several students openly wept. One student passed another a tissue and was thanked.
>
> Though Kasia's essay was very successful, Jeff showed his commitment to helping his students develop their abilities as writers by asking of the class what more Kasia could do to invite our participation and interest in her written world:
>
> Jeff: "I'd like to see more of the sister."
> Addison: "What happened on the way home?"
> Gloria: "I'd like to hear more of noises."
> Cecilia: "Did she go back to school?"
> Jeff: "Was it hard to go back to New York? Have you had nightmares?"

We raised several questions for Kasia to explore in a future revision, but we didn't expect her to answer these questions in class. She might have been unable or unwilling to answer these questions without prolonged and careful reflection. I didn't want to do anything to make her feel more anxious—and it's likely that some of these questions are anxiety provoking. Nor did I want Kasia to feel pressured into additional self-disclosure. What I did want to do was to create an empathic classroom in which she could write publicly, for the first time, about the most horrific experience in her life. That she was able to do so is a tribute to her strength as a writer. She maintained her composure while I read the essay aloud, and she was glad that she shared the experience with her classmates. Recall Lucy's statement that Kasia is "much stronger than she may give herself credit for." Lucy and her classmates listened respectfully and absorbed her words. Many were moved to tears. I don't want to exaggerate the importance of Kasia's self-disclosure and her classmates' response to it, but if the empathic classroom is a microcosm of the larger world, then some of her core assumptions that were shattered by September 11—the belief that the world is benevolent, the belief that the world is meaningful, and the belief that the self is worthy—were recreated, at least momentarily. No one can disagree with Kasia's conclusion that the world is now a more dangerous place, but we demonstrated that the world of our classroom is safe enough to write about traumatic experiences without being retraumatized in the process. That in itself is a remarkable event.

"Thinking Like A Writer"

Monday, February 25 and Wednesday, February 27

Many students used Assignment 4, on "Shattered Assumptions," to explore whether they should forgive those who hurt or abandoned them. Beth wrote about her anger toward a grandfather who had always disappointed her. Confiding this anger to her mother, Beth was surprised by the advice she received. "'Don't waste your time being angry when you should forgive.' I stared at her in shock for a few seconds, and I finally felt those tears come out from the depths where I knew they were. It is embarrassing for me to cry in front of people, even my own mother, but it felt so good." Javarro's admiration for his father changed to bitter disillusionment when his father left his family, largely because of a drug addiction. "All my life he had taught me that a man should always provide for his family, regardless of the circumstances. I soon realized this was not the case for all families." After a near-fatal heart attack, his father promised that he would never again hurt his family. "I must admit that he has been a man of his word so far, and today he is living a healthy and successful life."

Not all students, however, could find it in their hearts to forgive those who failed them. Nicholette wrote that she could never forgive her father, who deserted the family when she was three. "My heart is healing everyday, and there is not a day that goes by where I don't think about my father. I always think to myself, 'If he could see me now, I would like to tell him how he tore my world apart. . . . Then I would like to tell him how he means nothing to me and that I will forget him from this moment on, but [how] he will spend the rest of his life thinking about me.'"

Lucy's shattered assumption involved the realization that there is never enough time to say goodbye to those we love. "My uncle's sudden death caused this crazy idea of 'one last goodbye' to vanish from my mind. Now I live by the assumption that there will never be one last goodbye. Since my uncle's death, there is rarely ever a phone call to or from my family that has ended in anything but 'I love you'."

Kamilluh and Jacob read aloud their essays on "Shattered Assumptions" that stirred everyone in the class. Kamilluh's essay evokes pain, while Jacob's evokes shame, dark emotions that swept over all of us.

Kamilluh

Kamilluh's beloved cousin Mahogany had died the previous year, and this was the major reason she wanted to take Love and Loss. "My biggest loss thus far in my life has been my cousin dying at the age of 19," she wrote in her opening assignment. "I cannot even begin to put in words how I feel or what went through my head the day I found out she was not going to be here anymore. Perhaps that is why I decided to take this course." Mahogany was Kamilluh's first and best friend, the person to whom she confided everything. "I was my complete self with her. I looked up to her. She made life fun. She made taking chances natural, and we even considered each other halves of one another. So, in essence, when I lost her, I lost a part of myself, which is not anything easy to deal with." In Expository Writing, Kamilluh had written about her cousin's life but not about her death. She never attempted to "put in words" how she felt about the loss. Now she was ready.

A deeply religious person, Kamilluh listed God as her most important love. "He is the ultimate source of life and love, and my life is all the better since I have accepted Him in it." Kamilluh was dismayed when I mentioned last semester my religious disbeliefs, and she spent most of her first Love and Loss diary entry discussing how my appearance seemed to belie my words. "I never saw someone so comfortable with death that did not believe in God. I never saw someone who had such a spiritual demeanor not believe as well, not to say that people who don't believe are evil, but I see they usually have another demeanor to them. I cannot explain [this] right now." She had no doubt that Barbara was in Heaven watching me. Nor did Kamilluh doubt that sooner or later I would realize this. "He talks to her picture, but it doesn't serve her justice because she is not only in a picture. She is in the atmosphere, God-sent. He sent her just for him. I truly believe that he will see his wife again. There is so much more than just this earth. I believe that without a doubt in my heart. Hopefully, one day, he will too."

Kamilluh's discussion of my "spiritual demeanor" touched me. I seldom regard myself as a spiritual person, even though I often think about spiritual questions. Her comments did not make me into a believer, but they did awaken in me the same feelings I experienced when the nurses at St. Peter's Hospital, where Barbara was treated, would offer their prayers—I felt gratitude for their concern. Robert C. Solomon's (2002) characterization of spirituality defines my own beliefs as well:

> Spirituality embraces love, trust, reverence, and wisdom, as well as the most terrifying aspects of life, tragedy, and death. Thinking of spirituality just in terms of our terrifying realization of loss of control and impending death is morbid, but thinking of spirituality only in terms of joy or bliss is

simple-minded, a way of (not) thinking that is rightly summarized as 'la-di-da.' If it is passion that constitutes human spirituality, it must be the whole spectrum of human passions—and thoughtful passions—that we must consider. Thus when I have to summarize naturalized spirituality in a single phrase, it is this: *the thoughtful love of life* [italics in original]. (p. 6)

Kamilluh's loss of her cousin did not weaken her faith in God, but it did shatter her assumptive world, as she revealed in Assignment 4:

> For 14 years of her life, my cousin had what most people consider a normal life. She frequently made herself the center of attention. In school, she was one of the most popular children. She was one of the best dancers in her ballet and African dance classes as well. She was a cheerleader in junior high school. The crowd would erupt in applause when she participated in parades, her pom poms flying high in the air as she landed to perform a split, and reached her hands in the air to catch them. I watched her in awe. To me, she could do anything. I watched her try to be "grown" while boys our age would approach her. She handled them the best she could, her unique laughter and toss of her long thick Indian hair transfixing them. However, she did have flaws.
>
> Until the age of 12, Mahogany would wake up to a warm substance in her bed, [which] most toddlers potty training could not identify: urine. Mahogany peed in the bed almost every night. She had plastic placed on her mattresses, and at one time had a device hooked up to her waist so that when she had to go to the bathroom during the night, she would receive a slight shock to wake her up. I remember her getting constant beatings because she could not hold her bladder, and most people thought it was due to nerves or laziness. At around 13, she began to experience other problems with her body that included swollen feet and hands. After going to several specialists to figure out what exactly was wrong with her, at age 14, we found out the reason for Mahogany's "accidents" was because she was born with kidney failure.
>
> Can you imagine the first 14 years of your life, living fairly normally, and then finding out you have a terminal disease? It is unreal. They informed her mother that the normal life span for a person in Mahogany's case was three to five years. Of course there were many exceptions. The first time she went into the hospital, she was close to death. Her heart stopped three times. I was in a state of shock. But when I saw how she recovered, even after a kidney transplant, I assumed she would be able to live longer. After all, since the day we knew what a family was, we talked about our future together: going to the same college, getting married at the same time, having children around the same time, living next door to each other until we were old, and so forth. At a young age, we made ourselves blood sisters in a secret ceremony where we pricked our fingers and rubbed them against each other to sign the deal. She was going to be around forever, or at least I thought.
>
> When I look back on everything, sometimes I cannot fathom that in only five years, a disease meant for her since the time she was born, would end her life. It is one case to lose a parent, someone who raised you to be

who you are. But to lose a friend, a person who knew more about you than probably any guardian, who you shared secrets with, someone who completed your statements, is unlike any feeling in the world. Associates are easy to come by; however, a *friend* is amongst the few.

My assumptive world was shattered into a million tears as I stood at her wake, watching her lie in her casket. It was eerie to see how everything around seemed familiar, as if I had been in this scene before. She was the first dead body I ever touched. She was so soft that it was still tough for me to believe that everything we hoped for was now just one person's goals. I did not cry that day because she did not have to suffer anymore. I knew she would rather have been somewhere else than be on dialysis for the rest of her life. I was the last person to talk to her from a phone, and the last person to see her the day of her wake. It was crazy. I never thought I would have to take this walk through life on earth, in my own assumptive world without her, feeling utterly alone.

The first paragraph of the essay conveys Mahogany's uniqueness. Noting nonjudgmentally that she was an attention seeker, Kamilluh then transitions smoothly to her cousin's bed-wetting followed by the worsening of her illness and death. She remains remarkably composed in the last paragraph, an emotional restraint that heightens the impact of the last word, *alone.*

Kamilluh read her essay aloud, and several of her classmates commented on it in their diaries. "Kamilluh's story on her cousin Mahogany allowed me to understand the ways in which she brought her cousin back to life through writing," observed Jacob. "The effect of the words in the first sentence made me interpret death as feeling cold. The last sentence reminded me of moments during my childhood which helped me understand how one could cope with the loss of a loved one." The essay also affected Cath, Kamilluh's classmate last semester in Expository Writing. "I had only known the happy Mahogany [last semester]. This new essay let me see her sickness. It brought me closer to her. I could feel their pain. I felt their hearts break. I could see Kamilluh's hand touching the cold skin of her best friend. I could see her as a small child knowing that moment was going to change her forever." Cath felt sympathy, not pity for Kamilluh. "She was brave when everything was pushing hard against her. She faced problems many adults couldn't understand. I didn't feel sorry for her; I'm proud of her." Shannon was so moved by Kamilluh's essay that it "*scared*" her.

In her diary entry, Kamilluh admitted that her classmates' responses surprised her. "I am so used to hearing people's reactions to others' essays that I never would have expected to have people react to mine. I did notice with the essays I wrote about my cousin in the past that I have never exposed her death, and how I felt about it. I think that may have been the difference this time around." Kamilluh appreciated her classmates' comments. "They gave me encouragement to continue being who I am. So to everyone who commented, thank you."

Unlike Kasia, Kamilluh wanted to read her essay aloud. "When Berman reads aloud, I almost cringe. His voice is so dry, and his tempo is so slow that it is eerie. The mixture of the voice and the content of death forces me to be alert. There is dramatics behind it that gets to me." Kamilluh was glad that she was able to read aloud the essay about her cousin's death. "I was contemplating for a long time whether I should do it or not. If Berman had read it, I think I would have needed to walk out of the classroom. No offense, Berman, but when you read, it is effective."

I certainly didn't take offense, but I was nevertheless startled by her observations. I always try to read essays and diaries respectfully, but I seldom consider how my speaking voice affects my students. I try not to convey "dramatics" when I read an intense essay. If anything, I suspect that my voice slows and perhaps takes on a different pitch when I read aloud emotionally charged essays and diaries. In doing so, I try to make essays less painful to hear. I never realized that my voice might make someone "cringe."

Jacob

"When my father cheated on my mother," Jacob wrote in Assignment 1, "it created the death of a marriage and separation of a family. Ever since I was a child, I have always envisioned him as being a perfect man and father, but continually cheating on my mother, he lost my respect. After learning that he was not perfect and that there are flaws to his character, I managed to forgive him." Jacob returned to this subject in his Assignment 4 essay:

> When Raoul Ramirez first met my mother Maria Gonzales at a dance party in a New York City college, their friendship evolved into a relationship. The moment she became pregnant, they decided to give up their college education in hopes of seeking employment opportunities. Mr. Ramirez became a New York City Yellow Cab driver while Ms. Gonzales became a home attendant. When Ms. Gonzales, my mother, gave birth to me, the medical staff placed me in intensive care as a result of being born with swelled up eyes. She became devastated after learning my eyes were swelled up because she was diagnosed as having gonorrhea. It was the first time; she started to suspect my father, Mr. Ramirez, was cheating.
>
> Despite being too young to understand what was occurring as a newborn, there were moments during my adolescent years where I witnessed a power struggle between him and my mother. Whenever she challenged his authority in the household, he would try to physically overpower her. I experienced domestic violence when he took my favorite "Bugs Bunny" glass cup and threw it at her. She dodged the glass cup, and it shattered on my head. I remember him apologizing while drunk and chasing my mother afterwards.
>
> When she grew tired of his refusal to provide the key or combination to his metallic safe, she waited for him to leave the house to rip it open with a wrench. Upon opening the safe, she discovered naked pictures of all the women he slept with along with the phone numbers and dates. I was there when she decided to pick up the phone to dial the numbers to all these women and issue verbal threats. That night, when he arrived home, she locked him

inside the closet and warned him that she would leave. When my father found out she was pregnant with her second child, he punched her in the stomach and gave her a black eye. My mother, Ms. Gonzales, used to wear skin lotion and sunglasses to disguise her bruises.

For a long time after Ms. Gonzales decided to marry him and give birth to his four children, he managed to remain faithful until I graduated high school. After I started attending community college, he started to cheat more often. There were days where he would say that he had to work for twenty-four hours on the cab and leave the house in a suit and tie. There were moments where he would use the money he accumulated from work and send it to women in the Caribbean. During the days I was away from home and in college I felt miserable and powerless. I remember telling my mother over the phone that I wanted to punch him in the face and kill him. The drama at home was causing my grades to fluctuate each semester. I would often find myself having nightmares where I was being pursued by a dark force over the course of several months.

I became overwhelmed with rage after learning that my mother was calling my grandmother to provide shocking details about my father. I would always ask my mother to leave my grandmother out of the drama because she would not be able to handle the news. The worst feeling I experienced in the presence of my grandmother was seeing her cry while telling me that she did not fail to raise her children properly as a mother. My grandmother would say the moment they reached adulthood; they left and forgot who raised them.

Now, at the age of 24, I don't blame my mother for continuing to hold to some resentment towards my father. Ever since I was a child I tried my best to block out all the bad memories and envision him as being a perfect father. I believe one of the reasons that contributed to him cheating was the amount of hours he spent working as a cab driver while my mother was taking care of the children. He is a man who has a habit of remaining indecisive when it involves women and money. I would have respected him more if he would have told my mother that he wanted a divorce instead of cheating and playing with the emotions of others. I have taken my father's mistakes into consideration and have learned from them. I realize he was abusing certain privileges during my childhood upbringing such as committing adultery or engaging in domestic violence. I had a difficult time understanding why he didn't use the privileges that were made available to him responsibly after he decided to marry my mother. The advice I offer to children who have witnessed domestic violence at home is to use the experience to strengthen the relationships you have with other individuals in the future. If you feel the need to argue with your spouse, I would advise you not to do it in front of the children.

Jacob's essay is filled with the concrete details that allow us to see this domestic violence, almost as if we were witnesses to its horror. I have never witnessed domestic violence myself, and I was shocked when he describes the glass cup, hurled at his mother, that shattered on his head. No less startling is the description of his drunken father punching his pregnant mother in the stomach. We can understand his indignation when his mother shares the "shocking details" of this story with his grandmother. Given the shame he feels over his father's behavior, one can imagine how hard it must have been for Jacob to write the Assignment 4 essay on "Shattered Assumptions" and then share it with his classmates and teacher.

There is a formality to Jacob's essay, conveyed by the many references to "Mr. Ramirez" and "Ms Gonzales," that may be significant. Jacob is a member of a minority group, and as Sue and Sue (1999) point out, race, culture, ethnicity, and gender may affect communication styles. Members of minority groups may be reluctant to engage in self-disclosure when it involves painful or shameful confessions about one's family. Just as counselors need to be sensitive to multicultural clients, so do writing teachers need to be sensitive to multicultural students. In certain cultures, intimate revelations are shared only with one's immediate relatives and, perhaps, close friends. To share these revelations with strangers may be exceedingly difficult and require both formality and distance in order to maintain dignity and self-respect.

Jacob read his essay aloud in a hushed voice, without affect, and it was unclear whether he was not used to reading aloud in class or whether he was trying to detach himself from the essay's dark content. The most striking detail of his reading is that he stopped twice in his reading to change faulty semicolons to commas. I cannot recall another student doing this while reading aloud such an intense essay. No less striking is the contrast between the domestic violence in his parents' marriage and his determination to avoid such violence in his own future marriage.

Many of Jacob's classmates could not imagine what it must have been like to grow up in such a family. "One paper that immediately caught my attention was Jacob's," Lucy stated in her diary. "There was something about Jacob's story that was so chilling, and so unbelievable to me, because I have never had to endure such pain. It made me appreciate, so much more than I already do, my own parents, who never once fought in front of my brother and me, and who showed love to one another as well as to us." Lucy felt saddened but not burdened by her classmates' pain. "Each time someone reads a story of divorce or abuse, the death of a friend or a parent, I cannot help but feel their pain; however, I know when I walk out the door, my thoughts stay with them, but that pain turns into gratefulness." Lucy added that although she thought the course would help her recognize the loves in her life through her own writings of love and loss, she now realized that, as a result of the shared stories of her peers, she was able to find peace with her losses and a new awareness of her loves.

This was a challenging assignment for Jacob, as he reveals in his diary entry. "I found it difficult to write this assignment because it dealt with domestic violence, the separation of a family, and the death of a marriage. I often suppress these emotions whenever I see my mother and father. As I result, I have learned from these experiences. When I get married, I look forward to becoming a faithful, strong-minded and respectful husband. I want my children to have everything I was unable to have during my childhood." He made an additional comment in his next entry. "Despite finding it difficult to write about domestic violence and the separation of parents, I felt determined to read it aloud to the students in class. The power struggle that occurred between my parents is one of the reasons I choose to be a faithful and respectful individual toward my fiancée. I look forward toward being a parent in the future because I know I will be a positive role model in their lives."

Students like Jacob do not ask me whether they should forgive a relative or friend who has hurt or betrayed them, and even if they did, I would be reluctant to give them advice. In general I believe that it is better to forgive than not, but I'm wary of telling students how to live. In *Empathic Teaching* (Berman, 2004) I discuss the ways in which students confront the question of forgiveness in their lives. Of the many statements I have read about forgiveness, Jeffrie Murphy's (1988) is one of the most astute: "Each of us, if honest, will admit two things about ourselves: (1) We will within the course of our lives wrong others—even others about whom we care deeply; and (2) because we care so deeply about these others and our relationships with them, we will want to be forgiven by them for our wrongdoings" (p. 133).

Essays that focus on domestic violence are often more difficult to write and read aloud than those on dying or death because they are filled with shame, the most virulent of emotions. Shame compelled Jacob to ask his mother not to provide "shocking details" to his grandmother. Given his shame over his family life, it is ironic that he is nevertheless willing to disclose these shocking details to us. Nico also comments on this irony:

> The essay drew in the audience at once when Jacob revealed something that, in a post-secondary environment, may well have subjected him to scorn and ridicule. Jacob is a brave young man, full of earnest intention. That he felt comfortable enough to share this information shows the level of trust that has already, at this early date, been established in Jeff's classroom. The essay was also filled with the kind of crystalline detail that gives the reader the feeling of being present at a scene: a shattered Bugs Bunny glass, a drunken chase, a wrench on a safe lock. The only shying away from his subject of which Jacob may have been guilty is evident in his use of the formal "Ms. Gonzales" and "Mr. Ramirez" in place of his parents' first names, "Raoul" and "Maria." The use of formal naming perhaps allowed Jacob that small bit of distance necessary to unearth such painful childhood traumas. Jeff was very complimentary of the essay and encouraged his writer with true and kind words: "You can see his desire to be a good writer," he said. "He's thinking like a writer."

On Wednesday I spent several minutes talking about the venerable adage of showing rather than telling and, echoing Nico, making the reader suffer. This is what creative writers attempt to do. If one describes, as many students did when writing about loss, a friendship coming to an end, the writer must show us the developing tensions and arguments. I asked everyone to imagine the trivial reasons that might cause two friends to quarrel when living together: squeezing a tube of toothpaste from the wrong end, failing to place dirty glasses in the dishwater, clogging up a shower drain with one's hair, replacing a new roll of toilet tissue with the paper "up" instead of "down."

Writing teachers routinely advise their students to show rather than tell, but there may be a problem with this recommendation in a course devoted to love and loss. Students who write on traumatic topics—the death of a loved one, the breakup of one's family, the decision to have an abortion, the serious illness of a relative or friend, the horror of being in the World Trade Center on September 11th—may not be psychologically ready to provide us with the concrete details to understand their loss. They may still feel numb over these losses, unwilling or unable to recall those agonizing details they have been trying to forget. To survive a major loss, one needs to become detached, distanced from grief, but excessive detachment may prevent us from writing effectively about loss. The challenge is to find the right balance between involvement and detachment. I concluded by asking students in their future essays to make the reader feel their love and to reproduce in the reader the devastation, shock, and confusion arising from loss. I also asked them to discuss in their diaries whether they believe they have succeeded or failed in making their readers love—and suffer.

The writing in the course continues to improve not only grammatically and stylistically but also substantively. Nico thought that this week's classes were the most successful to date:

> It's hard to say why, precisely, but there was a feeling in the air once the period was over that the class as a group had broken through some previously unbroken threshold of expressive excellence. The feeling of success the class collectively experienced may have been due to the quality of the student writing submitted, though I hesitate to say that this was the only reason; it occurs to me that there are at times factors at play in a classroom that are beyond my ability to understand but that are, nevertheless, present. It can only be described as the feeling that, for a brief period of time, a group of disparate men and women, with disparate tastes, values, and experiences, has managed to achieve an equilibrium of purpose such that the majority of the group (if not everyone) feels an involvement in an important and shared journey. This feeling, so hard to pin down, is the very thing I'm after each time I teach. Jeff is very good at bringing it about by inviting his students to bring their lives and concerns into the classroom in an expressive and disciplined way.

I agree with Nico's observation that the class has reached a new "threshold of expressive excellence." How have we achieved this? Everyone in the class knows that invitations, whether they be inside or outside the classroom, can be respectfully declined. We have an explicit agreement that anyone can avoid writing on a topic that is too personal or threatening. Teachers who ask their students to write about love and loss must remember this. Students can be encouraged but not compelled to write about painful or shameful experiences. They must also be psychologically ready to write about these experiences, and their classmates must be ready as well. We are ready because of the protocols we follow during each class and also because we have established trust in the classroom—trust that helps to offset the darkest emotions. Each person is beginning to think like a writer, and the result is writing that is both expressive and disciplined.

"I'm Sorry, I Understand"

Monday, March 3 and Wednesday, March 5

We began on Monday in our usual way, doing sentence revisions, which the entire class seems to enjoy. I remind my students that, as Mark Twain famously observed, the difference between the right word and the almost right word is the difference between lightning and the lightning bug. There's always much laughter when we revise certain sentences, especially when I challenge them to improve on my own revisions of their writing. This laughter offsets the sorrow in the darker essays, helping to maintain a positive "smile-to-tears" ratio. After-wards, I handed out a copy of the following anonymous in-class writing assignment, which I then summarized the following class:

Bearing Witness to Suffering

Many of you have written essays about painful and sometimes traumatic experiences—losing a mother at an early age, enduring a brother's suicide, growing up without a father, experiencing the breakup of one's family, suffering from depression, losing a beloved grandparent or cousin, being in the World Trade Center during 9/11, and witnessing domestic violence. You are also reading the story of the death of my wife. These are wrenching experiences, yet no one has written in the weekly diaries, even during those weeks when there have been more tears than smiles, that the course has become morbid, depressing, or gloomy. On the contrary: many of you write in your diaries that this is your favorite course of the semester. A stranger learning about our course would almost certainly be surprised, perhaps shocked, by this. As writers, you seem to be disclosing without burdening; as readers, you are identifying without becoming at risk.

In a paragraph or two, please explain why, instead of feeling infected by an essay's dark emotions, you feel strengthened and inspired hearing your classmates' stories. Why does writing about a painful experience lead to relief? If I decide to write a book about this course, your comments here will be important to my readers.

I was relieved that no one feels the course has become morbid or depressing. Many people implied that their recognition of shared vulnerability has heightened their feeling of connection. "By sharing a pain of my own with someone I have never known, I discover that sadness does not mean loneliness. When I cry during a reading of an essay, I am not the only one feeling this way." Most people wrote about how impressed they are by their classmates' strength and courage. "Hearing these essays from my classmates has shown me how strong people can be, and how their problems or sufferings are not endured by only one person. Indeed, the emotions revealed through the essays help to make others with those same emotions feel normal." Some students commented on the therapeutic nature of writing. "Before you write that experience down, it just sits inside of you. The experience plays over and over again, like a bad record. But when you put it down on paper, it's like you are releasing it from your body." One of the most revealing statements came from a person who argued that "the class has taught me that I don't have to turn to women, drugs, or alcohol to deal with my pain."

In an empathic classroom, students expose their vulnerability without fear of criticism or attack. In the process, they become more rather than less protective of each other. I've never seen one of my self-disclosing writing courses become the kind of "pecking party" that Ken Kesey dramatizes in his 1962 antipsychiatric novel, *One Flew Over the Cuckoo's Nest*, where, under Nurse Ratched's baleful influence, the inmates in a psychiatric ward are reduced to a flock of maddened chickens who tear each other to pieces. Nor have I seen a writing class resemble the 1985 film *The Breakfast Club*, where students' angry self-disclosures lead to the humiliation of classmates.

Several students wrote about the importance of placing problems in perspective. "Hearing my peers' essays on loss helps me to appreciate what I have each day. It also helps me to realize that there are worse situations that can happen in life than a breakup with a boyfriend." Commented another, "When you think you have it rough, you look around and see people who are just like yourself, people who often suffer greater losses, and who can help you overcome your own."

Some students wrote about how the course has changed their thinking, and though they didn't have time to give specific examples, they implied that these changes may be far-reaching. "My classmates' stories have really changed the way I have been looking at life. I think about my classmates' essays on a daily basis. Their words are so real, and nothing is fake. I am so inspired about how much my classmates are willing to put themselves out there."

Significantly, students identified with each other without ignoring their differences. "When I look around our classroom," one person wrote, "I can see incredibly different people. We dress different. We listen to different music; we're involved in different clubs." And yet the same person felt that the similarities were greater than the differences. "We share experiences. We share feelings of love and loss. We sympathize with each other. Reading and writing allow our stories to be real again. Writing our stories allows our memories to be alive in the present, rather than a faded copy left in the past. And reading them aloud allows others to carry them into the future."

Finally, what makes the course unique, a number of students suggested, is its emphasis on unconditional acceptance:

> This is the first class where I have felt that the students all want to be here and that they weren't just going through the motions of watching the time fly by. Even though the students do not know each other, there is such a feeling of acceptance in the room and a true sense of nonjudgmental attitude. In my four years here I have never felt such a silent comfort with a class, a group of strangers who fill the room with compassion. I could not have picked a better time to take this class, and I am blessed that I got to experience such a fulfilling and interactive classroom.

Last week Assignment 5 was due, "Writing a Wrong," in which I asked students to write an essay or a letter in which they try to right a wrong that has been done to them or that they have done to another. The assignment encouraged students to discover how writing may be useful for healing wounds and problem solving. Daphne read her essay about a family crisis. She teared up while reading, and I completed it for her:

> By now I am sure many of you, my classmates, have heard the story that my grandmother died from pancreatic cancer in October, 2005. Since then, my parents split up, my childhood dog died, and I have moved seven times in the last three years. I lived with my aunt for a few months after I left my parents' home. This was just before my grandmother died, and I decided that with so many tragic endings in sight, moving into a home with some consistency would be a good idea. My mother had some serious trouble with me leaving. She felt that I had abandoned her; I felt that I had given her freedom. When I was an infant my mother was diagnosed with schizophrenia. Since then all of her decisions have been made for her either by my grandmother or my father. At the time they had both left her, my mother was forced to make her own decisions, whether they be financial, medical, or even emotional. Many people believe that it was my duty as the oldest child to do as my grandmother and father had done. I, however, knew that with independence my mom could learn to trust her own judgment and finally have her own life.
>
> This was a crazy time for me; I was too scared to leave and too stressed to stay. On the night that I moved out, my grandmother called me—she had just gotten back from chemotherapy. I picked up the phone with a shaky hand and my grandmother replied, "I have never been so disappointed in you." She hung up before I could explain myself. My family was angry because they thought I had chosen my father's side of the family, because my aunt and uncle are his relatives, not directly my mother's. I called back my grandmother's house in tears. My mother's youngest brother had picked up the receiver and began shouting at me. He explained his thoughts on my disgrace, my insolence, and the audacity of my actions. A few days later I went to visit my grandmother alone and as I walked in the door, she opened her arms and said, "I'm sorry, I understand." While my grandmother apologized, my mother's brother never did. I have never forgotten that phone call.

> Since my grandmother passed away, my mother has succeeded in many ways. She has gotten a job, her first in the last 20 years. She maintains her house with my youngest brother, who is still in high school. She is close with her friends and has managed a life of her own. My mother and I talk daily, and she once told me that she was proud of me and thankful that I had been strong enough to leave. She said, "It would have killed me to know that I kept you from succeeding in your own life, and now we're both moving on."

Daphne was surprised she began crying in class. "I just couldn't get past my own words in my essay," she stated in her diary. "I had read my essay earlier in the day for some of my co-workers, and I seemed to get through it fine. But my mind just broke down when I read it aloud to so many listeners." Daphne choked up when she came to the word *abandoned*. "It didn't help that we had just heard a sad essay. Those heart-crushing feelings were already surfacing themselves as I began my essay, and when I finally glanced at the word *abandoned*, I lost my focus and my tears made my vision blurry."

Several of Daphne's classmates commented in their diaries on her essay. "Daphne's essay about losing her grandma and the family problems that arose from it touched me," Chipo wrote. "Her essay reminded me about how fragile the relationship with my own family has become since losing my grandfather." Daphne's tears distressed Ayla. "It hurt my heart to see her cry as she was reading it. I understand her perspective on her mother and how she chose to handle the situation. I think that Daphne was very strong for giving her mother independence, and she should definitely be commended for it." Beth's observation is also worth reporting. "When Daphne was reading her essay about her mother and her confusing family situation, she could not help but cry. I was sitting about six seats away, and I felt like I was close enough that I could do something to help her. Before I could even get out of my seat, Isabella had given her a tissue and a pat on the shoulder."

Daphne appreciated her classmates' support. "Many people were nice—Gloria told me on the way out of class that it was hard for her too, and Faith later in the week made sure to tell me that she thought I did a good job. I thanked them both because it did help to hear their support." Daphne added that she wished she could have written something witty or funny. "I regret this because my life hasn't always been so sad, but I keep reflecting that in my work. However, I know that I do this, because this class is my one venue to really write about my feelings, especially on the dark moments of my life." Daphne said that her next goal is to "read my feelings aloud, the whole way through. I'm thankful for the opportunity to set these feelings free which I've kept hidden for so long, and I believe that's why they make me so fragile."

The class's supportive responses to Daphne's essay demonstrate the importance of creating a classroom community based on empathic understanding and fellowship. Nico's diary entry this week reveals the feeling of goodwill and camaraderie that has developed in the class:

I got to class a few minutes early and chatted with some of the students. It's always amazing to me how eager and ready they are to share aspects of their lives with their instructors and with each other. I remember my first year of college life, and the intense feelings of loneliness, isolation, and destabilization that accompanied it. Perhaps these factors explain why students are predisposed toward conversations that remind them of who they are outside of, and before, the college experience.

So I shared pictures of my dogs with Scotty, Shannon, and Lia. Scotty and Shannon pulled out their own dog shots. "These are my bitches," Scotty said, flashing a pic of two beagle/German mixes. Shannon showed off her Airedale. "Is it true that they're somewhat stupid?" I asked. Shannon was protective. "Not mine," she said. "He's very, very clever." We all laughed and in the confusion I drank Lia's tea, Shannon's Powerade, and then snuck a handful of Shannon's Cheetos. I think its important to steal food and supplies from our students. A sense of playfulness in the classroom is essential to bringing about in our students the ability for full expression.

"Sometimes I Feel Like An Outsider In This Class"

Monday, March 10 and Wednesday, March 12

While most students felt a strong connection with each other, one person did not. She used last week's diary entry to offer the first substantial criticism of the course. On Monday I read her entry in its entirety, anonymously, as I read all diaries, and I invited those who wished to comment on it to do so in their next entries:

> Sometimes I feel like an outsider in this class. This is for a couple of reasons. One in particular is because I'm a first-time student of Professor Berman's, whereas a bunch of students have had him before. I feel like the class is separated between these former students and the new ones. I feel like I'm out of the loop with a lot of what the professor has to say in regards to grammar, but those who have had him don't.
>
> Even though I know he doesn't mean to do this, I feel that when he pays special attention to his past students, and dotes on them more about their writing, that he considers them his favorites, and worthy of creating great writing. And that the rest of us have a lot of work to do to catch up to their level. I feel bad about writing this, but I feel like being completely honest. No holding back. I love the way he focuses on grammar, and how I've learned soo much already in this course. I used to love my writing, but now I find myself doubting every word I write. I think that each one of us in this class is great writers; it's just that some need more help getting it down on paper better.
>
> I was thinking about this when I was working in my kindergarten class (EDU 390 project). I thought that if I only put the exceptional work on the walls, week after week, what motivation would the other students have? I believe that everyone's work should be praised and showcased, not just for its beautiful end product, but for the effort and the love it took to make it. The process takes a lot of hard work, whether you're good at what you are doing, or are a beginner. And by praising this process, you're getting rid of any doubts that that student may have about what they are trying to accomplish, and instead, you are allowing them to succeed.

The criticism surprised me. I was not aware of a division between the new and returning students, nor was I aware that I was displaying favoritism. I agree with her about the importance of validation. I was glad that she felt comfortable enough to express a criticism that she knew might incur the disapproval of many of her classmates and, perhaps, her teacher. She trusted me to voice her criticism, just as I trusted her and her classmates to express their feelings and thoughts, even if they were not what I wanted or expected to hear.

I doubt the student would have expressed this criticism aloud, for almost certainly she would have felt self-conscious, and if her classmates disagreed with the criticism, she might have felt further isolated, if not stigmatized. By reading her diary entry anonymously, I voiced her criticism—and validated the seriousness of her comments, even if I did not necessarily agree with them. Many of her classmates used their diaries to disagree with her, as we can see in the following entry written by a returning student:

> In Monday's class we heard a diary that changed the mood of the class. The diary was by someone who felt like an outsider. They said former students of Jeff were treated different. They said we group together. They said they didn't feel welcome.
>
> I was angry. I was sad. I felt guilty. They had to be wrong. Maybe they were right. Did we section ourselves off? Is Jeff favoring us? No? No. Maybe? Who can say?
>
> I was angry because I don't think we group together. At least not intentionally. Maybe we do. We don't block anyone out. I don't. I just always sit on the same side, near the door, in front of the room. Always. And that's where a bunch of other people from other Jeff classes sit. And we talk. So, yeah, maybe we have grouped off. But not to push anyone out, just to say hi. Some of the kids are from previous Jeff classes, but sometimes not. Some of us were in the same classes, and some were not. I just met them. They just happen to be former students. I'm sorry we section ourselves off. I was sad because I thought everyone was growing close.
>
> I was sad because I thought we all had connected. I thought it was becoming a new family, again—like in former classes. My [earlier] feelings that this class wasn't going to be as close as the last had disappeared. I believe we were building a strong bond. But I guess my engineer's plans were flawed and their plans had lied—we're crumbling and someone feels alone. They must feel alone watching the parts of the building fall in clumps. The clumps are the people who knew each other. I guess.
>
> I felt guilty for getting angry. Why was I so offended by this? I was so offended because it hurt. It was as if someone told me I didn't love my siblings. The thing about siblings is, no one but they can understand their bonds. But you should be our sibling too. New siblings are just as good as old. We might not know each other from before, but we can know each other now. That's what counts: right now.
>
> Our stories are the same. When we tell our tales, they have no markings. We cannot tell who has been in class with Jeff before by their words. Their

pain and love and hope does not tell us if this is their first time. It is that moment that counts. And it makes me feel so uncomfortable that someone feels outside that moment. I want to bring them in. We should share it; it's here for us.

I quote the entire diary entry because it reveals the intensity of the conflicting emotions the above student felt upon learning of a classmate's criticisms. The two diary entries reveal strikingly different points of view, that of an "outsider" who seeks to become an "insider," and that of an "insider" who suddenly experiences an "outsider's" estrangement. Both students feel sadness and disappointment; both feel a disconnection that threatens to limit their participation in Love and Loss; both feel burdened by dark emotions. Given the title of English 450, it's ironic that their love for the course has turned into a feeling of loss.

As the above student recognizes, in many ways a class resembles a family, with the students feeling at times as if they are siblings. Trust, whether it be in the classroom or in a family, can be destroyed quickly—and I was dismayed by this unexpected development. If students are siblings, does that mean the teacher is also a parent figure? In some ways, yes. I believe that classroom dynamics reproduce many family dynamics. As hard as I try to de-center the classroom, to minimize the extent to which I come across as an "authority figure," I am still the person who is in charge, the person who confers approval (or disapproval) through grades, the person who enforces classroom rules and regulations, the person who is responsible for the success or failure of the group, the person whose experience and expertise are tested in every class. I don't want to exaggerate the claim that the teacher is a parent figure, but I believe that family dynamics are always present in the classroom, and that teachers who are aware of these dynamics are in a better position to control them than those who remain unaware.

How, then, should I respond to this unexpected crisis in the classroom? My first decision was to read carefully all the diaries, to determine how many students agreed with the "outsider." None did. The nine students who responded to that diary entry were as startled by the criticism as I was. I decided to read one of these diaries aloud, and I chose the following, mainly because of its self-mocking humor and pragmatic advice at the end:

> To the student who feels discouraged:
> 1. Humble yourself! I know this is a hard concept, especially for us English majors. We all have egos and we all think we are the best writers, but we all still have plenty to learn. Just because your grammar is not perfect does not mean you're a bad writer. When I took Jeff's Expository writing class, I felt discouraged too, but by the end of the semester, I became a grammar whizz—trust me!
> 2. Jeff does not favor certain students; he gets excited about powerful essays. Here is a reality that may hurt your feelings: Jeff's former students have become good at grammar because of his grammar lessons. In this class, I have also observed that they feel more comfortable participating.

Raise your hand and do not be afraid TO BE WRONG. It happens. As a former student and loudmouth in general, I love to participate in class, so Jeff is forced to call on me. He is a nice man and wants everyone to participate—former students or not.

3. Write your rant. Express in an essay why you feel discouraged in this class. Write about your shattered assumptions about this class. Write about why you think Jeff is an asshole and how he favors students. Write everyday! You will improve, I promise!

A second criticism of the course emerged from a diary entry this week, one that, like the first, caught me by surprise:

In response to last week's diary entry on Professor Berman's favoring his older students, I would have to disagree. I am a new student and I don't feel that I am being told to "work up" to others. I do understand why someone would feel that way, though, as his older students are very cliquey.

The cliquishness among our class didn't bother me at first. I came into this class to write for myself, not to make friends or be a part of a clique. What really drives me crazy, however, is how these certain people who seem to have gotten close continuously talk over others. Sometimes, Professor Berman will be correcting an essay, or doing sentence revisions, and these people have a conversation while his back is turned. While they might already know the correct answer, being older students of his, I do not always know the answer. I want to learn. I want to find out what's wrong. While this always annoyed me, it really made me angry when they did it during one of MY sentences. I had no idea what was wrong with it and how I made the mistake, and there was a large conversation in one half of the room. I find it incredibly rude to other students who are interested in learning, and I believe it's extremely disrespectful to our professor, who is truly trying to make his students better writers.

I don't know how many people shared this perception, but I read the diary aloud and then asked everyone to sit next to different members of the class for the rest of the semester. I have never made this request before, and I hope it will eliminate the problem of cliquishness. The same student wrote in her next entry that she is pleased I took her complaint seriously. "I hope that this diary will bring some change in the classroom. I think this class is an amazing, wonderful experience for all of us, but the chatting was really starting to get to me. I hope now that the problem will be eliminated and that I can love this class as much as I have since the beginning." Six of her classmates used their diary entries to respond to her criticism. Some were angered by the comment and thought it was unfair, but most were nevertheless agreeable to my request that they sit next to different classmates each class.

While we were on the subject of pedagogy, I asked everyone to write a brief in-class response to the following questions about the sentence revisions that we do at the beginning of each class:

How Do You Feel about Sentence Revisions?

Each class we spend about 15 minutes doing sentences revisions—revising a sentence, grammatically or stylistically, of every essay submitted that week. A visitor would probably find it strange that we place so much emphasis on sentence revisions in a course devoted to death education. Please describe in a paragraph or two how you feel about the sentence revisions: whether you like or dislike doing them, whether you find them interesting or boring, and whether you find them helpful or not. Have you ever done sentence revisions like this in another college class? Do you recommend that we continue the sentence revisions for the rest of the semester?

Without exception, everyone praised this part of each class and said that we should continue. Only a few students had done this for other teachers, never on a daily basis. Many were enthusiastic about it. "I love it! I have learned—finally—what a dangling modifier is. I told my friends, with great pride & joy, what a dangling modifier is and how to avoid it! I have done sentence revisions in other classes, but I have never seen a professor as dedicated to grammar as you are. I definitely want to continue this exercise." They gave several reasons for liking sentence revisions: they see significant improvements in their writing; they enjoy being paired with classmates; they realize that others make the same grammatical errors that they do; they see how clear writing helps them understand their feelings; and they find the exercise fun and challenging.

On Wednesday Nico taught class while I attended a signing at a local bookstore for the publication of *Cutting and the Pedagogy of Self-Disclosure* (Berman & Wallace, 2007). I mentioned the book at the beginning of the semester, but I didn't discuss it. The timing of the book signing was ironic for two reasons: Faith read aloud her essay on cutting entitled "To My Left Arm," a response to Assignment 5, and another student turned in an essay called "Love and Hate" in which she spoke about cutting herself in her junior year of high school after a painful breakup with her boyfriend:

> I had just clicked the off button on my cordless house phone and I snuggled in the big leather office chair. I had been talking to him. This was after our "official" break-up which apparently still gave us property rights over each other's lips. After about 30 seconds of hugging my knees into my chest and willing myself not to go to the bathroom, I gave in. I walked out of my room and into the bathroom, making sure to lock it once there. I was staring at myself through the medicine cabinet mirror. Lately when I would look into the mirror, I couldn't see me. I was no longer there on the surface but I knew that I had been lost somewhere deep in those eyes, screaming for help.
>
> I opened the medicine cabinet that hung over the sink and took out a bottle of shampoo. Behind the bottle I found my escape. I removed the folded paper towel, returned the shampoo to its conditioner and closed the cabinet. I paused as I always did, because I knew this wasn't the way. But time and time again I convinced myself that maybe it was *my* way. I placed the paper

towel on top of the sink and turned on the water so it could fill up the tub. I shed my clothes and sank into the warm water that prickled my skin. I allowed the water to devour me as it slowly filled up the tub. I turned the water off and reached for the paper towel once again. I look at the bathroom lock making sure, once more, that I had definitely remembered to lock my secrets away. I shook the paper towel open and the sharp, shiny piece of metal fell onto the edge of the tub. It was a small razor but it did the job. I let the water devour my left arm and then spit it back up to the surface. I sat up, bent my knees and placed the left arm, wrist up, on top of them. I moved my right hand on top of the other and allowed it to align with my wrist. And there I went. With each vertical movement of the hand, my tears and fears slipped away and only now I felt like it was going to be okay. When the movement would have reached almost up to my elbow, with deep, close-knit lines, I stopped. And I could once again breathe. I slipped my arm under the water and watched as the redness took over the transparency of it. It was leaving my body: the sadness, the loneliness, the guilt and most of all, the disappointment.

My self-destructive punishments, according to everyone else, were obviously because of him. It was black and white to them. I, of course, knew that he was a small part of it. Yes, he was among the reasons because the truth can only be said the way Mariah Carey sings in a song called "Breakdown." *"So what do you do when somebody you're so devoted to suddenly just stops loving you?"*

I think to really understand why I did what I did a person would have had to live my life, in my house, with my family and with my heart. The first thing you would have to know about me is that I admire strength. You get right back up from a fall, tears are a sign of weakness, and when you let a man bring you as well as your tears to fall, well, that was unacceptable to me. I remember all too well watching my mother and sister be destroyed by men in one way or another. Watching them cry and being so helpless. Back then, I would never have allowed that to have been me. So you see, when everyone else thought that he had made me do the things I did, the truth was that it was the disappointment, my disappointment for allowing myself to be in that type of situation. The love I had for myself turned into a form of hate, and I didn't know how to handle that. It may seem like such a small reason but to me, it was the biggest. He had great power over me, he treated me the way he wanted to and I just stood there and took it, like a defenseless dog that hadn't yet learned how to fight back.

The cutting was the only thing that alleviated the hurt and the only way my body would allow me to weep. What I needed to do was forgive myself. But back then I just couldn't.

How is an essay on cutting related to death education? People who cut themselves often feel as if they are not fully alive. They inhabit an ambiguous state of death-in-life in which they inflict pain upon themselves to prove they are human. Most clinicians believe that although cutting is a self-destructive act, it usually provides the cutter with a degree of welcome psychological relief, thus preventing a more serious self-injury. Many people cut themselves because they have lost their sense of self: notice the writer's inability to see herself as she looks into the bathroom medicine cabinet mirror. Writing about cutting allows her to regain visibility. By the end of the essay, the writer has increased our understanding of a dark period in her life.

The above essay was written only for me, not for the entire class, but I have received dozens of essays like this in other writing classes, and I know from experience that classmates sympathize with these writings even if many of them cannot imagine why a person would choose to cut herself. (And it is usually women, not men, who engage in this self-harming behavior). We respond to these essays the way we respond to all essays. We begin by listening empathically, sympathetically, nonjudgmentally. Such listening allows cutters to tell their stories and find solutions to their problems. If, as cutters believe, razor blades are their best friends, they discover, through writing, that pens or word processors are even better friends. We accept the validity of the cutter's emotions, thus offering unconditional acceptance. We offer a safe place where students can write on any topic, no matter how painful or shameful it is. We then open our discussion by singling out the best sentences (my favorite: "With each vertical movement of the hand, my tears and fears slipped away"), and then we revise those sentences that contain grammatical or stylistic errors. If we have time, we raise questions we would like the author to elaborate upon in a revised essay (my questions: when and how did she begin to forgive herself?). If an author asks me to read the essay anonymously, I do so, and there is no discussion of any kind. We never make judgmental criticisms, never psychoanalyze the authors, never give unsolicited advice. If I feel the author is in danger of harming herself or another person, I immediately contact the counseling center or the campus police. (Only a few times have I contacted the former, and never the latter.) When do I discourage essays on cutting or other dark subjects from being read aloud? Only if I believe the author is romanticizing or glorifying these acts, which is clearly not the case here, or if I fear the author is too emotionally unstable to hear the essay read aloud.

CHAPTER 9—WEEK NINE
"I Felt As If I Were Reliving That Day"

Monday, March 17 and Wednesday, March 19

Assignment 6, "Holding Two Opposed Ideas without Becoming Paralyzed," due on March 3, encouraged students to write about ambivalence, a word coined by Freud's contemporary, the Swiss psychiatrist Eugene Bleuler, to signify co-existing contradictory feelings toward a person, place, or thing, such as love and hate, attraction and repulsion, or fear and desire. This writing assignment was inspired by F. Scott Fitzgerald's (1945) observation in his autobiographical *The Crack-Up*: "The test of a first-rate intelligence is the ability to hold two opposed ideas in the mind at the same time and still retain the ability to function" (p. 69).

To be aware of ambivalence is to be aware of complexity, contradiction, and irony. Sitting on a bookcase in my university office lies a sign one of my Cornell students wrote for me in 1972, a year after I completed my doctoral studies: "Be ambivalent clearly." I can't remember why she gave it to me, but I have always cherished it. If we cannot resolve our ambivalence, we can at least remain aware of it, lest we find ourselves paralyzed by conflicting emotions later in life.

All of the Assignment 6 essays were serious except for Cath's, which brought smiles to everyone in the classroom. "I hate you. You leaked all over and left a big stain. I know you're old, but you can be careful. I even gave you time to heat up before we started; we didn't go that far, but you're so loud. Mom heard you last night. It's all your fault." Only when we reach the final paragraph do we realize that Cath's love-hate object is not her boyfriend but her aging car, which continues to break her heart.

We spent the entire week hearing oral presentations, which were based on Assignment 7, a discussion of a memorable essay written either by the student or by a classmate. Most students cited a classmate's memorable essay rather than their own, though in many cases they implied that their classmate's essay emboldened them to write on a topic they might not have otherwise chosen.

Isabella was the first to give her oral presentation, and she began by discussing Kasia's essay on September 11—which turned out to be the one that most students cited. Isabella then offered additional information about how her father's FDNY experience during September 11 changed her own life. She teared up during her presentation but was able to complete the reading:

Isabella

Kasia's vivid description of her experience on September 11, 2001 was beautiful yet disturbing. The words she used to bring her story to life made me feel as if I were alongside her and her sister, standing at the foot of catastrophe. I became trapped in her nightmare, a nightmare that is very real to me, as if I could hear the beating of her heart while fear took over her body. Her view of falling bodies, people running and screaming, and the smoke which turned the blue sky black, are all images my father witnessed. I never needed to be present at the scene on that day, because the horror and sadness which my dad experienced was present in his eyes. The horror and sadness that Kasia experienced is present in her words.

For seven years I have not discussed that day which turned our world upside down, not until assignment one for this class. I want to forget that day. I know Kasia wants to forget that day, and she similarly avoided writing about her experience. Yet, despite countless attempts to throw away the worst day of my life, the minute details haunt me. I always joke with my dad that I have horrible long-term memory and that there must be some herb that will magically help me to recall most of my childhood. I now wish there was an herb to help me forget the gut wrenching pain which sits in my stomach every time I think about the ironically, blue skied day of September 11, 2001. . . .

When I heard Kasia's essay, I felt as if I were reliving that day. I heard my version plus her version, an uncut rendition of horror, death, and fear. We could not censor the painful truth, because those are the details we think about before we go to bed at night, or each time the clock reads 9:11. Furthermore, the tragedy of that day did not end on September 12. I know it did not for Kasia. She will never forget the sight of falling bodies, or the pain in her legs after a four hour walk home. She will always thank her sister for being her strength.

September 11 affected many aspects of our lives as Americans and as New Yorkers. Kasia believes her former assumptions of the world came crashing down along with the two towers. She fears life itself. She is angry, and expresses that she "never felt such hatred until 9/11." I know how Kasia feels. My family knows how Kasia feels. My dad feels that hatred, but I find it harder to do so. We have discussed the current Iraq war; my dad agrees with the war, and he actually suggested that the United States should take more extreme measures. "Nuke 'em." I understand that he is just angry; he is not a monster. He knows I do not agree with him, and he thinks I am young and naive to think we have other options than to eliminate the race that killed so many innocent people. "Dad, stop. We cannot kill the world!" "Why not, we should just drop a bomb, and get it over with. That is basically what they did to us. They are cowards, and sneaky, and attacked because they know they cannot win a war against us." "But dad, think about how you feel right now: angry, and sad because so many people died.

The towers should have never fallen; the firemen should have never died. Think about their families. Think about us. Think about how dropping a bomb in the middle of Baghdad, which we have done, kills innocent people. We hit their towers too. We are doing no better. Do you think death is easier to deal with on the other side of the world? Do you think those mothers will cry less for their sons and husbands?" "I always knew you were smart, Isabella; I don't agree, but that was a really good argument." No one deserves to feel the pain of losing a loved one. I will never forgive or forget what occurred on September 11; however, I will also never wish for anyone else to have to feel or experience the pain which will forever be a part of my life.

Several observations are relevant here. First, Isabella identifies strongly with Kasia, an identification based on shared vulnerability and suffering. Kasia's essay has motivated Isabella to recall a traumatic experience she has tried to forget, but in doing so, the latter has reopened a wound. Kasia did exactly what I had asked all my students to do in their writings: she has made her readers suffer. Kasia's essay was "beautiful yet disturbing" precisely because it captured so much of the wrenching truth of Isabella's own experience, as she lived it vicariously through her father's experience. No less than Kasia, Isabella shows, not tells: To characterize Kasia's description as "beautiful yet disturbing" is to make an aesthetic as well as a moral judgment. Both Isabella and Kasia seek to write stories that capture the truth of their experiences and compel their readers' attention.

Second, Kasia's essay has enabled Isabella to tell parts of her story that we have not heard before, a story she has never shared with anyone. James Joyce's (1934/1961) observation in *Ulysses* that history is a "nightmare from which I am trying to awake" characterizes how Isabella and Kasia feel about September 11th. Their stories recall Dori Laub's observation that survivors need to tell their stories in order to survive. The two classmates' stories also remind me of Kafka's (1977) statement to a friend about a writer's need to "wound" readers:

> I think we ought to read only the kind of books that wound and stab us. If the book we're reading doesn't wake us up with a blow on the head, what are we reading it for? So that it will make us happy, as you write? Good Lord, we would be happy precisely if we had no books, and the kind of books that make us happy are the kind we could write ourselves if we had to. But we need the books that affect us like a disaster, that grieve us deeply, like the death of someone we love more than ourselves, like being banished into forests far from anyone, like a suicide. A book must be the axe for the frozen sea inside us. (p. 16)

Third, Isabella describes for us two strikingly different responses to September 11, her father's, echoed in the chilling words "Nuke 'em," a cry for revenge that lead us first into Afghanistan and then into Iraq, and her own, a response based on understanding and measured retaliation. Her use of dialogue captures not only the clash between father and daughter but also the tensions that have polarized a nation. Many of us can understand the father's desire for revenge even if we agree with the daughter's call for restraint. Even the father admires her, though her argument does not persuade him to change his mind. She is wise enough to know that this disagreement cannot be easily resolved. By refusing to turn grief and loss into the desire for revenge, she distances herself from the forces of irrationality and embraces wisdom and compassion. Her essay has particular value in a course on death education, for it heightens our understanding of the dangers, external and internal, that beset us at the turn of the twenty-first century.

Finally, Isabella offers us a portrait of a loving father who is at once heroic and irrational, a man who valiantly sought to save his fellow Americans' lives but who is now willing to kill innocent people in the name of vengeance. It is not easy to describe in a paragraph or two our conflicting feelings toward a parent, nor is it easy to convey briefly an irresolvable family tension. In paying tribute to Kasia's memorable essay, Isabella has written her own memorable essay, one that impressed her teacher as much as it impressed her classmates.

CHAPTER 10—WEEK TEN
"There Is No Preparation For A Sight Of Death"

Monday, March 31 and Wednesday, April 2

We returned from spring vacation, during which I received an email from Saverio telling me that his grandfather had died and that he was missing Monday's class to attend the funeral. I sent around a condolence card that everyone signed. Students began to read their essays on Assignment 8, "posttraumatic growth," which Tedeschi, Park, and Calhoun (1998) define as the ability to recreate one's life following a devastating loss. Posttraumatic growth includes changes in perception of self and in interpersonal relationships. Such changes allow us to see ourselves not as victims but as survivors. Kamilluh read aloud the following essay about her cousin, whose death remains the central loss in her life. One month earlier, we recall, she had written her "shattered assumptions" essay on Mahogany, but now she writes about how her cousin's death has allowed her to grow stronger in many ways, allowing her to rebuild her assumptive world.

Kamilluh
"Mahogany died at 3:14 pm. Milluh, I'm so sorry I couldn't be there to hold you." These were the words that were told to me the day I realized death was a reality, and that my life would never be the same again. The day that my cousin died, I was sitting at my desk at my job where I lived on campus. I forced my mind not to run into a million different directions by attempting to stare at a clock until it was my time to leave. My mom had called me approximately two times before that day to tell me that Mahogany's heart had stopped once again, and that they were trying to revive her. I prepared every element in my body for the next phone call I would receive, knowing full well that all of the preparations in the world would not come close to comfort. The phone rang and as my stomach dropped, I knew she was gone, and her struggle was over. I was the last person to speak to her by phone, which was about two hours prior to her death. She could not respond because she was unconscious, and so my aunt placed the phone to her ear. I told her I loved her and no matter what, God would end her suffering one way or another, as an effort to have her understand that whatever she decided to do, I would be okay with it.

I remember her wake like it was yesterday. I walked into the room slowly, my mother holding my hand, once again trying to prepare myself to see her dead. Someone forgot to give me the memo that there is no preparation for a sight of death, though. Flowers surrounded her coffin, as well as many pictures of her through the years, a good amount of them including me. My grandparents, her mother (my aunt), and my older cousin stood hesitantly watching to see how I was going to react. My grandfather had tears in his eyes. I never saw him cry before, or his eyes so blue. She had gained weight since her body retained a lot of fluid. They cut her thick long black hair. My mother cried and rubbed her arm. I had never been so close to a dead body before. My aunt stood on the other side of me, placing me in the middle, and all she kept repeating was "Oh Mahogany," as tears slowly crept down her face. I stared at her body. She looked as if she was sleeping. I wanted her to wake up, but I knew she wouldn't. I shed a few tears but I don't think it hit me just yet that she was gone.

At her funeral, I walked into the church where Mahogany (Hoggie) and I once ran up and down the aisles where we weren't supposed to, alive as Catholic school girls, being baptized together, and receiving our first communion. I would have never smelled death there. That was the first time I attended a funeral in that place, which now I had no choice but to remember differently. I stood next to my family members in the pew, crunched in tight because there were so many of us. Her coffin stood in between the middle aisles. I was not expecting it to be so close to me. The same priests, who baptized and did our first communion, were the same men whose voices echoed throughout the church, "Ashes to ashes, and dust to dust." I felt like I was in a nightmare, and this time I could not get out of it. I loss shortness of breath, and I my mind ran out of my body. As they carried her coffin out, my heart released itself from my body's attempt to control myself, and I broke down, screaming her name. At that moment, it hit me.

After her death, I had to force myself to rest, because I had been losing out on it for some time. I was so tired mentally, emotionally, spiritually, and physically that I could not move. I was thankful to God for allowing me to be able to have a being to believe in. I say this because if it wasn't for God, I think I would have gone crazy or did something out of my character in order to deal with her passing. I have this understanding that everything happens for a reason and life and death is in the hands and power of God. I have no control over her life, mine, or anyone else's. Life is promised to no man. She was 19 years old. I am 20 now. Who is to say I will see tomorrow? After her death, all I could think of was at any given time, anything can happen. I do have a great fear of dying young and the way that I am going to die. However, slowly, I am trying to deal with that fear by appreciating people in my life, because who is to say a rushed phone call with a loved one won't be the last phone call you will have with that person? I value conversation as well. I think when you take the time to talk to someone, even for a few minutes, you can change their life, small or large.

When I look back, I am so grateful for everything that has happened to me. Some believe this to be crazy. However, I beg to differ. A big part of me feels like last year is the worst that my life is going to get while I am in college. Everything that I have lost, God has restored in some way. I love where I live. I do not have to deal with any kind of drama. I had two beautiful internships over the summer and in the fall, with employers who loved what I contributed to their establishment. I received recognition for my efforts to empower my peers. I am comfortable with my love life, enjoying being single. And Hoggie, God rest her soul, does not suffer another day. Life is not so bad when you appreciate each experience. I would not be the person I am today, had each event never happened. People go through much worse, so who am I to complain? Not everything in life will run smoothly. As I've learned, it all happens for a reason.

Kamilluh's posttraumatic growth essay does not soften the grief she experienced during her cousin's funeral. Indeed, the emotional climax of the essay, near the end of the third paragraph, when she finds herself screaming her cousin's name, is so intense that she uncharacteristically makes two typographical errors, suggesting that she did not proofread the essay: "I loss shortness of breath, and I my mind ran out of my body." Nor does she describe regaining control of her life following the funeral. She discusses, in the three lengthy paragraphs I have omitted, other difficulties after Mahogany's death: the breakup of her relationship with her boyfriend, the loss of her job, and the spitefulness of her roommate. Nevertheless, despite the ordeal of writing, the assignment on posttraumatic growth has reminded her of the importance of gratitude, and the essay's affirmative ending is fully justified. Despite or perhaps because of the many misfortunes she has described, she retains her faith in God, a faith that makes possible her growth as a person.

I don't know how many college English professors encourage their students to write on posttraumatic growth, but I believe that such topics are useful because they remind us that psychological growth and development can arise from traumatic events. Kamilluh's essay demonstrates the value of such writing, both for herself and her classmates. The essay also confirms an observation made by Frantz, Farrell, and Trolley (2001): "Although one's spirituality and beliefs about God and the universe are often upset by the betrayal of death, the altered belief system that emerges from bereavement is frequently stronger" (p. 193). They cite a study in which 80% of the 300 adults who had lost a loved one felt strengthened by their religious or spiritual beliefs. One need not share Kamilluh's religious beliefs to appreciate the importance of faith in her life, which is one of the sources of her courage and optimism.

Saverio returned to class on Wednesday, and I gave him the condolence card signed by everyone in the class. He explained in his next diary how he felt upon receiving our condolence card:

> I returned to class last Wednesday after the death of my grandfather. When I walked into class, I was greeted by Professor Berman: "Welcome back, Saverio," were the words that he spoke. As I looked around the room

there were a lot of people smiling at me. Some of them also welcomed me back. As I sat down, Berman handed me a card. I knew what the card was for. I thanked everyone in the room, and was greeted with "your welcome" from other members of the class. I did not want to look at the card until I got back to my room. I was not ready for what was inside the card.

On Mondays and Wednesdays I have a routine. When I get out of Berman's class, I go to the campus center to get something to eat. That day I got Wendy's, but I wasn't thinking about if I should get the number two or nine. I wanted to see what was in the card and could not wait to get back to my room.

I swiped my card to get into my building as fast as possible. I hustled down the hallway, barged through the door, put the food on the table and headed straight to my room. I sat on my bed, opened my bookbag, and reached into it for the card. I took the card out of the envelope and pulled out the card.

On the front of the card were the words, "With Sympathy to Your Family." When I opened the card, I saw that everyone in the class had written me a message. Each person sent their condolences to myself and my family. There was one that caught my eye as soon as I opened it. It was from Chipo. I, like the rest of the class, know Chipo's story. We all know about his mother and his grandfather because of the beautiful words he had written about them. His words were elegant. At the end of the message he wrote his phone number down and told me that if I needed to talk, do not hesitate to call him.

When I finished reading all of the messages, I sat on my bed, with a smile on my face and tears in my eyes. People who I do not know that well sent their sympathies to me. They cared. It was a beautiful sight to see.

I want to thank all of my classmates. In a time where I needed someone, you all went out of your way. Something as simple as a card made me feel so much better. I will keep this card, and I will never forget all of you. You were all so nice to me that first day back. The little smiles and a simple hello, made my world less dreary.

Saverio's response reminds me of Gorer's (1965) observation that "the grateful acceptance of spoken condolences is the most reliable single sign that the mourner is dealing adequately with his grief" (p. 62). Saverio's response also reminds me of the gratitude I experienced when I received hundreds of condolence cards following Barbara's death. As I acknowledge in *Dying to Teach*, "I valued every expression of sympathy, regardless of how it was expressed. . . . Cards with handwritten notes were always better than those without handwritten notes. Many began their brief notes by writing that 'there are no words to express our sadness,' but in doing so, they were, paradoxically, finding the language to convey sadness, even if only formulaically" (p. 209). Small acts of kindness can have unexpected significance, and I suspect that years from now, when Saverio reflects upon Love and Loss, he will remember his classmates' heartfelt condolences.

Scout remarked on my absence from class a couple of weeks ago. "When you were not in the room by 5:45, the entire class panicked. Why was Berman late?

Was he not coming to class? Was everything alright?" Scout added that when Nico told the class that I was going to be absent from class that day, "there was a mixed feeling of disappointment that you would not be there and of excitement over the possibility that class might be canceled. We asked Nico to let us out early, and we said we would not tell you. (The weather was nice that day, and I know that I for one would have loved to run while the sun was still out.)" Although everyone wanted to enjoy an afternoon off, by the end of class Scout realized that my absence "had in effect made the class come together more, thus making the class worthwhile." Nico offers his own perspective about that class:

On Impersonating the Bermanator
This past weekend presented a unique challenge for me. Jeff could not teach class on Wednesday and asked me if I could stand in for him. After extorting some cash off him, driving the price up, and extorting some more, I agreed.

I was then faced with a series of questions about how I should proceed. For one thing, Jeff wisely did not tell the class that he would be absent on Wednesday, knowing full well the opportunistic fickleness of the under-graduate makeup, and not wanting to subject me to an hour and twenty minutes of sitting in a nearly empty classroom while mumbling to myself about "the fucking TAs just don't get any respect." But as it was, almost everyone showed up on Wednesday, and I pulled a little prank on them by playing coy with the whole situation, waiting until a few minutes after start time, speculating about "What's wrong with Jeff? Doesn't he know it's not kosher for a teacher to be late?" and finally, positioning myself behind the desk command post, throwing my bag dramatically down, and yelling, with zeal-filled eyes rimmed with the glossy red of insanity, "I'm in charge here!"

This was followed by a slew of "seriously?[s]" and "you must be jesting, sir[s]," to which I responded, "just try me." I'm half kidding, but here really was a period of adjustment, in which I had to transition the class's view of me from that of colleague to that of the instructor. The students kept asking me where Jeff was and I told them, "he's fine. He's tied up in a safe, comfortable place." The switch might have been smoother, but the students were further disoriented when I asked them to stand up and prepare to throw stuff around the room, whereby I produced a multicolored vinyl juggling ball and told them to get ready to learn everybody's first name. It surprised me to learn that none of the students knew all of their classmates's names, especially given the convivial and warm tenor of the class, and so I was happy that an exercise intended mostly for my benefit turned out to be quite useful for the students as well. We played the name game for 10 minutes, and I gradually introduced two more balls, followed by two bags of jelly beans. By the end of 10 minutes, the students had just about mastered each other's names, and had consumed enough sugared pectin to fuel a rhino's Saturday sex romp, and we moved on to the usual business of class.

As I conducted sentence revision, I found it extraordinarily difficult not to mimic Jeff. I found myself parroting almost verbatim some of his grammatical maxims, while pushing my glasses back up onto my nose, and being seized by a strong desire to speak powerfully and earnestly about my wife. (I have no wife so this may come across as strange.) I'm only half kidding; it was truly eerie to feel that I was both myself and possessed by the spirit of the Bermanator. I had trouble inserting myself into the classroom as a me that I recognized. At first this was jarring and disorienting, but after a few minutes I stopped noticing what I was doing altogether, a testament to the powerful influence our mentors have on us.

CHAPTER 11—WEEK ELEVEN
"I Love You Too Much"

Sunday, April 6

Today I went to the cemetery to mark the fourth anniversary of Barbara's death. Arielle and Jillian came with me, along with their families. It was the first time Jillian has been to the cemetery since her mother's death. She was so strong when Barbara was dying, helping me to care for her round-the-clock, but after her mom's death it was too painful for Jillian to think or talk about her. I haven't pressured her to visit her mother's grave, but I think it will now be easier for her to work through loss. I've learned that everyone grieves differently. I'm at one extreme, talking and writing about Barbara incessantly, while Jillian is at the other extreme. It may be that my public grief—teaching courses and writing books on love and loss—has compelled her to withdraw into private grief. But she was ready to visit the cemetery today. We stayed for about an hour. Arielle and Jillian and their husbands Dave and Alex stood near Barbara's grave and quietly talked while I played with our grandchildren a few feet away. The kids thought we were in a playground, and they ran and tumbled on the wet ground, instantly muddying their clothes. We picked up small stones and put them on the gravestones, as is the Jewish custom at cemeteries. I tickled the kids and turned them upside down, causing them to squeal with delight, and then I swung them from their arms and legs as if we were acrobats at a circus. I love playing with them, and I realize how much I miss seeing them everyday. While we were having fun, Jillian nursed Max, who is only three months old. The cemetery is peaceful and serene, and the grass was beginning to turn green. It was a time of renewal and rebirth, and I was aware of the profound intergenerational connection when grandparents and grandchildren are together, especially at a cemetery.

The cemetery visit allowed me to reflect on my characteristic way of grieving. In *Men Don't Cry . . . Women Do*, Martin and Doka (2000) describe two distinct patterns of grief, "intuitive" and "instrumental," and a third pattern, "blended," which combines elements of both:

> The intuitive griever converts more of his or her energy into the affective domain and invests less into the cognitive. For the intuitive griever grief

consists primarily of profoundly painful feelings. These grievers tend to spontaneously express their painful feelings through crying and want to share their inner experiences with others. The instrumental griever, on the other hand, converts most of the instinctual energy generated by bereavement into the cognitive domain rather than the affective. Painful feelings are tempered; for the instrumental griever, grief is more of an intellectual experience. Consequently, instrumental grievers may channel energy into activity. They may also prefer to discuss problems rather than feelings. (p. 31)

Those with a blended pattern, which constitutes the vast majority of individual grievers, choose adaptive strategies "that are more evenly balanced, reflecting the greater symmetry between the cognitive and affective responses of the individual" (p. 32). Those who are "dissonant" grievers express grief differently than they experience it, and are thus "truly at war with themselves" (p. 58).

Martin and Doka are careful to point out that there are many ways to experience and express grief. "No pattern is superior or inferior to the other. It is the individual griever's choice and implementation of effective adaptive strategies that determine how well he or she adjusts to his or her loss" (p. 35). This is an important conclusion because of the cultural "bias toward affective expression": the widespread belief among counselors that affective expressiveness is more therapeutic than cognitive or behavioral responses. Martin and Doka also observe that patterns of grief exist along a continuum; it is rare to find someone who is either a "pure" intuitive or a "pure" instrumental griever.

According to Martin and Doka's classification, I exhibit characteristics of both patterns of grief. I score high on "intuitive griever" questions such as "I am more emotional than most people I know" and "It is easy for me to cry and show my feelings"; I score high on "instrumental griever" questions such as "I find that solving problems associated with loss helps me." Like most intuitive grievers, I experience intense feelings of loss and sorrow, and I usually tear up when hearing my students cry over their own losses. I also experience grief as "waves of affect," another characteristic of intuitive grievers. Martin and Doka cite Shakespeare's words in *Macbeth* to describe intuitive grievers—"Give sorrow words, the grief that does not speak knits the o'erwrought heart and bids it break"—a quotation I cite often in my teaching and writing. My belief in the talking cure, the writing cure, and the teaching cure reveals my commitment to facilitate the expression of emotions, an important adaptive strategy for intuitive grievers. I want and need to discuss my feelings with other people, a process that helps me work through my grief. Unlike most intuitive grievers, I don't experience prolonged periods of confusion, disorganization, or disorientation.

Like instrumental grievers, I strive for self-mastery and engage in problem-solving as a strategy to control my feelings and environment. Instrumental grievers find comfort and solace through activity, especially memorializing the deceased: "Carving an urn, digging a grave, chiseling a tombstone, planting a memorial tree, and beginning a memorial fund or scholarship are just a few of the ways action becomes mourning" (Martin & Doka, p. 49). My main activity after Barbara's death has been teaching courses and writing books on love and loss. I identify with the instrumental griever's efforts to "do something" to deal with loss. Like other instrumental grievers, I have experienced grief physically as augmented energy. My desire to learn as much about bereavement as possible, in an effort to heal myself, is a characteristic of the instrumental griever. Interestingly, Martin and Doka suggest that many people who enter the field of thanatology "as a result of, perhaps even as a way of dealing with, their own losses" (p. 134), are instrumental grievers, a generalization that certainly applies to me. And yet unlike instrumental grievers, I am not reluctant to talk about my emotions, nor do I elevate thinking over feeling. According to Martin and Doka, most men are instrumental grievers and most women are intuitive grievers—a gender stereotype that is untrue for me. Given my responses to the twenty-five questions of the "Grief Pattern Inventory" in the Appendix of *Men Don't Cry . . . Women Do*, I am a blended griever, committed equally to both emotional expression and cognitive processing.

Martin and Doka observe that counselors need to become aware of their own grief patterns so that they avoid projecting their own biases onto their clients. Counselors also need to know, as Sue and Sue (1999) point out, that "different cultural groups may be more receptive to certain counseling/communication styles because of cultural and sociopolitical factors" (p. 91). Regardless of whether death educators are ministers, therapists, or literature professors, they should remember that there is no "correct" way to grieve: each person will experience loss and recovery in a unique way. There are many ways to respond to grief—emotionally, cognitively, spiritually, and existentially—and each person will choose adaptive strategies consistent with his or her life experience.

After we left the cemetery, we had lunch at McDonald's, and Arielle told me that Nate, who will be five in August, and the only grandchild whom Barbara saw, said, "Baba Jeff should write a book about Grandma Barbara so we can remember her." Arielle was flabbergasted by the comment, as I was. Perhaps he heard us talk about the book—I had showed him the photo of himself and his mom that appears in it—but his remark seemed to come from nowhere. The wisdom of children. During lunch I said, "Nate, I love you too much." "Why?" he asked. I didn't answer.

Monday, April 7 and Wednesday, April 9

Assignment 9, "Write to Life," was due last week, and toward the end of Monday's class Scout read aloud her seven-page essay about visiting her grandfather at Montauk, a small hamlet on the easternmost part of Long Island that is thronged with beach lovers during the summer. She teared up at the end of the essay, and I completed the reading. I include the opening and closing sections of the essay:

When I signed up for this class, I invariably knew that I would write about my grandpa. In fact, I thought that I would write about him sooner, or in more essays. This assignment is the ninth, and aside from the paragraph I wrote on him for our first assignment on four loves and four losses, I have not chosen to write on him for any other essay. When you handed out this assignment, however, I knew right away that *this* was the assignment I *needed* to use to write about my grandpa. When I read over the assignment, I suddenly realized that the reason I had not written sooner about my grandpa is because I feel I am slowly forgetting everything I remember about him. He only died five years ago this past January, but to me, it seems like I saw him eons ago.

Most of my memories of my grandpa are him on the beach; this is where we spent the most time together. He lived in Montauk, New York, and my family and I would make weekend trips out to see him during the summer. We did not even need to call grandpa when we arrived in Montauk; we simply knew to park the car on Essex Street, unload our beach chairs, toys, cooler, and dad's surfboard, and walk down onto the beach by the Terrace hotel. Grandpa would be sitting there in his chair, under his umbrella, wind blocker protecting him, mini cooler handily next to him. His white hair looked even whiter, next to the dark Ray Ban sunglasses he wore. When he would go into the sun, he would put a cap on to protect his face. I remember him wearing bright colored swim trunks—two pairs distinctly stand out: a solid blue pair and a solid yellow pair. He would sport the trunks either bare-chested showing his sun-tanned slightly potbellied stomach, or wearing a sweatshirt, depending on the intensity of the wind and time of day.

By the time we arrived at the beach, usually around eleven Saturday morning, he would have his cutting board out with a hunk of cheese, crackers, and big purple grapes. His glass of red wine was at his side at all times. Being a true Italian, he was usually drinking a bottle of Chianti. This vivid memory, the one of him relaxing on the beach that comes to mind any time I think of grandpa, makes me wish that I could be with him now on the beach—talking to him over his cheese and wine while looking out to sea. I can picture his lighthearted, Italian accented voice, making jokes about this or the other. If my dad was by us, I am sure we would poke fun at him. We would probably sit there for hours enjoying his fresh cheese, drinking multiple bottles, talking about life, or just sitting there watching the waves. Although I was young, just from my memories of him always with a goofy smile, content with sitting and enjoying the beach scene, I know that being in his company as an adult would have undoubtedly been a great pleasure . . . .

Although I was 16 when he died, looking back now, I realize I was still too young to fully comprehend what was going on. I was too young to know what cancer actually meant, and to grasp that I would never have a grandparent again. Looking back now I clearly see that I was actually, despite my beliefs, too young to understand the situation, and to understand how to react to the situation of losing a loved one. He was the first and only family member that I was alive to meet and then lose; he was the only grandparent I ever had the chance to get to know. When I was born in 1987 all of my other grandparents had already died: my father's mother from emphysema, his father from pancreatic cancer, and my mom's mother had died from an overdose of anaesthesia she was administered during a simple operation when my mom was only five years old. Being the only grandparent I would ever know, I wish I had realized what his loss meant at the time, and what it would mean in the future. I wish I knew how easy it would be to forget certain memories or features about a person after he or she died. I wish I knew that I would miss him still today, and this loss would be intensified by not being able to remember him fully.

Before I started writing this essay, I had a couple of days that were free, so I decided to take a trip out to Montauk to visit my grandpa's grave. I thought that by being there, a flood of memories might pour back into my head. I was wrong. The only thing that struck me hard when I went to visit him was the date he died, and that he was gone—unable to help me realize childhood memories spent on the beach with him. When I visited his grave, I reacted much like you describe in your book *Dying to Teach*, and like Philip Roth's (1991) observation in *Patrimony*, "I find that while visiting a grave one has thoughts that are more or less anybody's thoughts, and leaving aside the matter of eloquence, don't differ too much from Hamlet's contemplating the skull of Yorick. There seems to be little to be thought or said that isn't a variant of 'he hath borne me on his back a thousand times.' . . . What cemeteries prove, at least to people like me, is not that the dead are present but that they are gone. They are gone and, as yet, we aren't. This is fundamental and, however unacceptable, grasped easily enough" (Berman, 2007, p. 188; Roth, 1991, pp. 20–21). Indeed, there I was looking at his headstone, knowing he would never again be down the beach by the Terrace, and that I would never be able to sit on that beach with him to have a serious talk about life, while enjoying his wine and cheese.

Like Scout, I find myself slowly forgetting details about a lost loved one, details that become shadowy through the passage of time. Writing these details down, when they are still vivid, helps to preserve them. Writing is, as Thomas Larson (2007) suggests, a "prophylactic against forgetting" (p. 96). Many of the details we think we have forgotten spring to life through the act of writing. Thus the "Write to Life" assignment. Scout may have forgotten much about her grandfather, but her verbal portrait is detailed enough to allow us to see him. Writing heightens her connection to him—so much so that she visited his grave in order to bring him to life in her essay. The visit to the cemetery may not have resulted in any epiphanies, but I suspect that she will long remember and appreciate her loving words.

On Wednesday Addison read her essay about her brother's suicide. It was the first time she wrote about him since Assignment 1:

Addison
My brother Mick died on June 7, 1992. I was six at the time. I have a few memories of him, but for the most part, I never knew him very well. What I

know now is through stories that my sister or my mom have told me. When I was little, I thought he was so much older. Now I'm the same age he was when he died, and I can see just how young twenty-one is.

Up until I was 10, my parents refused to be clear with me about what had happened. I remember the anger and humiliation I felt when my peers would ask how my brother died. I would shrug and say, "I don't know." When I was six, this was acceptable. By the time I was 10, I was beginning to get teased about it. When I look back on it, I wonder why the kids were still concerned about something that had happened four years earlier, but the fact is kids are cruel.

After begging my parents to tell me what happened, they did. I realize now that I was too young, even at 10, to understand what happened. I can also see now that maybe my mom didn't tell me right away because it was too painful for her. She sat me on her lap and asked me if I knew what suicide was. I did, but I told her I didn't because suicide was scary and I didn't want to think about it. She explained that suicide is when a person kills themself, and that's what Mick did. With a gun in the backyard.

After that, I didn't ask questions about Mick for a few years. I was afraid to approach the subject now that I knew how shocking and terrible his death had been. Eventually, however, I began slowly asking my mom more questions about what Mick had been like while he was still alive. My mom would only be able to talk about him for a few minutes before her eyes would fill with tears and she would shake her head and turn away. As the years passed, my mom was able to talk about him more and more. Now, she can share a story about him, laugh, and move on with her day. However, it took 16 years of grieving before she was able to do this.

Ask anyone who knows my mom—she is the biggest Rolling Stones fan you'll ever meet. She can answer any question you throw at her. There is a sticker of the Rolling Stones tongue on the back of her car. If she wasn't afraid of needles, she would get a tattoo, and it would be that tongue. Seriously, she knows the Rolling Stones better than you know yourself. My mom's undying obsession with the Rolling Stones is what gave my brother his name. The first time she told me my brother was named after Mick Jagger, I couldn't help it—I rolled my eyes. It was just like my mom to name her first born after a rock and roll legend.

My mom loves telling me how Mick loved to drive her and my dad crazy. She told me about one day when the house suddenly went very quiet and she realized I had disappeared. Frantic, she looked out the front window to see me sitting in the driver's seat of Mick's car, on his lap. I was steering the wheel as he pulled the car into the driveway. The next few minutes were a blur of "What were you thinking?!", "She's only five, SHE CAN'T DRIVE!", and "Do you know you could've killed your sister? DO YOU?!" He almost succeeded in giving my mom a heart attack.

I think about my brother a lot. Even though I didn't know him very well, I often wonder what he would have been like now. I wonder what he was like then. I feel kind of sick for thinking about it, but I like to think he killed himself outside as a favor to my mom. So she wouldn't have to clean up or anything. If that's true, that would mean he was caring, empathetic of what my mom was about to go through. Of course, if he was really thinking hard about sympathy for his family, he just would have gotten help.

My mom has offered to let me see the note my brother left. I have refused. I feel as though I would be violating him if I did. The note was not left to me; it was left to my mom. If he wanted me to someday read it, maybe he would've written one to me too. But he didn't, so I'm not going to intrude on something that was only meant for my mom. Sometimes I think about going back in time. What would I say to him? I've always said that I wouldn't change the past even if I could, but I think I would change this. It would completely alter the lives of everyone I know, but I think it would be worth it.

In the process of learning about my brother, I have also learned a lot about my mom. As it turns out, my mom is the strongest woman I know. Losing a child is the worst thing a parent can go through, and my mom didn't even have a chance to grieve. She told me she wanted to stay in bed and cry and never get up. But she couldn't and she didn't, because she had other children that needed her. She had me and my brother, who was only four. We needed a mommy. She had an older daughter, only 19, who is now suffering from the same depression that ultimately killed my older brother. My mom could not mope and cry, for our sakes. Two days after her eldest son committed suicide, she came to my dance recital, and she went to my younger brother's pre-school graduation, and she did it all with a smile on her face. She comforted my sister and tried to make her feel better, even though she couldn't make herself feel better.

In my attic, there is a cardboard box with Mick's things. My mom has always been a bit prone to dramatics, so she planned on going through it on his fifth death anniversary. She wasn't ready. She said she would be at 10. She wasn't ready. Then one day, 12 years after my brother passed away, she was in the attic, getting a suitcase for my dad's business trip. She saw the box in a corner, and opened it. She pulled out the jerseys, the dice that hung in his precious car, the CDs and movies he had collected in his bedroom. She smiled at each of them, and carefully put them back in their place. She got downstairs and felt an overwhelming sadness fall upon her. She cried a little, but she has told me that she knows he is gone and there isn't anything else she can do. She grieves on his birthday and his deathday. She thinks about him everyday. He is her baby, her first child. He will always hold a special place in her heart. My mom has accepted his death, although she will always miss and love him. The blame is gone. I hope that one day I can be as strong of a woman as she is.

Miller and Rotatori's (1986) observation—suicide is considered a "taboo topic" by Americans (p. 24)—is still true. Suicide remains one of the most stigmatized forms of death, overwhelming relatives and close friends with dark emotions—guilt, grief, anger, betrayal, and confusion. Addison's essay focuses less on her brother's suicide than on its continuing impact on her family, the anguished aftermath of suicide, including, though she doesn't use the term, disenfranchised grief. Her essay is at once insightful and emotionally expressive.

We learn about the anger and humiliation she experienced as a child when her friends asked about the details of her brother's suicide, details she was unable to convey at the time but that she now discloses in her essay. Suicide was so "scary" for her that she tried not to think about it while growing up, but now she does, and the result is a well written essay that helps us to understand one of life's most shadowy acts. (We recall Chipo's statement that his mind "went blank" when Addison told him about her brother's suicide.) She carefully controls the mood and tone of the essay, capturing her mother's sadness, her comic obsession with the Rolling Stones, and her exasperation over her daughter's early driving lesson. Never sentimental or maudlin, the essay honors not only her brother's memory but also her mother's strength and courage, qualities that we see in her daughter as well. The essay demonstrates that although the grief arising from a loved one's suicide is never-ending, one can still find meaning and happiness in life, an insight that is often forgotten when tragedy strikes.

Like Jillian's visit to her mother's grave, Addison's essay reveals the role of time in the process of bereavement. One must be ready to talk about a loved one's death, just as one must be ready to visit a cemetery. Each person will be ready at a different time. Writers must also be ready. Addison disclosed in the first writing assignment that her brother had committed suicide, but she was not ready to write about it until 10 weeks later. I don't know whether she shared her writings in Love and Loss with her mother, but I suspect her mother would have responded to her daughter's last sentence with the words, "You already are."

"We're Taking Risks In A Safe Place"

Monday, April 14 and Wednesday, April 16

Last week Assignment 10, "Reading *Dying to Teach*," was due. This week we discussed Assignment 11, "What if Love Doesn't Work Out?" Beth found it one of the hardest topics of the semester. "When I asked my mother what she thought her life would be like without my father, she was actually disturbed by this idea." Nor was this a topic Beth felt comfortable writing about; she thought to herself, "You still haven't found love, and you don't know what it is yet." Several students remarked in their essays that one of their biggest fears is falling out of love with the person they marry. "I'm very cautious when it comes to relationships," Bianca confessed, "and I never get involved with someone if I can't see myself spending the rest of my life with that person." Addison admitted that her greatest fear is her boyfriend's death. "When I think about what would happen if he died, I cannot look past my immediate actions. I imagine I would crash to the ground, curl in a ball, cry until my throat went raw and my eyes dried up. I think I would lie in bed for weeks."

On Monday I gave an optional, anonymous take-home assignment on crying in the classroom. Eight of the sixteen students who turned in responses indicated that they cried while reading aloud an essay in the course: four of the eight were surprised that they cried. The frequency of crying ranged from once to several times. All eight felt that it was acceptable to become emotional while reading an intense essay. No one who cried felt judged or criticized by a classmate. Significantly, seven of the eight people who cried while reading their own essay aloud responded in the same way when hearing a classmate's essay. All eight students who cried felt that the course has increased their empathy for classmates. Seven of the eight who did not cry while reading aloud an essay also felt increased empathy. Several people felt sad over hearing a classmate's essay, but this sadness soon disappeared. Three people made noteworthy comments. One wrote, "Crying is a very natural and significant reaction to all of the topics we were asked to write about. I do not regret any tear that I have shed, and I'm glad that I was comfortable enough to show who I really am and not be embarrassed." The second observed, "At the beginning of the semester, you said that this class was not a replacement for therapy. I think, however, that this class has helped most if not all of us. We have become a kind of support group, whether we wanted this to happen or not." And the third noted, "Some of the essays take the risk of uncovering a pit of anxiety. But uncovering it allows us the chance to fill it in. We're taking risks in a safe place."

My students' acceptance of the value of crying reminds me of an observation made by Maimonides, the twelfth century Jewish philosopher: "Those who grieve find comfort in weeping and in arousing their sorrows, until the body is too tired to bear the inner emotions" (in Moffat, 1992, p. 100). Nico made a telling observation about the number of students who cried while they were writing or reading aloud an essay. "That made me feel good, not because I like to think of these lovely people as grief-stricken, but because I am impressed by the idea of students having such a profound engagement with their writing. This, I believe, is the hardest and most essential thing to do: get the students to want to write, to see writing as worthwhile, to imagine themselves capable of writing in such a way that their words will reach out to their classmates."

To date, four women out of 25 students, or 16% of the class, have written about their experiences cutting themselves, This percentage is nearly identical to Whitlock, Eckenrode, and Silverman's (2006) research indicating that 17% of the more than 8000 students studied from two northeastern universities, which the news media identified as Cornell and Princeton, engaged in self-injurious behaviors, three-quarters of whom engaged in these activities more than once. A student began this week's diary begins with the following paragraph:

> I remember the power of cutting. I remember holding a silver exacto-knife; I remember cleaning it with antibacterial wash to make sure it was always clean. I remember holding it tight and staring at my partial reflection. I remember running the water extra hot and watching blood dot up and then become streams. I remember watching blood pour down my legs and swirl around my feet. I remember watching how the water darkened and how the white of the shower turned quickly to crimson. I remember the first time and how I wasn't sure if I was a terrible person. I remember bending down to where the blood met my ankle, and moving my hand slowly up my leg, pulling the blood upward and toward the smooth cut, trying to return every ounce to its home. I remember letting it go and watching it all run right back to my foot, this time lighter and more dissipated. I remember feeling a relief.

This is a haunting description of cutting, as aesthetically powerful as any I have read in a published novel or memoir. As if unconsciously confirming the power of the contagion effect, the author remarks that she began to rub her arms when she heard me read aloud a classmate's earlier description of cutting: "I rubbed them hard trying to make old memories disappear." Elsewhere in her diary she reveals how she was always afraid people would see her scars and that she now struggles to resist the urge to cut. "I wonder how many people Faith and Lia have told their stories to. I am proud of both of them for sharing their stories with our class. I believe that if there is any group of people that would be so accepting of these honest stories, it would be our class." From this the author concludes that her class is an "amazing" learning experience. "This class is a hope that there are better ways to cope. This class has proved that. This class continues to prove that. I hope that everyone finds strength somewhere, and a productive way to cope. I hope others can avoid the crimson swirl, and I hope that with all my heart."

"Write As If You Were Dying"

Wednesday, April 23

There was no class on Monday, and much of Wednesday's class was spent with sentence revisions, reading several diary entries, and passing out information about the remaining two weeks of classes.

Assignment 12 was due today. I took it from Annie Dillard's (1980) book *The Writing Life*: "Write as if you were dying. At the same time, assume you write for an audience consisting solely of terminally ill patients" (p. 68). This is an intimidating assignment, to be sure, but it inspired several important essays. Beth wrote about the two traumatic experiences that have shaped her life: suffering from anorexia when she was 11 and being diagnosed with cervical cancer in 2004, when she was 18. "Even though I did not consider myself as being at risk for dying, it was the closest I have ever come to my own death, and it was very real. . . . The greatest gift cancer has given me is a sense of fearlessness. If I can handle cancer, I feel I can try anything."

Lucy imagined that she was writing her boyfriend for the last time, urging him not to dwell on her impending death. "You have helped to make my life as wonderful as possible. You are the love of my life. Continue living, and continue loving; life is nothing without love. I won't ask you to remember me always, because I know you will. I only hope that you can find in yourself the strength to push memories [of our love] aside and make room for new ones."

Jacob wrote a letter to his dying grandmother in which he expresses a secret wish: "'Do you remember the moment I told my mother that when grandma dies I want to be buried in the same coffin?' I remember you smiling during my hospital visit and you telling my therapist that I had two mothers. I have always perceived you more as a mother than a grandmother. I am grateful for pouring your whole heart, knowledge, and soul into me."

Saverio imagined writing a letter to his family in which he describes his love for them. The letter is tonally restrained, but his diary entry records how emotional he became during the assignment. "I cried writing it. I never cry. I'm not ashamed to cry. It's just that I have not come across anything so far that drew tears. I cannot believe I cried writing this assignment. It really shocked me, but then again, it didn't. We all have people we love to death and would do anything for. I am glad that I realize what I have today." Saverio stated that he intended to allow his family to read his letter. "I hope they like it. More importantly, I hope they see how much they mean to me."

Kamilluh expressed her undying gratitude to God. "If it were not for your mercies and grace, I would not exist, nor have a purpose, nor have my name written in the Book of Life. You have stayed with me and guided me through this life, and I cannot wait to meet you in the next one." Kamilluh believed that God's love is eternal. "What I want to thank you for most is remaining faithful. You told your people that you would never lead them astray, and that when temptation presented itself, you would provide a way out of it. You said that you created every creation out of love, and that might be the greatest explanation of why I never felt you left me, even in my most dreary times."

"I Used To Cry In The Middle Of The Night and Contemplate Suicide"

Monday, April 28 and Wednesday April 28

This was the last full week of the semester, and we began with Javarro's essay about depression, which we didn't have time to hear last week:

> The experience of depression is one I will never forget. I had my most recent encounter with depression back in April 2007 when I was in a motor vehicle accident that changed my life. Before being in this accident, it seemed as if everything was just going so well for me, and in an instant everything that I worked so hard for had just vanished. I can remember this day as if it was just yesterday.
>
> It was a Friday afternoon, and the sun was shining as if it was a spotlight. I had just come from picking up residents from work and taking them to the bank so that they could cash their checks. Everything was so marvelous. As my residents and I were enjoying one another in conversation about our plans for the weekend, we were sideswiped by an eighteen-wheeler. Fortunately, everyone was all right. Everyone, that is, except for me.
>
> Initially, I was fine and happy to be alive. However, about an hour after the accident I started getting sharp pains down my side, and I was rushed to a healthcare center in Saratoga. Once arriving there, I was given numerous X-rays and once the X-rays came in, the nurse directed me to the waiting room while the doctor reviewed them. As I sat, patiently waiting to go home, I was surprised with some news that I didn't expect to hear: the doctor told me that I had fractured my C5 bone in my back. But that was not even the worst news of the situation. The doctor also informed me that by fracturing a bone in my back the way that I did, it was possible I could become paralyzed.
>
> God must have been watching out for me because I was not paralyzed, but it still did not keep me from having to do four and a half months of rehab. It also prevented me from being able to have a chance at playing football after all of the training that I had gone through in order to prepare myself for the season. Not only did this accident take me away from sports, but it also caused me not to be able to work and take care of myself like I usually was able to do. Unable to play sports or work, I felt as if I was less of a man because I couldn't physically or mentally take care of myself.

> Depression is a serious issue that is overlooked many times. It easily lowered my self-esteem and made me feel as if I was nothing. I never knew that anything could make me feel so useless because I was so used to being active. My mother told me, "this accident was just a warning from God to you that you need to slow down because you are living too much in the fast lane." When my mother first told me this, I didn't pay her any attention because I knew that she was just trying to make me feel better. But now as I look back on my life, I can understand what my mother was saying because I was living my life too much in the fast lane, only consuming myself with the thought of money and sports: I wasn't cherishing my youth while I was still young.
>
> Due to this accident, I can say that what I learned from personally experiencing depression is that no matter how busy I feel that I am, I always need to make time for myself. I also learned that everyone who says he or she is your friend isn't your friend because a true friend will always be there for you, regardless of what obstacles you are going through.

Javarro's early writings were unusual because he wrote about a childhood that many of his classmates never experienced: growing up in a dangerous inner city, being part of a "hood," and trying to avoid becoming one more victim of a senseless crime. He wrote movingly about seeing some of his friends wounded or murdered by rival gangs. In one memorable essay, he writes about his successful struggle to free himself from this violent world. "I have lost a lot of soldiers in my life. They are either incarcerated or dead, so I hope I can reach at least one child from the younger generation and help change his life." These early writings were powerful, but they were also filled with grammatical and stylistic errors, many of which he had made the previous semester, when he took my Expository Writing course. We had gone over these errors last semester, and he learned to avoid them, but then they began to reappear in his writings during the beginning of this semester—a phenomenon I have noticed with many students. And so I was pleased that his essay on depression was technically polished, showing the improvement of his writing skills. It is not easy for anyone to write about depression, which remains socially stigmatized, and it must have been especially difficult to acknowledge that he "felt less of a man." Javarro's essay would be stronger if he showed, as specifically as possible, how and why he felt less of a man. Javarro's essay emboldened Nico to write about his own experience of depression, and he supplies us with the concrete details to help us understand what it is like to suffer from a mood disorder:

> Javarro's essay had a strong emotional impact in me. Several years ago, I started to experience incapacitating, severe back pain. If you've never had nerve pain running down your legs, you can't imagine how horrible it can be. The pain causes your muscles to lock up (this is called the pain reflex arc), and the muscle tension itself becomes worse than the nerve pain. After a few months of this condition steadily worsening, I could no longer put on my fucking right sock on my own. It was terrifying. I used to cry in the middle of the night and contemplate suicide. I saw scores of doctors. I felt totally

powerless and felt that my life was spiraling wildly into an abyss from which there was no return. In short: it sucked ass. And it was depressing. I felt like less of a man. I wasn't able to have sex with my girlfriend, or participate in physical activities. In the end, however, sappy old adages prove true, and I can honestly say that the back pain fiasco led me, through the weirdest, most circuitous route, to leave law school and pursue my true love, which is literature, by enrolling in grad school. I wrote my grad application on yellow legal pads, lying on my back on my futon couch. After a few months in the doctoral program, doing the things I was truly meant to be doing, my back pain dissipated until it was only a bad memory. Like Javarro, I found that hard times can make you slow down and carefully consider what in your life matters most.

I was very impressed with Javarro's reading. The sensitivity and openness with which he wrote about a personal issue were especially touching because it seemed at odds with who he outwardly appears to be; he's a big, strong, handsome black guy, and generally he doesn't give the slightest indication of worry or weakness. Hearing Javarro read his essay made me see him in a different light. I'd known from previous essays that he was a gifted writer, but I had never suspected he was capable of making himself so vulnerable in front of his classmates. . . .

After class, I walked back to the Humanities building with Jeff. We talked about the tenor of the class in recent weeks, about how brutally emotional many of the student essays had been, about how many students had been unable to read their own work because it was too painful. I told Jeff that my girlfriend Erica's visit to the class two weeks prior had produced an odd reaction in me, in that her visible emotional reaction to emotionally charged student essays caused me to reflect upon my own inability to experience a similar reaction. Why is this? I asked. Am I incapable of relating to the sad experiences of others? Am I heartless? Or is it that I've spent so long reading fictional prose that everything, true or untrue, strikes the same emotional register? But then I had a realization that I wasn't heartless, but that, instead of putting myself in the place of the author, I am a caretaker, as is Jeff.

I appreciate Nico's characterization of me, but I would qualify his last sentence by saying that I was a caretaker, or caregiver, only for Barbara, when she was dying, not for my students. One can be caring without being a caretaker. I make this distinction because the "pedagogy of self-disclosure," as I practice it, requires a caring, empathic teacher, not a caretaker, which is defined by the online dictionary "Answers.com," as a "person who is legally responsible for the person or property of another considered by law to be incompetent to manage his or her affairs." Teachers are not caretakers—they cannot and should not be required to perform the weighty and often burdensome responsibilities necessary to care for people who cannot care for themselves. My students know that I care about them, as I believe they care about me, but we are not each other's caretaker. Caring for another person may sometimes become burdensome, but more often than not, when we care for others, they care for us, a reciprocal act that is mutually beneficial.

Now that the course was almost over, I wanted to know whether the students felt that the two problems that emerged last month were solved, and so I asked them to respond to the following questions:

Problems with Our Course

As far as I know, there have been only two problems with our Love and Loss course this semester, both of which you conveyed to me through your diaries, and which I then read aloud: first, the tension one person felt between my new and returning students, and second, the frustration another person experienced when the returning students would talk among themselves during sentence revisions. To solve these problems, I asked you to sit next to a different classmate during each class. No one has mentioned these problems again, and I assume, though I don't know for sure, that these problems have disappeared. Would you comment briefly—and anonymously—about whether you also believe these problems have been solved. Have there been other problems in the course? If so, please explain.

Nearly everyone felt that the two problems were now solved. "I never thought it was a problem at all," one person wrote. "It is only natural to talk to people in the class whom you already know. I did. It definitely helped us to get to know each other. As far as I know, there have not been any other problems. Out of all my classes, this class has the nicest people and most welcoming. I would like to consider us all as 'old' students now, and I'm very grateful to have met these people and shared stories amongst one another." Another person agreed. "I think people still talk, but now the old and new students are talking together. I never had a problem, and whatever problem people may have had has been solved."

Most people liked the suggestion to sit next to different classmates. "I think that having us sit next to a different person every class turned out to be a wonderful idea. I have to admit that I wasn't too thrilled when you first suggested it because I like to sit in the same exact seat all the time. However, sitting next to different classmates gave us the opportunity to talk to different people when we worked on sentence revisions" Another person agreed. "It became a fun game to see where everyone would sit. One day while shuffling around, I heard someone say, 'I don't even realize who is a *new* student and who is an *old* student anymore.' I think everyone would agree with this. It makes me smile." The same student observed, "I almost wonder if Jeff made up this story about someone being disturbed by this 'old/new' student issue. I wonder if he did it to see what would happen."

I didn't make up these two problems, neither of which I was aware until I gave students an opportunity to tell me how they felt about the course. I knew that it would be tricky to disclose these problems to the class, for there was the possibility that relatively minor problems would become more serious if they were debated out loud, with some students later withdrawing into silence, perhaps less willing to self-disclose in the future. We avoided these serious problems by giving everyone an opportunity to express a point of view while remaining anonymous.

Had these problems continued, the trust that had developed in our classroom would have been compromised, at least for some people, making self-disclosure problematic. Trust is, like empathy, essential for self-disclosure. Although the teacher-student relationship is asymmetrical, it is based on both trust and empathy. As Solomon and Flores (2001) observe, "trust is not merely reliability, predictability, or what is sometimes understood as *trustworthiness*. It is always the *relationship* within which trust is based and which trust itself helps create" [italics in original] (p. 6). They quote Kierkegaard's famous statement that trust involves a "leap of faith" (p. 46)—one that is necessary if students are willing to write about love and loss. Solomon and Flores also remind us that care is "perhaps the most essential ingredient of authentic trust, not only care about the immediate outcome but care about the relationship" (p. 105).

Several people suggested that I should make a greater effort the next time I teach this course to help students learn their classmates' names, as Nico did when he taught the class. There were two other suggestions: announcing before I read an anonymous essay that anyone could leave the room if the essay was too disturbing to hear, and writing an essay about a situation that made you cry but that now makes you laugh.

What were the funniest moments of the semester? I asked students to jot down some of these moments so we wouldn't forget them. Many people cited Cath's essay about a love-hate relationship to what we first thought was a person but was, in reality, her aging car. Saverio began his essay on "Writing a Wrong" with the sentence, "I am definitely going to make a few enemies amongst the ladies with this story." The story involves dating two women who find out about the other's existence and then revenge themselves on him at a movie theater, where he has taken one of them only to find the other waiting to ambush him. As he was reading his essay aloud, the women in the class reveled in his embarrassment. "I was glad that I made everyone laugh, even though it was at my own expense." Two of Gloria's funniest moments involved her teacher's cluelessness:

> One of my all time funny moments is an incident that happened to you, Jeff. It was an extremely windy day, on a Wednesday night. You blew into class right at 5:45. Most of us were there already, sitting in our semi-circle, awaiting your arrival. As you entered the room, we couldn't help but notice your hair had become slightly windblown. We all sat there giggling until Scotty yelled, "Hey, Berman," and motioned you to slick it down. It was so funny. You looked like a cockatoo. Another funny moment again caused by you was a story you shared with us, twice! It was the story about your grandson and how you told him, "I love you too much!" It was an adorable story and I am so glad you shared it. But the funny part about this story is that the next class we had, you were very excited to share the same story with us. You retold it, as proud as you were the first time. Again we giggled but let you enjoy the moment.

"I Am Not Alone In This Battle"

Monday, May 5

Monday was our last class, and we began by having everyone fill out the university and department evaluations of the course. I handed back everyone's writings along with final grades. Afterwards, a few students volunteered to read aloud their Assignment 13 essays, "Learning from a Classmate." Beth singled out Javarro's recent essay about depression. "I wanted to give him a standing ovation because I had no idea he went through that kind of struggle; it takes a special person to overcome those struggles." Jacob's essay "The Death of a Marriage" impressed Nicholette. "While reading the essay, I made one powerful realization that has helped me to start my healing process: I don't know if I will ever be able to talk about my father and not shed tears, but I know that I am not alone in this battle." Jacob taught Nicholette that "despite all of the hardships from his father's domestic abuse, he came out of that situation with strong intentions to take his father's mistakes into consideration and learn from them."

Assignment 13 was a summing up of the semester as well as a leave-taking. "I've been telling my mom a lot about this course, and what I'm writing, which usually doesn't happen between the two of us," Maggie stated. "She asked me a question the other day that I still can't seem to answer. 'What do you think you'll remember the most from that class?' My answer is still, 'I have no idea.' I don't think I'll remember whole parts of this class, but rather bits and pieces will randomly come to mind." Maggie singled out "Chipo's laughter after hearing a funny line of an essay, Lia's tears while reading her essay on her grandpa, the way she wrote so beautifully about my own grandpa, and the goose bumps that formed while I was listening to Faith's essays." Isabella concluded her essay with an Italian proverb: "L'insegnante e' quello come la candela di cera au da la luce a tritto, e si brucia," which she translated as follows: "The teacher is like the candle which lights others in consuming itself."

I find Isabella's simile intriguing, I told my students, but I believe that my own candle burns brightest when I help light their candles. In helping students, I help myself. The more I give, the more I receive. I have never felt, even after a difficult class, that teaching has extinguished my light. The opposite is true: teaching is for me an inexhaustible source of energy. That's why I love teaching and cannot imagine retiring. Now that the semester is over, I can say that Love and Loss is the best course I have taught—a statement that becomes more significant because I have enjoyed all of my courses in 35 years of teaching. But this course is special in so many ways. I have never felt so close to my students as I feel toward them, never experienced such intensity of emotions during every class, never seen so many people willing to share their stories of love and loss with teacher and classmates. Just as my students have learned so much about my life from reading *Dying to Teach*, I have learned so much about theirs. We have all grown as writers and people. In many cases, the growth has been dramatic and profound. We have seen how the course itself has become a part of each person's life. We have heard about our love for relatives and friends, and we've also read about the deaths of beloved parents, grandparents, siblings, nieces, and cousins.

Psychoanalysts talks about the end of a long analysis as a mourning, a feeling of grief for both analysand and analyst. We have seen a version of this mourning in the last two weeks. Many people have written about the sadness they experience now that the course is over. The sadness may be stronger for those who are now graduating. Based on the final assignments and diary entries, I believe we all love each other. This is not romantic or transgressive love, which would be dangerous and unruly in the classroom. Nor is it sentimentality, inauthentic love. Rather, what we feel is pedagogical love, the love that arises from teaching and learning from each other over a period of several months. I am not being naive when I use the word love, because our feeling is, like all types of love, focused as much on the other as on oneself. Our hearts go out to our classmates when we hear their stories of love and loss. We have been there for each other when someone has cried during the reading of an essay. We have been there for each other when we have praised a classmate's reading. We have been there for each other when we have wished a classmate good luck before a reading or patted a classmate on the back after a reading. And we remained there for each other despite where we were sitting. These acts of kindness and maturity testify to our pedagogical love for each other. I have never seen so much love in a classroom.

PART 2

Breakthroughs

The contagion effect is a ubiquitous if largely undocumented pedagogical force in all classrooms, but it is especially potent in a course on death education. My students' writings on love and loss demonstrate that sadness, anxiety, and grief are emotions that are easily spread to others in the classroom. Emotions, like viruses, are "communicable"—in our case, spread through students' (and teacher's) writings as well as their facial and vocal expressions. "It doesn't take much in people's expressions, voices, or actions for others to pick up on what they are feeling," Hatfield, Cacioppo, and Rapson (1994) observe. "Researchers have found that teacher expectancies and affect toward students can be determined from brief clips of teachers' behavior" (p. 129). The good news is that by the end of the semester, everyone concluded that the positive emotions—courage, strength, hope, optimism, perseverance, and gratitude—were far more powerful than the negative emotions. The students experienced their classmates' sorrow and distress but also their happiness and joy, and they felt solidarity and engagement with each other.

Our pedagogical experiment has, I believe, intriguing implications for what has become called the "positive psychology movement," a term adopted by Martin E. P. Seligman (2002) and popularized in his book *Authentic Happiness*. My students' writings affirmed the qualities emphasized by the positive psychology movement. These qualities are particularly important in a course on death education, for they remind us of the possibility of living a self-fulfilling life in a world beset by so many problems. The positive psychology movement has been criticized for failing to pay sufficient attention to the dark emotions of human life, but anyone who reads my students' writings on love and loss will conclude that these emotions are well represented.

Indeed, dark emotions appear in the writings of Chipo, Lia, Shannon, Faith, and "Anonymous," all of whom write about the way in which death has touched their lives. In what follows, I discuss how each student experiences a breakthrough as a result of Love and Loss. The darkness of the essays distressed everyone in the classroom, and yet, paradoxically, the essays were inspirational, conveying more hope than sadness. I conclude with a discussion of how my students responded to reading *Dying to Teach*, a book that moved them in expected and unexpected ways.

"I Have To Turn My Shattered Reality Into A Livable Dream"

Chipo's writings are noteworthy for several reasons. First, they show that students must be ready to write about their losses. He was not ready last semester, when he was a member of the Expository Writing class. He was ready this semester in Love and Loss.

Second, his early writings about his mother in Love and Loss were vague and tentative. In his first essay, "Writing about Four Loves and Losses in Your Life," he gave few details about her death. As he gained self-confidence, however, he began to write in depth about the impact of loss on his life, and his later essays are filled with concrete details, funny and sad moments, and rich expressive content. We can see his development as a storyteller. We can also see how the verbal portrait of his mother allows him to honor her memory and bring her to life to everyone in the classroom.

Third, his writings reveal the shattering of his early assumptive world, including the belief that his mother would be around forever, and the construction of a new assumptive world in which he recognizes the necessity to survive on his own without his mother and grandfather, though they are never far from his heart. This new assumptive world represented a shift in his understanding of his own life story. Writing about his new assumptive world helped him to construct a meaning for his mother's death, exploring, in the process, the relationship between the living and the dead. We can see in his writings the process of meaning-making and the construction of a new identity.

Fourth, contrary to his fear that he would not be able to share his writings with classmates, Chipo read these essays aloud, and they had a powerful effect on everyone. They were able to identify with his situation and empathize with his loss. His willingness to write about his mother's death emboldened his classmates to write about their own losses. His story became a gift that he shared with his fellow students, resulting in their own gifts to the class.

Fifth, in the assignment on "Write to Life" Chipo imagined reconciliation with his father, from whom he had long been estranged. We can see how writing serves as a form of both problem-solving and healing, in this case, repairing a broken relationship, enabling writers to probe their feelings and find solutions to problems that once appeared intractable.

Finally, Chipo's writings dramatize the intersubjectivity of the empathic classroom, where students teach and learn from each other. And what they remember are life lessons about courage, strength, hopefulness, and endurance that will help them confront challenges in the future.

"Love like the four leaf clover is rare in Chipo's life." That's how he opens his Assignment 1 essay, written in the third person point of view. A few paragraphs later he tells us that "Chipo never really knew what loss was until he lost the precious people in his life that money, time or deeds could not replace." He then elaborates on his major loss. "He had this lovely bond with his mother. She defines caring in his book, so much so that family members suggest that she was overprotective toward him. His second love is for his grandpa, whom he calls 'Dad.' His love for his grandpa fulfills a fatherly bond in his life that he did not have with his biological father." Notice that Chipo still uses the present tense to describe his feelings toward his grandfather, suggesting he has not yet adjusted to the reality of the recent death. Chipo spends less time discussing love than loss—and he writes less about his mother than about his grandfather. He devotes only five sentences to her death. "When he lost his mom in a car accident, it was too surreal for his fourteen-year-old mind to grasp. He had lost the closest person to his heart. He had always thought no matter the circumstances, his mom would be with him. Unfortunately, by the time she was pursuing a college degree, while crossing the street with his sister, they were hit by a car and his mother was killed. After losing his mom, Chipo was frightened because he now saw how harsh the world could be first hand." He reveals that harshness in the next sentences:

> He was locked out of his apartment by his sister's father at the same time he insisted that Chipo stay with him. He decided to live with his grandfather, who had been retired from [the] sanitation [department] since Chipo was born. Dealing with the loss of his mom was tough in 2001, but being able to build a solid relationship with his grandfather made the tears come through his eyes easier with someone who could understand his pain. He had lost his guardian angel, and his grandpa had lost his youngest daughter. Throughout the tough times his grandpa had seemed to gain a new vigor for life. But six years later, his grandpa got sick and passed away. Chipo had found out during CPR training when he was in college at Albany. He was in CPR training because he thought he needed to prepare to help his grandpa if necessary. Unfortunately, he did not make it in time.

Chipo states at the end of the essay that he "enjoyed writing as a way to express his feelings." Writing about love was easier than writing about loss. "He soon realized that he could never cherish the love until his circumstances made him realize he had lost people that were irreplaceable like the earth losing its rain-forests. He believes he has more loves because every time his heart is consumed with the sickness of death, he is usually given a dose of special medicine: two tablespoons of understanding, three cups of wisdom, four ounces of empathy, and a quarter cup of love made from scratch."

I sensed at the beginning of Love and Loss that Chipo was preparing himself to write about his mother's and grandfather's deaths. We can see from his first essay and diary that he compares his losses with those of his classmates, a comparison that is not a competition. Nowhere in any of his early or late writings does he imply his loss is greater than his classmates' losses or that he has a feeling of entitlement, the belief that he deserves special treatment. Nor does he use his classmates' stories only as an opportunity to talk about himself. Rather, he listens attentively to his classmates, reflects on their losses, and then affirms his connection with them. The empathic classroom encourages students to identify and sympathize with others without blurring the distinction between self and other. He is interested in his classmates' stories of love and loss for their own sake, because he finds them interesting and enlightening; at the same time, he sees how their stories relate to his own life. He is also sensitive to the ways in which his classmates express themselves through writing, hence, through the art of storytelling.

Students who have lost a parent to death or to divorce seldom realize that classmates have experienced similar losses. But this knowledge soon becomes evident in a self-disclosing writing course, as we see from Chipo's observations in his first diary entry. "My first class in Professor Berman's English 450 class was a unique experience. He read several of my classmates' reasons for joining the class. Their reasons reaffirmed why I knew it was a good choice for me to make a conscious effort to get in his class." Chipo singled out two students who made a strong impression on him. "One student said her father left a note saying he left [his family], and when she came home that night their mother and brother were showered in tears. I felt goose bumps on my skin trying to imagine how that pain must have felt. The other student mentions the loss of their grandfather in October. This stood out to me because I lost my grandfather in December, and it makes me curious to hear if that person is going through a similar time like I am dealing with in the loss of my grandpa, who I had a close relationship with."

For Assignment 2, "Writing about One of Your Classmate's Loves or Losses," I paired Chipo with Gloria, who read aloud her essay on his mother's death. Cecilia describes her reactions to hearing Gloria's essay on Chipo. "That was the essay that touched me the most. I remember last semester when Chipo disclosed to the class that his mother had passed away. After that essay he never mentioned her again. I always wondered why." Cecilia assumed, correctly, that Chipo was not ready to write about maternal loss. "I have to say that if he is ready to make that step in coping with it, then he found the right time to share. I look forward to hearing him express how he feels because I know from his previous work that he is a very talented writer and that he will do his mother's memory justice."

Nowhere is Chipo's connection with his classmates more striking than in his next diary. "The third class of English 450 was intriguing. I remember Shannon wrote a story about Lia's grandfather. She said 'her grandfather is the glue that stuck her family together.' I felt like those words came from my mind because my family situation is similar. My grandfather was an intricate part of my family. When my grandfather died in December, the glue began to dry up. Now I am feeling the effect of him not being around. My family does not spend the holidays together and only occasionally speak to one another. The situation is sad; I hope my family will reconcile." Chipo then discusses an essay about a classmate's divorced parents. "Cath's relationship reminds me of my relationship with my father and my sister's father. My relationship is not good, not how a father and son relationship should be. Similar to Cath's distance, I am not far from him, but from the amount of time we spent together to build a relationship, someone would be right to think that he lived in another country. On the other hand, my relationship with my step-father is like Cath's relationship with her step-father. He says he cares, but he would not hesitate to make communicating with my sister difficult to hurt my feelings." Chipo closes the diary on a positive note. "This class was interesting. I find myself captivated by my classmates' personal stories. They are well written and express a sincerity that shows the human heart. I can't wait to listen to the next story in the next class."

One of the many benefits of students learning about their classmates' loves and losses is the discovery that everyone struggles with life. Each adult, no matter how fortunate or privileged, has experienced loss, whether it is the breakup of the family, the death of a relative or friend, the failure of a relationship, or the loss of health. We all have dark secrets that we assume others cannot understand. When we learn more about each other's life, however, we recognize kinship, an unexpected connection that makes us feel less lonely, isolated, and hopeless. Sociologists call this phenomenon "normalization," the process that makes something "more normal." Normalization is often associated with *Discipline and Punish* (1995), Michel Foucault's influential account of repressive disciplinary force, but it has another, more positive meaning: the recognition that we all have conflicts, fears, and problems that are more widespread than people realize. As the distinguished American psychiatrist Harry Stack Sullivan observed more than half a century ago, "We are all much more simply human than otherwise." Before we can appreciate our differences with each other, it is first necessary to understand our commonalities.

Chipo and Addison were partners for Assignment 3, "Writing about How an Experience of Love or Loss Has Changed a Classmate." These essays were written only for me, not for the entire class, but I was so affected by Addison's essay about Chipo that I emailed both of them for permission to read it aloud, which they granted:

> Tragedy can strike anyone. Death rarely seems just, especially when a person loses a parent at a young age. Chipo lost his mother in a car accident when he was just fourteen. Her death devastated him.

In his essay, Chipo explains that he "had always thought no matter the circumstances his mom would be with him." This sentence struck a chord in me, as I feel the exact way about both my parents. I cannot imagine a life without them, and Chipo felt the same way before his mother passed away.

His mother's death "frightened" Chipo, as he soon realized "how harsh the world can be." It stunned him—he could not understand how or why his mother had to be taken away from him. She was the love of his life; the woman he could rely on forever. She raised him and taught him every value he had. She was "the closest person to his heart."

Chipo put a lot of blame on himself after his mother died. He explains, "I thought I could have been a better son. I could have done the dishes, done the laundry, gone to the store for her." It was only through living with his grandfather that he was able to come to terms with her death. Before leaving him, Chipo admits, "I would try not to cry." He discussed with me how he would purposely hold his tears back and swallow his emotions. He had dreams in which he would cry and cry, and wake up with dry eyes. Living with his grandpa helped him to not only overcome his fear of crying, but also helped him to accept his mother's death as an accident, and not something to be blamed on himself. He now realizes that her death is not something he can take responsibility for. He has come to understand, however, just how much his mother did for him, and how much responsibility she had as a parent.

I asked Chipo how he copes with her death at this point in his life. He tells me that he "thinks about her often," every day. He told me he has written poems, stories and songs about her. It made me smile when he said that, overall, he copes with her death by trying to appreciate her *now*. At 14, we often overlook the responsibilities our parents have and the many sacrifices they make for us. Chipo is able to appreciate his mother's sacrifices and hard work now that she is no longer with him.

During our interview, Chipo explained to me that this is his second time taking a course such as this one. (The first was with Professor Berman as well.) When asked how he feels about the course, Chipo explained that he finds the class very helpful for him. He uses the class as an outlet to talk about his feelings for his mother. Chipo feels that taking the class is a way for him to keep his mother's memory alive—by putting his emotions on paper, he will have his words when his memories begin to fade. He also told me that he has found enthusiasm for talking and writing about his mother with the help of this course.

A loss such as the one Chipo experienced can tear a person apart. I imagine one of my parents dying, and the thought of having them suddenly taken away from me at the young age of 21 would be cruel and unfair. Chipo was even younger; however, he managed to turn his loss into something positive, by allowing the loss to teach him to love and appreciate those he is lucky enough to have in his life.

Addison's essay reveals valuable new information about Chipo's response to his mother's death that is not included in his first assignment or in Gloria's essay. She tells us, for example, that he felt he could have been a better son, information gleaned from her telephone conversation with him. She tells us that he had tried not to cry over his mother's death by "swallow[ing] his emotions." She also tells us that he has written poems, stories, and songs about her. We had not yet discussed "posttraumatic growth," the topic for Assignment 8, but Addison informs us about Chipo's ability to recreate and strengthen his life following a devastating loss.

Traumatic loss has affected both Chipo and Addison, one suffering the loss of his mother through an accident, the other the loss of her brother through suicide. Each is sensitive to the other's loss. Each raises questions that elicit significant new details about the other's story. I read Addison's essay aloud and singled out one of her observations in the penultimate paragraph: "by putting his emotions on paper, he will have his words when his memories begin to fade." Addison's sentence, I told the class, captures exactly how I felt when I was writing about Barbara. I reread sections of *Dying to Teach* whenever I find my memories of our life together beginning to fade. Years ago Chipo, Addison, and I could not imagine life without our mother, brother, and wife, respectively, yet the three of us have survived our losses and honored the memories of our loved ones by writing about them.

"Shattered Assumptions" was the next assignment, and Chipo offers for the first time the concrete details of his multiple family losses:

> A shattered reality is all that is left of my family assumptions. My assumptions come from my thoughts about family. My thoughts were my truths and those truths I held as self-evident. Growing up, I would lick the plate; my mom's dishes were delicious. Her soul food would never spoil, but I would because I could get away with not washing the dishes. I did not know her hugs would not last forever, the warmth continued after her hugs were over. I did not know the toys would stop coming. I was a Toys-R-Us kid after all, and Santa came for Christmas. But I didn't know how he got in, we didn't have a chimney. My father was not around at all, but I had grandpa, and my whole family called him "Dad." In my eyes I still had the American family. The only difference was I had a hamster and lizards instead of a cat or a dog. I would find the nerve to sing when mom played her Sade or Mary J. Blige. I was living heavenly in the projects.
>
> My mom was an advocate for my success. And my success was the gift that made her smile from ear to ear. The day I graduated from junior high school, she whispered in my ears before a photo shot, "I am so proud of you"; her words still echo in my heart today. That success would not be possible, if not for her. When I was five years old, she had bought writing and reading books. After work she would teach me how to read and write. And before the good night kiss, she read a story for me to fall asleep. My success is a tribute to my first teacher, my mom.
>
> When I was younger, I would get upset when I did not get what I wanted. But in my friends' eyes, I had everything. I had several crates full of toys. I was a Teenage Mutant Ninja Turtle fanatic. My mom took me to see all the movies, I had all the games and the sheets too. My friends would call me

the "secret of the ooze" to make fun of me. I would become angry over the teasing. But that temper simmered away because to mom I was "sweetie." I did not mind the name until my friends started using it.

During junior high school, I had been in an altercation with several boys that hung around my school. This particular day I was walking home with my two friends and a boy who was with his two friends asked me for 50 cents. I did not know him but I knew he was trouble. I refused to give him any money and told him to go buy his own chips. He felt disrespected. He rapidly took off his shirt to prepare to fight me. I did not know what to do. I thought about fighting him, but I was afraid his friends would intervene. I looked at my friends but they did not give me any signal that they were going to help; so I decided to run. I did not run home because I did not want to be known as a "runner." Instead, I ran in a different direction, in hopes I could isolate the boy. The plan backfired. He and his friends chased me down. When they captured me, I was frozen in fear. I told them "You're going to regret beating me up." They ignored my attempts to scare them away. Instead I had to block the onslaught. I could not keep count of the many punches and kicks that came my way.

My mother found out later that day I was jumped on my way home from school. My mother was concerned about my well-being. In an effort to cheer me up, she bought a Sega Dreamcast for me. The following day she and I went up to the school. While at school, we found one of the kids hanging around a nearby store. She yelled at him until I was frightened for him. She told me if need be I better pick up an object to defend myself. I was amazed. I had never seen my mom fired up before. My mom did not miss a second in my life despite several months later giving birth to my sister.

I began to attend high school, and three days into adjusting to being a freshman, 9/11 happened. I had seen the planes crash on TV. I heard many people had died. No longer would I see the twin towers from my window. But I did not understand what it all meant. I was not immediately affected because no one I was close to had died. My grandmother had told me a family member was killed but I had never met that person. But three months later, December 11, 2001, close to noon, while my mom was coming from Pathmark with my sister, a car that was being driven by a 19 year old caused a freak accident. His car slammed into a van and the van sped out of control and hit my mom and sister, who was in a stroller, in the middle of crossing the street. He was never tested by the cops for drugs or alcohol. This freak accident instantly killed my mom and left my sister in critical condition. What saved my sister was her being trapped in the stroller. My mom and sister were speedily taken to the hospital. But only my sister was able to fight for her life. The doctors thought if she lived she would be mentally disabled for life from the head damage she endured. It was a horror story covered by the local news. The world was no longer heavenly but hell.

That day two cops had revealed the news to my family and me. I had arrived home from school, and outside my door they were waiting for me. They did not tell me anything. But they insisted I get an elder; I went to get my aunt. The only thoughts I had at the time had been, "why are they being so rude to me" and "a terrible incident must have occurred." I had come to find out my twin towers had fell, my mom permanently and my sister who struggled for life for 64 days. The assumption that my mom would be around forever was gone.

Who would I turn to now? Would I turn to my father. I did not know whom to turn to. My father came around, but living with him was not an option. My grandmother offered her home and so did several of my aunts. But I decided to live with my grandfather. He lived down the block from where my mother and I lived. Despite living a nightmare, I was overwhelmed with support. My family made the effort to take care of me. My family was the best. Now that my mom was gone, they would be there for me. My new assumption became family cares for one another and will be there for each other in times of need.

My sister's father had successfully completed a hostile takeover of my mom's place. I now had limited access to the place I called home for several years. But living with my grandfather made my life better. He wasn't strict. He didn't help me with my homework like mom. But he would make sure I was up and ready for school everyday. In the morning, he would hit my door, clap his hands and in some cases sprinkle water on me. All these tricks to wake me up in the morning, I hated. But they did the trick. He would leave a few dollars on the table for me, and off I was to school. I did not ask him for much like I did my mom. I think it was because I asked my mom for the impossible. Even though he made sure I had. He cooked but his food wasn't like my mom's. But more importantly he supported me.

One day I had to go to a new doctor. I did not know where the doctor's office was located. Ever since my mom passed, dad would come with me to the doctor. This day we got off the bus at the wrong stop and we had to walk 10 blocks. He was in his mid-70s at the time. I was grateful he walked with me; but concerned he worked himself up over me. Since then he would always talk about the day I walked him to death.

During college, Dad would help me pay for my books. One day, I had asked him for a few hundred dollars. He agreed to help. The problem was we had to go to the bank to get it, and dad wasn't feeling well. I was subtlely aware because my grandfather is the type of person who will not tell you what is bothering him. He wasn't feeling good but he was adamant about getting this money for me. We made it to the bus stop, and by then I felt bad and I didn't want to go anymore. To him if I didn't get this money, it would be harder for me to be successful in school. We made it to the bank, met up with my uncle, and retrieved the money needed for the books.

But my grandfather continued to worsen. He was not taking his medicine as he was supposed to and as a result developed a bad cough. His condition was manageable as long as someone was with him. But I was attending college, and he was often left at home alone. I had managed to set up a nurse and home-aide to come and see him. This made his condition better. But in about a year, according to the nurse, he was well enough to be taken off the program. All while I had begun to hound my family about going to see my grandfather consistently. He needed someone to be with him, and I was afraid that desire was not being met.

My grandpa was stubborn and he insisted it would be alright. Even though on separate occasions, a relative had taken him to the hospital and I took him twice. But I started to think that my family was not doing their best to make sure he would be alright. My family would come over to make sure he was eating. I wanted them to make sure he was taking the medicine he needed and have someone to keep him company. I no longer knew how to contribute because I was away. When I went home it was for a couple of days at a time. That was not enough time for me to do anything. Then one day while I was in CPR training at school, I received a text from my cousin to call him. When I did, he said, "Dad is dead."

I immediately was confused. I did not want to believe it. Did my family let him die? Did he want to die? Or was it just his time? On several occasions he had said, "if it wasn't for me, I would have been gone a long time ago." In my mind, that made me feel like my family did not do enough. I waited two days to go home because I felt I was going to argue with my family in a hopeless attempt to resurrect him. I was not ready for him to die. I went home and found out his obituary was not complete but his funeral was the following evening. I put my heart into writing his obituary. But from that point on, my family was no longer a lifeline to be there for one another in time of need. I decided, I have to be able to survive on my own. My new assumption is to make life better, I will finish college. I have to make my mom proud, my grandfather proud, and to be a role model for my sister. I have to turn my shattered reality into a livable dream.

Chipo's "shattered assumptions" essay includes many new details about his mother's and grandfather's deaths, including his confusion following the latter's death and the belief that his family was no longer a "lifeline" for him. After he finished reading it, we went around the room and each person chose a favorite sentence. Some students chose the same sentence, but there were more excellent sentences than there were people in the classroom. My two favorites were his response to his mother's nickname, "sweetie"—"I did not mind the name until my friends started using it"—and the comparison of his mother's death to the destruction of the World Trade Center. (I dutifully pointed out, after citing the sentence, that the verb should be "fallen.") After discussing the best sentences in Chipo's essay, we revised those that contained a grammatical, punctuation, or stylistic error. We then raised questions on which we wanted Chipo to elaborate—my question was how he now felt about the surviving members of his family.

Several people remarked in their diaries on the shifting mood of Chipo's essay. "I loved how he made the class laugh and want to cry," Kasia wrote. "He did an amazing job bringing his mom back through his words. It's really inspirational to hear the personal stories in the class. I have never felt so comfortable in a room filled with strangers." Cassie was surprised that Chipo's essay was simultaneously funny and sad. "This is the complete opposite of what I expected from his essay." Scout stated that the essay demonstrates the power of writing about love and loss. "As I watched Chipo read his essay aloud with laughs and smiles, it hit me. THIS is why we are writing. THIS is why we are sharing: we are giving a voice to ourselves, and we give a voice to the ones or the objects that we love(d) and/or lost."

How would an outsider from the class react to Chipo's laughter on such a serious essay? Educators such as Carra Lea Hood (2003) who criticize self-disclosing writing courses claim that students cannot write on traumatic topics without being retraumatized in the process, that students are manipulated into writing what their professors want to hear, that personal writing is not truthful, and that such writing cannot be therapeutic because writing teachers are not trained therapists. None of the members of the class, however, believed that these problems occurred in Love and Loss. As the responses to Chipo's essay indicate, students felt saddened but not traumatized by his mother's death. They never doubted for a moment that he wrote the essay voluntarily, and they never questioned that the essay was anything but truthful and heartfelt. They believed the essay was as empowering for him to write as it was for them to hear. Further, as their professor, I never felt that my students were writing what they thought I wanted to hear or read. I valued funny and joyful essays as much as the painfully sad.

Chipo's diary entry explains how he felt when he read aloud "Shattered Assumptions." Notice how important it is for him to improve his writing skills and how attentive he is to his classmates' responses to his reading:

> In our last class I read a difficult essay to write. It was about my mother. Usually when I write about her I write a few sentences. But this time most of the paper was about her. It was about the good times we shared while she was alive. It was also about the last day she was alive. I was scared to read it. The essay also contained information about my grandfather. I recently lost him. It was just as tough. While reading the paper I tried to be funny. It made the paper easier to read. The paper represents parts of my life I wish never happened.
>
> After reading the essay Professor Berman said I was a "diamond in the rust [rough]" with my ability to write. I appreciated the compliment. But it made me think how do writers deal with the suffering of their life experiences? I want to continue to improve as a writer. But I'm afraid that reliving personal experiences will be as challenging as being creative with my words. While I was reading my paper, I heard sniffling coming from my class. I was wondering if my classmates were crying. I was about to stop reading and say "don't cry" because then I would cry. But I made it through. I am not saying this like it is a problem with crying. I just believed if I started crying I would have shed tears for the rest of the class.

If I had time in class to respond to Chipo's question about how writers deal with their own suffering, I would point out that, with few exceptions, they find such writing psychologically helpful. "Art is created against death," Donald Hall (1978), the former U.S. Poet Laureate, boldly affirms in *Goatfoot Milktongue*

Twinbird (p. 16). As I suggest in *Companionship in Grief* (Berman, 2010), a constant theme throughout Hall's long career is the therapeutic value of work, in his case, writing. I can cite many other writers who have made similar observations, including John Gregory Dunne (1989): "Clarity only comes when pen is in hand, or at the typewriter or the word processor, clarity about what we feel and what we think, how we love and how we mourn; the words on the page constitute the benediction, the declaration, the confession of the emotionally inarticulate" (*Harp,* pp. 15–16).

"Shattered Assumptions" was Chipo's most striking essay to date, and he used it as the basis for his class presentation during the middle of the semester:

> If my heart was a journal, the essay about my mother, grandfather, and sister would be the cover story within its pages. The headline would read, "buried within tears, Chipo shares." My essay was about the shattered assumptions I held about my family life. How one day I would not have my mother to go to movies with or how I would not have my grandfather to come home to during college vacations. I was surprised how my family responded to losing them. When my mother died, I don't know if I cried for me or my sister but I know I still have not cried enough. And the loss of my grandfather is so recent the family dilemma is current.
>
> This essay was not easy to write. I mean putting the words down on paper was not a problem. But reading the words and thinking about them was devastating. There were more smiles than tears. When I wrote the stories, I would smile remembering the details. It was funny to think about those times with my mother and grandfather. But the more I thought about the moments I shared with my loved ones, the more tears started to show. I don't think I cried when I wrote my mom's story because it has been six years now. But when I combine losing her with my grandfather I couldn't hold back anymore. When I read the essay out loud it hit me. I did not even want to constantly reread for errors like I usually do because I had to let the paper breath[e].
>
> The strength of the essay was my ability to show my experiences with my mother and grandfather. The words I used to convey my emotional state. And the picture I painted from the stories. The weakness of the essay was that I tended to jump around. I did not want to go straight into losing my mother and grandfather. I had to say something that showed our relationship. I think I could have better transition[s].
>
> I have not spoken about the essay to any relative or friends. I did not think about sharing it with them at this time. I don't know how they would react. After I wrote the essay, I felt that I could open or close this section of my journal because my heart has recognized I need to embrace the experience to heal.

Students who write on the most important people in their lives usually spend great care with their writing, for they want to do justice to these people. Sometimes, however, the challenge of writing on emotionally charged topics is so overwhelming that they cannot proofread their essays. Chipo's essay contains several grammatical and typographical errors. It was for this reason that I said during our class discussion that he was like a "diamond in the rough." But I also said that despite his technical roughness, he is a more gifted writer than I am. He has the gifts of characterization, dialogue, and metaphorical language that I lack, along with the ability to recall early childhood experience. At its best, his writing is haunting and evocative, playful one moment, plaintive the next. We can see these gifts in his next essay, written for the assignment "Writing a Wrong." In his early writings he hints that he was overprotected and spoiled, but now he elaborates on this in an essay aptly entitled "Tears":

"Tears"

Growing up, my mom would go to great lengths to make me smile. If it was a game I wanted, I received it. If I wanted to go to the movies, she took me to Busch Gardens in Virginia. I was 10 years old and entering the fifth grade. The night before we left my mom assisted in packing my bags. She told me to pack "shirts, shorts, socks, draws, a brush, a toothbrush, and pajamas." But all I wanted was to pack my toys. We left home. We took the subway to Penn Station to catch the Amtrak train. We made it on schedule. My mom carried her bags inside the train, and I dragged until my mom said, "Pick the bag up before you rip it." I did. I dashed towards the nearest two empty seats. "Mommy, can I have the window seat?" "Go ahead," she said. We rode the Amtrak for about 10 hours to go to Virginia. When we arrived in Virginia, the sun was beginning to set. But the smile I had could shine in the darkness. My mom produced a miracle in my eyes. We checked into our motel but before she could discuss our plans, I was out the door. We had five hours before the park would close. I could not wait. I ran to the park as if once it closed it would not open again.

I could not wait to go on the rides. I insisted on going on the rides that were dangerous to my mom. I had to get on the Escape from Bam Bay. It was a ride that had a 50 foot drop into water. "Mommy, can I go on this ride?" "No, it is too dangerous, sweetie," she said. "Can we go on this ride together?" "No, the ride is too high up for me," she said. "Can I please go, mommy, pleassse, I will be careful." "Fine, I'm going to wait by the exit and take a picture." I zoomed to, through, and past the empty line. I was next. I jumped in the cart, and I was strapped in by the usher. The ride started. As the cart crept to the tip of the 50 foot drop, I became nervous. Suddenly, my heart dropped, the cart was shooting down. I splashed into the water and I saw a flash; my mom captured the moment. For the rest of the night, we went sightseeing.

The next day we woke up early. While my mother made breakfast arrangements, I turned on the television to discover I could not find the x-men on its channel. We went to a restaurant for breakfast. After breakfast, we went back to the park. We went to see the animals at the zoo. I gave a sheep some seeds to eat but the sheep chewed my shirt. Flash! My mother captured another moment. Next, we played some water games. I shot the water into the clown's mouth fast enough to win my first prize, a big gold fish. My mother encouraged me to go on rides with her because I wanted to go on all the high rides. We went on the bumper cars. I slammed into my mom and drove off before she could catch me. We went on a ride that spun around twice as fast as a merry-go-round. The view from the Ferris wheel showed us tons of rides. My trip to Busch Gardens was amazing.

About two years later, I graduated from public school. When I read my speech on stage during the graduation ceremony, I made my family proud. My grandmother, grandfather, and mother were present. We left the auditorium. My grandmother went back to work. The rest of us walked towards my grandfather's place. Outside my grandfather's place we took pictures. I took a picture with my grandfather, my friends, and my mom. But my friends left to go eat with their parents. I wondered why I was not going to eat. But my mother and I had to go home. We arrived home. "Can we go out to eat," I said. "No, I don't have the money," Mom said. In what seemed like a few seconds, I broke my mother's heart. "I never get what I want. I'm always being denied. Why can't we go? All my friends are going. How could you?" "You keep that up and you won't get anything from me anymore," she said. "It's not like I ever get what I want. I will just end up disappointed anyway," I said. I struck a nerve. I made her cry. As soon as the tears started flowing, I felt like a fool. I was spoiled and I knew it. Tears began to fall down my face. "Mom, please forgive me. I never meant to make you cry." But the damage was done. If I could right this wrong, I would never have made her cry. "I need to make amends. The next time she walks through the door," I said to myself from that day. But I never did. The time was never right. I was not ready, just like the day she died. It has now been six years. And I still wait for her to come home to apologize.

Chipo's essay is masterful in its evocation of childhood innocence and delight. The mood becomes increasingly somber, however, as the young boy grows older and encounters the problematic world of adulthood. The mother is no longer the fairy tale figure in "Shattered Assumptions" who embodies infinite love, support, and gratification. She is now a more human figure who worries about her son's safety, sets realistic limits that he cannot understand or accept, struggles with the problems of being a single parent, and frets over the lack of money. The "I" in the story, a younger version of Chipo, cannot fathom why she denies his request to have lunch with his friends. Nor can he anticipate the consequences of his actions. "Tears" concludes with an elegiac epiphany suggesting that the writer will always be haunted by his tears over maternal loss. "Tears" remains, in my view, Chipo's most effective essay of the semester—of *both* semesters. With its excellent diction, clear organization, steady narrative distance, and unsentimentalized emotion, the story reveals a writer who is firmly in control of his material—a writer who knows how to cut and polish a diamond. Significantly, maternal loss is the catalyst behind his most artistically successful writing.

In his next diary entry, Chipo repeats a statement I had made in class: "Professor Berman said, 'make your reader suffer.' In other words, he wants us to write in a way that we show more than we tell our experience. But as a writer I feel like I have to relive the experience the more I show. For a brief moment I can connect with the dead. But is that reconnection worth losing a loved one twice?" Excellent question. In writing about the dead, we seek to bring them back to life, to make them alive and palpable, to endow them with the qualities we loved when they were alive and part of our lives. We know, however, that we cannot succeed in bringing them back to life. The best we can do is to create a verbal portrait, a simulacrum, which is not a replacement of the dead—the dead can never be replaced. Nevertheless, this linguistic creation can provide pleasure, beauty, and comfort to others and ourselves.

Chipo continued to reconnect with the dead during the second half of Love and Loss. Four of his essays written during this time are noteworthy. His essay "Leaving," written for Assignment 6, "Holding Two Opposed Ideas without Becoming Paralyzed," describes how his love for summertime began to change after his mother's death. He still played with his high school friends, still enjoyed many of his old games and activities, but something is now different. "One of my friends stopped coming outside. Another ended in jail. And another friend nearly lost his life from a bullet. I went to the hospital to see him, and he said that I was one of his few friends to visit. I was amazed he could speak because his family said 'he was not expected to survive.'" This was the turning point in Chipo's life. "I could no longer stand being home. I no longer was in love with the summertime. I decided I was leaving home. . . . I told my grandfather I wanted to go away for college. He respected my decision. And I left home to find a better life."

Chipo's essay for Assignment 8, on "Posttraumatic Growth," offers new information about his devastation over his mother's death. "The traumatic shock of losing my mother did not run its course. Even though it has been six years, it still presently affects my life. How did I go on? If I just gave up, how would my mother have felt? What is going to happen to my sister? I was 14 at the time. I never met death before losing my mother. Back then, I couldn't tell you about death. I couldn't tell you about the initial denial, agony of acceptance, the fear of tomorrow, the regret of the past, and the pain of the present. 'Is it all a dream?' I said. 'NO, it was a nightmare!' I confirmed."

Chipo tried, unsuccessfully, to sleep the pain away. "When I had lain down that day, to get a good night's rest, I told myself, 'mom will be here soon to eat baked ziti with me.' She had cooked baked ziti before leaving for my sister's doctor and Pathmark, a grocery store." He ends the essay by writing about his efforts to improve his relationship with his father. "My grandfather, who is my mother's father, and who I credit as my dad, always encouraged me to get to know my father. Dad would always point out that my father made mistakes but that he was not a bad person. One day, I met up with my father in Manhattan to grab a bite to eat. It was one of the rare moments we spent together. I am now finishing up my junior year in college. My life has become a work of art that my mother drew. I just give this picture a vision, a story; I dare myself to dream true."

In Assignment 9, Chipo imagines his mother writing a letter to him on her deathday. He uses a rhetorical device called prosopopoeia, the imagined speech of someone who is absent:

Dear Sweetie,

I just finished cooking baked ziti. I know it is your favorite dish. I took the day off from college today to take your sister to the doctor for a checkup. Gary left for work already, and I decided to write you a letter. I do not know if this letter will reach you. I don't know how old you will be when you are able to understand what I'm writing. However, I'm sending this letter into the future and I hope this letter finds you in good health.

When I raised you I sent you to your room when I had grown folk conversations. You are not aware of the family friction that damaged our family bonds. I know you are aware that your father is not around and I am raising you with the help of my father. I never had anything against your father. At one point in time, I loved that man. But one day I found out he was no longer faithful to me and that forever changed the bond he and I shared. I don't keep you away from him. If you are wondering what happened to him being a father to you, ask him.

Now I don't know how much you know at this time. But I never knew my mother. I was told that my mother, your grandmother, died several weeks after giving birth to me. My mother's sisters in Barbados and St. Vincent wanted to raise us. But your grandfather, Dad, decided to keep his children together. He raised five kids with the help of many of his friends who[se] sons and daughters grew up with me. Now you know their kids and they are like family to all of us. In other words, do not take offense when people take an interest in your life. They knew you before you knew yourself.

Remember that time we went to your Aunt Patsy's for the holidays? Well, that was the first day you seen a crack in our family foundation. You were actually in the bathroom when the argument started. All I told you was that your other aunt and cousin had some tough words for each other. Those words were enough to break the family bond our family shared since your grandmother died. I'm glad your ears did not hear the conversation. It would have done nothing but confuse you. My hope is our relationships do not interfere with the bonds our children have yet to form. That's why I bring you over to my brother and sisters' homes because I wanted you to form your own relationships. I know you and your cousin are close. That's a reflection of his mother and my relationship.

But more than anything, I want to show you how much I love you. I don't know if you understand how much I love you. I could not help but tell my girlfriends about you. How we shared a bond since you were in my womb. Do you know why you like to eat Frosted Flakes in the middle of the night? I would eat Frosted Flakes at night when I was pregnant with you. In no time, you were born on May 4th, 1987 at 1:19 in the morning. I was so proud to be a mother. I did not even think twice about putting you before my wants. I spoil you because I want to give you everything I did not have and more. I bet you don't remember when you were two years old and broke your arm. You rolled off the bed. I had to fire your baby sitter because she was not doing her job.

I know what you're thinking. Why do I still treat you like a baby? You will always be a baby in my eyes. You always make a big deal over me calling you "sweetie" around your friends. You are a child but you want to be a man around your friends. I'm glad I took you to Busch Gardens. I needed a vacation. And we spent quality time together. I'll never forget how your face lit up like fireworks on the fourth of July when we arrived in Virginia. I thought it was not a good idea to go to Busch Gardens with half the day gone. But I went with my heart and you and I had a blast.

I never understood why you question me so much. Are you attempting to rebel? Or was it your young mind trying to get a better understanding of life? I believe it is some of both because despite how much I do for you, I can't teach you how to be a man. I do my best to show you how to be accountable. I make you wash the dishes, take out the trash, hang up your clothes, and go to the store to give you responsibility. I will not be here forever, and I want you to remember. You will not always get along with those you love, but finding common ground to build on is important for any relationship to prosper. Look after your sister, she will look toward you for guidance. Do not forget you have family you can depend on. Most importantly, do not forget your dreams are reachable.

 Love,
 Mommy

Chipo succeeds in creating a character who is older and wiser than he is, and who can peer into the future to see what her son needs to do and know to have a good life. She is a highly sympathetic figure without being idealized or senti-mentalized. She casts no blame on her son for being spoiled, and she makes no reference to the regret he feels for having made her cry. She reminds him that she will not be around forever without making him feel guilty over this. She accepts the inevitability of her death and thus makes it easier for her son to accept her death—and perhaps his own in the future. She is, like Chipo, articulate and at times eloquent, as we can see in sentences such as "They knew you before you knew yourself" and "You are a child but you want to be a man around your friends." Sometimes grammatical errors mar her language, as when she refers to the "day you seen a crack in our family foundation." She speaks like a mother when she tells him that his love for Frosted Flakes arose in her womb, when she would eat the cereal. Small details like this lend authenticity to her letter.

Indeed, what is perhaps most remarkable about Chipo's write-to-life assign-ment is that he creates a realistic letter that a mother might write to a 14-year-old son. If I had come across a fictional letter like this in a creative writing course, I would have suspected that it was written by a female student—one who was herself a mother. The letter sounds authentic in every detail, as if he had just come across it in his mother's desk. He not only creates a mother who refers to him as "sweetie" but he also addresses the letter to a son who is on the verge of manhood. She is a wise and compassionate figure, and though she is distressed that her son's father is no longer in his life, she avoids turning her son against him. Referring to the "family friction" that she knows her son cannot yet understand, she affirms the importance of intergenerational continuity. She knows that finding common ground is the secret behind every enduring relationship. She reminds him of his responsibilities to his sister, who will "look toward you for guidance"—especially when their mother will no longer be around. Finally, she urges him to fulfill his dreams, a fitting conclusion to a letter filled with undying love.

Chipo's essay "If I Died," written for Assignment 12 during the week of his twenty-first birthday, reveals his new awareness of death education. The essay is too long for me to include in its entirety, but the opening paragraph reflects the seriousness of his effort: "I have made a list of 11 goals I plan to do before I die. My 11 goals are to spend time with my sister, travel to Egypt or Barbados, have a child, write letters to my loved ones, graduate college, acknowledge those who have impacted my life, fall in love and, if time permits, marry her, establish a family tradition to strengthen our bonds, publish a memoir or poetry collection, establish a scholarship or project in my mother's name, and learn my family history to pass it on to the next generation." He then makes two promises: first, to create a scholarship in his mother's memory to be given to a woman who, like his mother, has children while pursuing a college degree; and, second, to create awareness for driving safety by sharing his mother's story. Following these promises, he writes letters to nine relatives and friends, including the following:

> To my sister: I was afraid mom would not love me the same when you were born. But that did not matter because I couldn't help but love you since the day I met you. You have this crazy sense of humor. Unfortunately, you were not able to know mom as well as I have, but she was a beautiful lady inside and out. I hope you discover the writings I have saved on my computer and learn about her. I was upset when I learned that your father moved away to North Carolina because I wondered if I would see you again. Fortunately, I did. I went to visit [you] when I came back from South Africa. Remember [when] you wanted to go bike riding, and I did not want to go. After a while you convinced me to bike ride with you. We rode for five blocks and you became tired and you wanted to go back. I couldn't believe it. How about that time I took you to the movies and we both fell asleep. We were tired. I would become sad when I brought you back to your father and it was hard to watch you cry. But I kept my composure to show you that everything was going to be OK. Stay strong, I love you, and follow your dream.
>
> To my step-father: I know losing your girlfriend, your fiancée, my mother, was hard for you. My reaction might not have been the best. Even though I was only 14 at the time, I will not make an excuse for my actions. I wanted to take whatever made her feel alive to me. You took me to an NBA game. I can't remember who was playing, but it was fun. I was happy you bought me sneakers for me on my birthday. You even bought me a computer. Despite

the complications that followed the computer, I appreciate the thought. It must be tough raising my sister by yourself. But I commend your effort. I hope you find happiness.

To my father: I'm not mad at you. I'm upset our bond is not what a father's and son's bond could be. But I do acknowledge you tried several times. You did call me a handful of times. And one day after school we ate lunch together. I hope whatever struggles you are going through, whether it is drugs or a mid-life crisis, you are able to overcome and be happy.

As Chipo notes in his final diary, the "If I Died" assignment represented a valuable summing of what he has learned in Love and Loss. "The assignment was not tough to write, but writing the essay made me look at life as if I did not have much time left to be alive. It made me prioritize what was important to me in my life. It also made me grateful to all the people that impacted my life. At first I did not expect the essay to be long, but once again I found myself writing from the heart to the people I hold dear to me. I am happy I wrote the essay but I do not think I will share it with my family at this point."

Chipo also learned that the best classroom experiences are those in which students teach and learn from each other. "What have I learned from this class? I have learned that everybody has a story to share and if you get the privilege to listen, share your own. That way, when the conversation is over, each person has learned from the other's experience. How else can I know how a woman feels about abortion? How it feels to be a son or daughter to live through their parents' divorce?" Chipo vows to take these experiences and apply them to his own life. "In an early journal I asked whether reconnecting with the dead through writing is worth losing them again. I did not know how to answer that question until now. If writing about my mother and grandfather can put a smile on my face every time, I might never put a pen down."

By the end of the semester, Chipo achieved all of the educational goals he had listed during the first day of class. He expressed his feelings about the two people who were dear to his heart, kept their memories alive by writing about them and sharing his writings with classmates, and created a substantial body of writings to give to his sister, so that she can remember her mother and grandfather. These were the three goals he mentioned on the first day of the semester. But he achieved other goals as well. The letter he wrote to his father, whom he hasn't seen in years, may help them to repair their broken relationship. The essays he wrote throughout the semester inspired his classmates to write about their own loves and losses. And the essays and diaries he submitted each week demonstrated a consistent improvement of his writing skills.

Chipo's writings reveal a striking change in his attitude toward self-disclosure. On the first day of the semester he was afraid that he might not be willing to share his writings with classmates, yet he read several of his most personal essays aloud and allowed me to read aloud his diary entries. To judge from the number of times his fellow students referred to him in their essays and diaries, his writings were the most cited and influential in the class. We learn from Addison's essay that since his mother's death, Chipo has written many poems, stories, and songs about her; but the first time he shared his writings about her with classmates was during our Love and Loss course. Opening his life to his classmates encouraged them to open their lives to each other.

In the beginning of the semester, we learn only the factual details about his mother's death, but in his later writings Chipo creates a vivid portrait of the mother-son relationship, one filled with love tinged with regret, guilt, and tears. He takes us on a journey from maternal loss and shattered assumptions to a new assumptive world filled with hope, courage, and strength. At the end of the semester, he imagines his own death and tells us how he intends to express gratitude to the relatives and friends who have helped him. His last writings reveal that he has become the man his mother had hoped when he was still an adolescent. One suspects that his imagined leave-taking would make her proud.

Rereading his writings eight months after the course ended, Chipo experienced many emotions. "I was sad because when I reread my story about my mother taking me to Busch Gardens, I knew that it was one of my fondest memories I could never have again. I felt angry because my relationship with my sister is dependent on her father's feelings. I felt happy because I was able to accomplish my goal of writing about my mother and grandfather. And I was relieved because I got to express feelings about love and loss in my life that had a positive effect on others. I also learned a lot from listening to my classmates' stories." He also realized that it was important for him to rebuild his relationship with his father. "I think our relationship has taken a step in the right direction by just communicating with each other. I think the important lesson I took from Love and Loss was that no one's life is paradise but a beautiful struggle that allows us to grow as human beings."

"Instead Of Minimizing My Struggles, I Wrote About Them"

"When I signed up for Expository Writing my junior year," Lia states, "I received much more than discussing my emotions. At the time, I was going through a divorce—it was my parents' divorce, but it always becomes everyone's divorce contrary to its supposed pure form. In a nonjudgmental setting, I wrote more honestly than ever before; I expressed many thoughts, dealt with pain, and experienced love. So, with a pit of anxiety filling my stomach, I signed up for more growth and obstacles."

Lia's determination to take Love and Loss was followed a few weeks later by her decision to begin psychotherapy. Whether these two decisions were causally linked remains unclear. Two years earlier she had seen a psychiatrist, who prescribed medication for her anxiety and depression, but she was now ready to speak with a therapist about her problems. After beginning therapy, she decided to write an essay about the extent to which the two losses in her life, the death of her beloved grandfather "Poppy" in 2005 and the wrenching breakup of her parents' marriage a year later, contributed to her ongoing struggle with mood disorders. The essay explores the serious conflicts in her life, including her dependence upon marijuana and prescription drugs. She read the essay, part of which contains an account of her first therapy session, to the class near the end of the semester. She never confuses her Love and Loss course with psychotherapy, yet we can see from the essay how both the "writing cure" and the "talking cure" are parallel efforts toward self-understanding and self-healing.

"Poppy is my grandfather on my mother's side, and I am still devastated from his loss," Lia observes in Assignment 1. "I wrote a piece on him for Jeff's Expository Writing course last semester. Since then I expanded on my story about Poppy, and it now spans almost 20 pages long." Many of the essays and diaries she penned in Love and Loss produced a "pit of anxiety" in her stomach, but the anxiety turned to relief when she read aloud her essay on Assignment 4, "Shattered Assumptions," in which she discusses, with characteristic wit and sarcasm, her depression and abuse of prescription medication:

"Just take one of these and you should feel better," the psychiatrist assured me and handed me two sample packs of Lexapro. "This is a selective serotonin reuptake inhibitor, an antidepressant. It treats depression and anxiety."

"You think that's the problem?" I inquire although I know I suffer from both disorders.

"Concerning your breathing problem, yes," she responds and smiles.

Regardless of her grins and caring demeanor, I know she thinks I'm crazy. Due to my countless chest X-rays, EKG's, blood samples, heart ultrasounds, and lung/chest X-rays with contrast—which means the evil nurses at the hospital forced me to gulp three half liter bottles of this white crap that tastes like, well, crap—my file in her office is thicker than the special edition of *Moby Dick*.

"I won't become addicted to this stuff, will I?" I ask.

"No, you will not become dependent on this medication," she responds and then squints her eye into a glare. "You're not self-medicating again, Lia, are you?"

"Just with marijuana." *LIE.* "There's nothing wrong with the sweet cheeba plant." *LIE. LIAR. YOU'RE A BIG FAT LIAR. In reality, it's more like marijuana, Xanax and Vicodin. Throw a little Oxycodone in there and I'm ready for rehab.*

"Well, that causes lung cancer—just like cigarettes. You should stop smoking those too. I am your physician. I care." She spoke with a motherly tone.

"We all have to die from something, right?"

"Yes, but I think that's a morbid way of looking at life. Don't you want to live a long and satisfying life?"

"I am not sure if it would be satisfying."

"Just take the medication, please. Call me if you feel more depressed or anxious."

"You got it, doc," I quip as I smirk at her and escape from the plain white walls and sterile smell of the doctor's office.

On that day almost two years ago, I knew I made the wrong decision. I knew I needed to talk to someone too, but I found excuses to avoid the whole therapy confrontation. I did not want help; I wanted to swim in my puddle called misery. My parents divorced in 2006, a year after my grandfather's death; by the time of my visit to the physician in 2006, I already abused numerous types of prescription medications. I preferred to feel numb instead of facing the unbearable pain.

In the notorious college ghetto of Albany in which I live, access to addictive pills is never denied. Someone is always selling some sort of med, and he/she lives two blocks away at most. By that time, I knew I was in trouble. I knew I was in trouble because I needed to eat at least four Vicodins to feel an effect from the painkilling drug.

When I began popping a 10-milligram Lexapro once a day, I felt better for awhile. The vicious pit that once filled my stomach with anxiety and depression disappeared. Without the help of the medications I abused, I finally slept soundly; I stopped bursting into tears at the thought of my dead grandfather and my parents' divorce. Without ripping posters and pictures off my wall to express my anger, I enthralled myself in my studies and wrote more than ever before.

As I entered my senior year this fall, I stopped feeling the beneficial effects of my medication. In response, the psychiatrist increased my dosage to 20 milligrams once a day, but this only helped me slightly.

I thought Lexapro would cure me. I thought that for the first time in over two years, I would no longer suffer from sleepless nights and daily crying sessions, and I thought my jaded and cynical view of life would disappear with the swallow of this 10-milligram pill—but, like the rest, this miracle drug failed me too.

We live in a society infatuated with instant gratification where our Internet must load in one second or it's shit, and where every element of our daily lives is fast-paced. We expect all medicine—illegal and legal, whether it be Xanax, Vicodin, Lexapro, or some other cocktail of pills—will solve our problems, when in reality, when we wake up in the morning or come off our highs, our merciless conflicts come right back; these medications cover symptoms, but they fail to reach the root of the problem.

Today, I continue taking this medication, but attend talk therapy as well, which is working out and will hopefully continue to work out.

Lia's essay proved to be a psychological breakthrough, as she recorded in her diary entry that week.

After I read my paper aloud, I felt like the merciless emotional weight no longer rested heavily on my chest. A couple of nights prior, I felt like a loony bin after writing about my experiences with abuse and Lexapro, and I was surprised at my classmates' compassionate responses—not because I think they lack compassion, but because I let my insecurities overpower my rationality. Throughout the short time this class has spent together, the group has always showed an extraordinary amount of compassion and empathy.

Lia remarked that in the Expository Writing course she took with me, she penned many essays about her parents' divorce, her grandfather's death, and her depression and anxiety, but she always left out certain details. "These grim and brutal details were unbearable to me to express at the time, and with my essay 'Shattered Love for Instant Gratification,' I felt, for the first time, that I was not only completely honest but vulnerable." Although Lia viewed her emotions as negative, she realized that she should not feel ashamed to suffer from anxiety and depression. "These feelings of shame hindered my desire to start therapy, and left me untreated for several years. I am petrified of my self-disclosure, but I know there is someone in this class who can relate to my experiences, and I hope my essay helped them in some way."

"Shattered Love for Instant Gratification" reads like a short story, and for that reason I asked Nico, who is a fiction writer, to suggest how Lia might develop it further. He made several recommendations for revision, which he then expanded in his diary entry:

> Lia's revealing essay on her struggle with anxiety, depression, and the psychiatric process sparked off a spirited discussion of the way in which narratives are constructed. The greatest strength of the essay was probably its honesty—an endearing trait in any work, basic or advanced—and it also displayed Lia's continuing development as an author capable of structuring her work in effective ways. Her use of extensive dialogue peppered with inner monologue made for a brisk pace; her avoidance of dull exposition was commendable. Jeff asked me, as a creative writer, to comment on the piece. I offered that I would edit the dialogue to make it sound more dynamic. I pointed out that, in every exchange between people, there are different motives and agendas at work, and that it is rarely the case that both people in a conversation are on the same page. Dialogue should duplicate the connections and disconnections of discourse. Characters should hedge, avoid, lie through omission, misunderstand. I illustrated a few ways in which this might be done. The psychiatrist, in particular, reads as overly wooden. Lia defended her creation by saying that the psychiatrist is, in actuality, very wooden and literal-minded in her interactions with patients. Yes, I countered, but if that's the case then you will have to do more to show the reader that you're looking to create an effect, rather than settling for reportage. Since words on a page do not live and breathe, I went on, you have to go beyond mimesis to achieve the illusion of reality.

Lia wrote three essays in Love and Loss that represent her ongoing efforts to understand the relationship between her grandfather's death and her struggle with mood disorders. She was apprehensive about her self-disclosures, but her classmates' sympathetic responses to "Shattered Love for Instant Gratification" encouraged her to reveal additional details in her last major essay, ruefully entitled "Saved by the Element of Denial: The College Years," which she read aloud late in the semester:

> **Part I: Poppy and the Pit**
> My grandfather was a jolly man with a round belly and wide smile. He was of German, Russian, and Italian heritage, but was proud to be American born. I loved him; I was his little Lia Jean the jelly bean, and he was my Poppy. As far back as I can remember, my Poppy had three "girlfriends" besides my Nanny (his wife and my grandmother): my cousin's golden retriever, my cousin, and me. I know this may sound creepy, but he did not refer to us as girlfriends in the normal definition; he used the word *girlfriend* as another term to express his love for the women in the family.
> Poppy was also a Korean War veteran, and although he did not graduate from high school, he was one of the most intelligent men I knew. To support his wife and three children, he drove a truck, tended the Parkchester baseball field, the property on which they lived, and ran the Parkchester Baseball League. After his death, the city of Parkchester created a memorial for him for his work with the Little League program. His charm, handsome features,

dark skin, and vivacious blue eyes won the hearts of many women in his neighborhood, but my Nan won his. Even as an elderly man with a pot belly and large, circular glasses, his attractive qualities still shined through. He was an avid hat collector; by the time he passed away, he acquired no less than two hundred hats. He loved Frank Sinatra, the Four Tops, and Donna Summer. During family gatherings, while holding his hands on his round belly, he would sway back and forth to the music. At times, he also added a little twist with his small but hefty body.

Although Poppy's heart was full of warmth and love, this organ was void of full physical strength. At age 40, he suffered his first heart attack.

It was kind of good, well, not good, but it was better after he had the first heart attack," commented my Nan when I asked her about my Poppy's heart condition. "He had to stop drinking with his friends every night." She laughs at this memory, but I learned of his callous side through my mom.

"He was physically abusive to Nan at times," she asserts. "I was too young to remember all of it, but I know he was terrible at times. He was a hardcore alcoholic then, much different from his sober, jolly, and caring personality."

Throughout his lifetime, he suffered five heart attacks but survived. After the fifth, his doctor suggested that a quadruple bypass might help his condition. During this time, Poppy's health was deteriorating, and this could be his last help. I was 15 at the time, and failed to understand the seriousness of his condition; I thought his surgery would cure his heart disease.

After the surgery, he lost weight and nearly withered away in size over the next three years. Even though he still expressed his love, he was agitated easily, and not as talkative. During my freshman year in college, he battled with his heart condition; his visits in the hospital were frequent and alarming. When I came home from college, I refused to believe Poppy could be dying. I visited him in the hospital every week; the hospital always smelled sterile, but the stench of urine and bile lingered in this environment at the same time. I hated seeing him in his weak condition; his movements were restricted to his hospital bed, and because he fell in and out of consciousness frequently, conversations with him never lasted more than 10 minutes. This was not my Poppy; *another man must have possessed his body*, I thought.

On July 12, 2005, Poppy lost his endless and fierce battle against his heart condition. His passing was the first death I understood; I was devastated. At first, I was in shock, and would cry myself to sleep every night. Because I was one of the older grandchildren, I helped with the preparation of the wake.

When I walked into the funeral home, I observed his body in the casket. He looked serene; he wore a black suit and his face was powdered white. His arms were crossed over his thin belly. I glanced at him several times to see if he would wake up, as if some miracle would bestow upon him, but he was dead. As my mother put her arm around my shoulders, I excused myself for a breath of fresh air; I needed a cigarette badly. As I puffed the nicotine stick, I sat on the cement sidewalk and hugged my body; the thick tears fell, one after the other, on the pavement from my eyes.

I remember my other grandpa's wake, and wished Poppy died then. I was a naive, pure, pudgy, round, cherry-cheeked eight-year-old who failed to grasp the concept of death. The dim, depressing lights in the funeral home contrasted with the pictures of happy faces in better times placed on the tables next to the entrance. My grandpa suffered from Parkinson's disease and Alzheimer's, and I cursed myself for failing to remember a time when he knew who I actually was; he always referred to me as his daughter.

My father, his eyes red and bloodshot, escorted me to the creme-colored casket. "Say a prayer for grandpa," he said softly.

Like Poppy, grandpa's face resembled that of a woman from the Victorian era: his face painted white, his thin, wrinkled lips colored, probably from make-up, in a light red. His colorless hands crossed over his chest, and his necklace, which bore a modest gold cross, rested motionless on top of them. I attempted to cry because everyone around me sobbed, but I felt more curious about the stoic corpse in front of me than sad for my grandpa's death.

Over the next three days at Poppy's wake, I sat in the funeral home in a daze. I grew to despise the word "sorry," because that was all that people would say to me. This word would not bring him back; my Poppy was dead. Poppy symbolized the glue that stuck our family together, and after his death, family gatherings became less frequent; the closeness we shared almost diminished.

Part II: Denial

After his passing, my mother observed, "Isn't it kinda funny that after Poppy's death, everything started to spiral apart." She used the word "funny" to lighten the situation and make me feel better, but I still felt horrible. Inside, I was falling apart, and before I returned to school in the fall, my regular physician diagnosed me with an anxiety disorder and suggested I see a therapist. By spring 2006, my mother divorced my verbally abusive father. Even though my father lost his job when I was 16 due to his alcoholism, money did not become tight until that year. I became financially responsible for myself in most respects; this sudden change exacerbated my anxiety, which led to full blown depression.

In summer 2006, I knew I was no longer the same person. My house, once filled with furniture, family photos, and togetherness, was nearly empty. In court, my mom won most of our possessions and moved into an apartment nearby with my little brother. When I returned home for the summer, I lived with my father and older brother in my old house. The emptiness of the house escalated the feeling of emptiness I felt inside. I self-medicated with marijuana; if I did not, on most nights, I cried myself to sleep. I worked more to distract myself and to exhaust my body to battle my insomnia. On weekends, I slept rather than partied with friends. My best friends were concerned about me, but I assured them I could handle myself. I used humor to shield my depression and anxiety, my strongest and most effective defense mechanism. I smiled when I felt like crying, and prayed for my last day on this Earth; I wanted to be with my Poppy in heaven.

I never tried to kill myself, but I became obsessed with death at times. Due to my anxiety disorder, I sometimes convinced myself that I would die soon. I know I am no longer suicidal because death petrifies me to no end. My feelings, however, contradict themselves at times when I feel plagued by depression. The *Merriam-Webster Dictionary* defines depression as a "psychoneurotic or psychotic disorder marked especially by sadness, inactivity, difficulty in thinking and concentration, a significant increase or decrease in appetite and time spent sleeping, feelings of dejection and hopelessness, and sometimes suicidal tendencies." This definition describes my feelings accurately, but I define depression in other terms; depression is the annoying pit in my body that extends from the top of my chest to the bottom of my stomach. Irritation, infuriation, and anguish fill this pit, and no matter how hard the sun shines down on me or how favorable my life may be at the time, this horrible pit remains and refuses to leave my body.

With the word "therapy" comes a terrible stigma. I needed help? Me? The straight A student with a countless number of friends?

"The problem is that you are a perfectionist," stated my mother before I left for Albany this past August. "I'm also afraid you've become cynical of life. I feel, well, I hate to say it, that you've become sort of jaded. You used to be an optimist."

"Optimism is overrated. I like to think of myself as a pessimistic optimist," I explained as I smirked at my mom.

"Smart ass," she responded. "You need to make an appointment at school."

Appointment for what?" I tried to sound like I had no idea what my mother was suggesting, but I knew her implications well.

She glared at me and smirked. "You need to see a therapist. You can't just take the Lexapro. You told me it wasn't working as well as it used to."

"I know, I know, I will," I responded with reluctance.

I kissed her on the cheek goodbye and hopped into my black Civic, wondering when I would find the time to or if I would make the time to see someone for my mental health.

Part III: Acceptance

"Hi, I have a 4 o'clock with Catherine," I say solemnly. *This whole therapy idea is starting to freak me out.*

"Sure . . . yup," the male secretary scans the appointment book on the gray desk. "Just take a seat and she'll be right with you." *I wonder what he thinks about me—maybe something like, "Yup, there goes another crazy one."*

I thank him and sit down on one of the generic red office chairs. Like most doctors' offices, the waiting room smells sterile and the walls are painted white. Two Ansel Adams photographs line the wall to my left; there is one from his Yosemite series and one of a waterfall. I study the black and white photos while waiting for what seems like an eternity. I fidget in my seat, and shake my legs and tap my fingers together.

A tall, thin, blonde woman walks out of the wooden door in front of me a few feet away. Her hair is pulled back in two French braids, and she smiles warmly at me.

"Hi, I'm Catherine," she grins. "Just follow me back here and we can start getting acquainted."

"Hello," I respond hesitantly and follow her through the long white hallway. When we make a right, I observe several rooms in the hallway; we enter room 133.

Contrary to the plain white walls of the waiting room, this room is a light midnight blue. A miniature wooden coffee table separates the space between two comfy blue chairs. A box of Kleenex tissues with aloe vera and a small green plant in a dark blue vase sits on the coffee table. *This must be part of the whole relaxation aura,* I chuckle to myself and take a seat.

When I began therapy on Tuesday, February 26, 2008 at the University at Albany Psychological Services Center downtown, I was hesitant at first. My Lexapro failed me, and I felt discouraged and depressed about all aspects of life. Therapy was my last hope; I was ready to cut the cord on my life.

At the center, SUNY students pay only $5 for each visit, which, for a broke college student like myself, is affordable. Since the UAlbany psychology program runs the center, PhD students meet with clients and videotape each session as part of their research. After each session, they consult with a supervisor who is a licensed psychologist. I see this set-up as a win-win situation; you help them with their research and they help you feel better.

I wanted to discuss time management with her in regards to how I can make more time to do more activities, but she felt we needed to talk about time management in regards to how I can make time to relax. When she stated this, I thought, *Wow, I never looked at it from that angle. These psychology people are so smart.* I always thought I knew everything, but so far, therapy has made me realize that I do not know everything nor do I have to, and that is A-okay.

I continue to see her every Tuesday, and I am starting to learn how to cope with my feelings in healthy ways. She provided me with a progressive muscle relaxation CD, which helps me fall asleep and alleviates my anxiety. Right now, I am working on breaking my cutting cycle. For the past two months, I have cut nearly every week. In order to break this vicious cycle, I made a list with Catherine of other activities I can do when I feel low, which include going to my friend's house around the corner, calling my mom, hanging out with my two best friends/housemates, exercising at the gym, and listening to optimistic music.

Therapy is a long and difficult process, but I am learning to look at the positives in my life rather than the negatives. After discussing my feelings about my parents' divorce and Poppy's death, I am learning to cope and accept my feelings. I know that it is normal to feel this way, but with the techniques and advice Catherine has and continues to provide, I am starting to move on.

With therapy, I am also attempting to wean myself off my medication because I do not want to rely on a pill for happiness. Although this relaxation helped me by alleviating my anxiety, and therefore preventing panic attacks, I hope I can stop consuming the pills soon.

With the help of an unbiased third party, I am learning I am strong and I can overcome the numerous obstacles I face on a daily basis, and most importantly, I am learning that I was brave in taking the step in the right direction, realizing I needed to seek help instead of taking a razorblade to my wrist.

As "Saved by the Element of Denial: The College Years" reveals, writing an essay, diary, or story allows students to identify a problem and then imagine ways to solve it. Writing encourages multiple perspectives. Thus we see Lia's characterizations of her psychiatrist, mother, and psychotherapist, all of whom seek to help her solve her problems. Characterizing these three people enables Lia to see that they all offer useful advice for her. Unlike speaking to another person, which sometimes does not give us sufficient time to pause and reconsider a statement, writing allows us to stop, reflect, revise, and reformulate a statement. Writing requires revision, rewriting, and reauthoring of one's story. That's what Lia does in her essay. Her early version of this essay contained only "Poppy and the Pit," but as a result of the questions raised by her classmates and Nico, she wrote the next two sections, which helped her to continue the story of her educational and psychological growth.

In the first section, Lia evokes Poppy's colorful personality, his zest for life, and his love for his three "girlfriends." She does not idealize him, for she informs us about her mother's statement that he had a "callous" and "abusive" side. Seeing him in the hospital, his body almost unrecognizable from five heart attacks and severe weight loss, Lia can hardly recognize him. "This was not my Poppy; *another man must have possessed his body*, I thought." She captures, in barely more than a dozen words, her shock, disbelief, and horror. She recalls in abundant detail how he looked in death and then contrasts him to her other grandfather, who died when she was eight. Poppy's death, she implies at the end of the section, has resulted in the loss of her innocence and the end of her intact family.

In the second section, "Denial," Lia conveys her life spiraling out of control. She is brutally honest, describing her feelings of sadness and loneliness, her abuse of marijuana, and her growing obsession with death. She hinted at these problems in "Shattered Love for Instant Gratification," but now she probes beneath her sarcasm and cynicism to describe her underlying fears. "Denial" was the side of her personality that she sometimes projected during class discussions in the two courses she took with me. She always empathized with her classmates, but she cultivated a "smart ass personality" that can be seen in the discussion with her mother and psychiatrist.

The third section, "Acceptance," reveals not the resolution of her psychological distress but an acknowledgment of it. One recalls in this context Chekhov's distinction between the solution of a problem and a correct presentation of the problem: Only the latter is obligatory for the artist. The cynicism, sarcasm, and flippancy present in the first two sections are replaced by a seriousness befitting the gravity of her situation. There is nothing forced about this seriousness, nothing preachy or inauthentic. She knows that therapy is a "long and difficult process," and she remains positive in her outlook but not pollyannaish. She provides information about the Counseling Center that will help her classmates avail themselves of this important college service. She ends by telling us that she is "strong" and capable of overcoming the many obstacles facing her.

All three sections reveal Lia's meticulous attention to detail. Her eye records every detail of her therapist's office, ranging from the generic red office chairs in the waiting room to the Ansel Adams' photographs. Many people who begin therapy are too depressed or self-absorbed to notice these details—depression tends to constrict one's thinking and point of view, making concentration difficult—yet she seems to see everything. She captures the outward details of her therapist's reassuring personality and contrasts it with her own anxious personality. She is discreet about the content of her therapy session, never revealing anything that might compromise her own or another person's privacy. Her main goal is to narrate the beginning of her therapy, yet at the same time she provides helpful information for others who may be thinking about beginning therapy themselves. The graduate student therapist is a sympathetic figure, neither idealized nor demonized.

Like Lexapro and other antidepressants, writing seldom produces "miracles," but it can be effective for those who suffer from mood disorders. Writing rarely provides "instant gratification," mainly because it requires hard work, mental concentration, and seemingly endless revision. Hundreds of students, not all of whom were English majors, have told me during the last 30 years that writing is a powerful tool for problem-solving, self-discovery, and self-healing. "The work of writing is my therapy," admits Donald Murray (2001) in his memoir *My Twice-Lived Life*. "As I write, defining and describing my fears and joys, anxieties and satisfactions, I begin to understand them and reduce the terrors to the manageable. It is the unknown that truly terrorizes" (p. 77). Writing produces far fewer side effects than medication, requires no prescription, and is certainly less expensive than prescription or non-prescription drugs. One can write anywhere, anytime, in almost any mood. Writing preserves a record of one's feelings and thoughts. "How do I know what I think till I see what I say?" E. M. Forster famously said. Sometimes writing may be sufficient to control a mood disorder, while at other times, as in Lia's case, writing works best in combination with medication and psychotherapy. It is true that writing heightens vulnerability when one shares one's essays and diaries with others, but writing also strengthens one's immune system, as James Pennebaker (1990/1997) has demonstrated in *Opening Up*. Writing may become "addictive," yet almost always it is a healthy addiction, in the service of creativity and self-expression. It is possible for writers to "swim" in their "puddle called misery," as Lia sardonically admits, but more often than not, writing allows one to escape from this puddle. Many authors have commented on the therapeutic benefits of writing. "One sheds one's sicknesses in books," D. H. Lawrence (1981) writes, "repeats and presents again one's emotions, to be master of them" (p. 90).

Lia presents us only with the first therapy session, and she leaves the reader with many questions unexplored. How did Poppy's death affect her parents' divorce? To what extent did his death remind her of her own mortality? How did his death shatter her assumptive world? Has she formed a new assumptive world? Has she experienced posttraumatic growth? When—and why—did she begin cutting herself? These are all therapy questions—and writing questions—to be explored in the future, when she is ready to explore them.

In describing some of her risky behaviors in college, Lia lays bare her pain and shame, thus exposing her vulnerability. Anyone who writes about depression, anxiety, and cutting opens herself to criticism, if not attack, from her classmates and teacher. Such writing carries with it both benefits and risks. "It takes courage to be self-revealing, to be truly known to others," Sidney M. Jourard (1971, p. 17) asserts, even as he reminds us that self-disclosure makes us vulnerable. Barry A. Farber (2006) lists the many benefits of self-disclosure in therapy, including "Experiencing a greater sense of emotional closeness," "Being known and affirmed by another," "Gaining greater insight into oneself," "Expanding one's sense of self," "Achieving a greater sense of authenticity," and "Relieving the physiological and psychological pressures of painful and/or shameful experiences." Farber also lists the many risks of self-disclosure: "Being rejected by the recipient of our disclosure," "Burdening another with our secrets," "Creating undesired impressions about ourselves," "Feeling regret for not having shared the secret earlier," "Experiencing increased vulnerability," and "Experiencing a sense of shame" (pp. 13–15). Farber's bias is toward self-disclosure in therapy; mine is toward self-disclosure in writing. The benefits of self-disclosure in writing may be seen in Lia's essays. She experienced a greater sense of emotional closeness with her classmates and teacher, heightened their understanding of her, gained greater insight into herself, expanded her sense of self, achieved greater authenticity, and relieved the pressures of her painful and shameful experiences.

I would be remiss, however, if I did not acknowledge the dangers of self-disclosure in the classroom, especially when teachers manipulate students into self-disclosure, grade their students on the degree of their self-disclosures, or transgress boundaries and dispense psychiatric advice. These risks have been discussed in detail—and, in my view, sometimes exaggerated—by Swartzlander, Pace, and Stamler (1993). I provide students with the opportunity to write about their lives, and when they sign up for Love and Loss, they know in advance that it will be an emotionally fraught course. Those who engage in "risky writing" often feel a "pit of anxiety" in their stomach, as Lia did, but such stress is probably inevitable. No one dropped the course once it began or implied at any point that it was too intense. No one felt betrayed by or regretted a self-disclosure. Nor did anyone object to the writing assignments or the class discussions. I am careful to put into place protocols that minimize the possibility that students who write about traumatic events will be retraumatized. Encouraging students like Lia to write about her struggles poses undeniable risks, but they are far outweighed by the many benefits of such writings.

Lia admits that her feelings "contradicted themselves at times," but this was a contradiction she saw herself, not one that a classmate or her teacher made during class discussion of her essay. I have found that the less a teacher analyzes the content of self-disclosing essays, the more willing authors are to offer their own self-analysis. This paradox is easily explainable: students are less threatened by their own interpretations than by a teacher's or a classmate's. Lia's self-interpretations throughout this essay are significant. The structure of her essay, beginning with "Poppy and the Pit," moving through "Denial," and ending in "Acceptance," dramatizes the movement of her journey toward self-understanding and self-healing. The mood of Part I of her essay is anguished, mirroring the depth of her grief and depression; Part II is sarcastic and cynical, conveying her refusal to acknowledge a serious problem; Part III is calm and resolute, befitting posttraumatic growth.

There is no mention of the "pit in the stomach" in the third section of the essay, and yet, not surprisingly, Lia was anxious about reading the essay aloud, as she admits in her diary that week:

> This essay reveals even more about my obstacles and my troubles with coping. I hope no one will judge me, but I am afraid of crying during my reading. I try not to cry in class because I do not want to bring attention to myself, which is part of my guise: looking okay on the outside to cover my feelings within. On Monday, I sat in my chair with this familiar pit of anxiety in my stomach. *When is it going to be my turn to read?* I thought. *Can I just get this over with already?* I never knew I would react this way, but there's this uncomfortable feeling that still sits in my stomach that I know will stay until I finally let it all hang out for my peers to see. I hope my essay will help others in the class who relate to me. I feel it is important for me to read this essay, regardless of my mind and body's resistance.

Despite Lia's fears, she remained composed throughout the reading, and the class responded sympathetically. Had she cried during the reading, her classmates and teacher would have remained compassionate, and she would have appreciated their support. Of this, I am confident.

"Saved by the Element of Denial: The College Years" was Lia's most important writing of the semester—of *both* semesters, if we include her work in Expository Writing. At the end of the essay, the narrator, the "I," is different from the person who begins the story. This difference reveals what she has learned about herself as a result of both the "talking cure" and the "writing cure." For all the differences between her experiences in psychotherapy and Love and Loss, there are intriguing similarities. The decision to reveal to her fellow students and teacher her depression required an empathic and nonjudgmental audience that she found in Love and Loss. In effect, our class became like her therapist Catherine, willing to listen empathically and support her efforts to find her own solutions to her conflicts. Lia stated, on the first day of the semester, that although she was anxious about taking Love and Loss, she "signed up for more growth and obstacles." The growth, it turned out, involved writing about these obstacles. And write she did, essay after essay about the many obstacles in her life. Writing for the first time about the "grim and brutal details" about her depression enabled her to begin confronting her demons.

Lia began many of these essays with a familiar "pit of anxiety" in her stomach, but she felt a "pit of pride" when she completed her writings and read them aloud in class. The demons did not disappear, but they became less fearful to her. She was willing to write about these demons largely because of her classmates' self-disclosures. "Hearing other students' brave admissions makes me more comfortable sharing my own," she observes in an early diary entry. Weeks later, she identified with Scotty's anguish over his parents' divorce. "I too 'escaped' to college when my parents were at their worst and 'abandoned' my little brother, leaving him to witness my parents' wars alone. However, my little brother did not overcome these obstacles like Scotty's brother; now 19, he struggles and has anger issues. I feel guilty for abandoning him. I hope our family will start healing soon." The death of Chipo's mother distressed her, yet she felt it was important to hear about her classmates' loves and losses. "At times, stories about a parent's death makes me feel uncomfortable because I am terrified of losing my own parents. I look forward to hearing my other peers' stories—the good and the bad." She identified closely with Daphne's essay about her grandmother's death. "When Daphne struggled to read her essay in class, I wanted to cry with her. However, as part of a defense mechanism, I stopped myself; even when I want to let this emotion out, I cannot. Chipo showed his growth and strength through not shedding tears, but I feel Daphne illustrated her strength through her vulnerability and honesty."

All the students commented in one or more essays or diaries that they felt close to their classmates, a bond that was both a cause and effect of their trust for each other. The empathic, self-disclosing classroom created bonds among the students that became stronger each week. Many students emailed me after the semester ended, telling me that they still felt close to their classmates. The class felt like a nurturing, supportive family, the opposite of the kind of splintered family that has depressed and wounded so many of my students. Lia felt especially close to her classmates who had lost a parent to death or divorce. It is impossible to exaggerate the importance of an empathic, nonjudgmental classroom atmosphere. Without it, students like Lia would never have been so self-disclosing. The feeling of camaraderie, community, and connection in the empathic classroom allowed her to expose her vulnerability without fear of being judged or criticized. She reaches an important insight in a late diary entry: instead of feeling like a "crazy person," she now knows it is "normal" to feel the way she does as a result of multiple losses. The pit of pride she experienced at the end of the semester revealed both her educational and psychological growth.

Tellingly, Lia's self-representation—the way she characterized herself—changed during the semester. In the beginning she was excited about taking Love and Loss but fearful of disclosing the full extent of her pain and shame. As she conceded in her "Shattered Assumptions" essay, in the first writing course she took with me, she had left out "certain details" about her parents' divorce and her grandfather's death, as well as her anxiety and depression. Many of these details appear in "Saved by the Element of Denial: The College Years." The three sections of her essay reveal her psychological journey, beginning with grief over her parents' divorce and her grandfather's death, moving through denial, and ending in acceptance. This acceptance implies not the completion of her journey but a recognition of the hard work that lies ahead of her. Her early and late writings are different in their attitude toward life. She began by revealing a "morbid way of looking at life," in her psychiatrist's words, a "jaded and cynical view," in her own words. She ended the course with the viewpoint of a person who is learning to "look at the positives in my life rather than the negatives."

In a brief preface to "Saved by the Element of Denial: The College Years," Lia informs us that many of her feelings about herself have changed as a result of revising and developing the essay. "I have grown immensely from this experience since the first draft." She elaborates on this statement in her last diary, which she signs as "Almost UAlbany Alum"—she was graduating in two weeks. "I started out as a pompous junior in your Expository Writing course. I thought I knew it all, but my grammar was crap and so was my attitude. I was intimidated at first, but after the semester ended, I was a grammar whiz. However, grammar is not the most important element I have learned from you. I know this may come as a shocker, especially since grammar is crucial to the clarity of my writing. I finally became honest with myself about all the obstacles I have faced in the past four years. Instead of minimizing my struggles, I wrote about them."

Lia feared at first that she was "drowning in a pool of self-pity," but she discovered something important. "You made me realize that grief is not always such a bad feeling to recognize. I have learned it is okay to grieve, just as long as I pick myself back up after. If I reflect, I can learn. If I reflect, I can start to move on, and by writing about my situations, I have started to throw those weights that have weighed so heavily on me off my shoulders."

Writing about anxiety and depression is, to use Lia's term, a "win-win situation," for not only do students often achieve educational and psychological breakthroughs but they also educate their classmates—and teachers—about urgent mental health issues. As reported in *NEA Higher Education Advocate* (2009, June, p. 3), "in the 2008 National Survey of Counseling Center Directors, more than 95 percent of the responding directors reported that students with significant psychological concerns continue to be a major problem on their campuses." For the past decade, the number of college students seeking treatment for serious psychological disorders has increased: "Recent studies found between 25 and 30 percent of students report significant signs of depression" (p. 3). Noting that two recent studies demonstrate the effectiveness of counseling centers, the article concludes that the challenge is "how to reach more students, especially with increased demands on the counseling center staffs." I believe that teachers can play a role in their students' mental health and, indirectly, in their students' academic success, by encouraging them to write about their experiences with anxiety, depression, and suicidal thinking. Lea's essays eloquently reveal how such writing can help to destigmatize both mental illness and psychotherapy.

Lia has continued to reflect on her life, as we can see from her responses to reading this chapter six months after the course ended:

> After reading my own essays, I felt overwhelmed with all different emotions. I felt proud of myself for disclosing my situations, and I was joyous because I had overcome all of these obstacles, but I also cried. I cried because I am so different from that person in the essays. My writings became a form of therapy for me—my own form of expression. From the time I was in grade school, I always kept a journal to clarify my thoughts and cope with the sometimes terrible process of growing up. Without this "terribleness," I would never have grown up, and I would have never written about these apparent traumatic events, which included my first kiss (sloppy-ew!), my first period, and my first heartbreak (which wasn't really that heartbreaking at all). Of course, these events are far from traumatic in reality, but they were devastating for a teenage girl.
>
> In college, I faced more severe struggles, and without my writing, I may have never overcome them fully. Those four years were the best years of my life so far, but at times, felt like the worst. I have never loved and lost so much as I have during this confusing and challenging time. In the end, I had to move away from people who have become my family and deal with my first serious breakup with my first love, which I am still coping with today. And of course, I am writing about this, and I am writing about this situation furiously.

"It's Hard For Me To Express Emotion"

"I'm taking this course for three reasons," Shannon asserted on the first day of the semester. The first reason is that she took an earlier course with me and did well. "My writing improved substantially, and I hope it will keep improving with this course." The second reason, which is "both a gift and a curse," is that for most of her life she had not experienced loss or tragedy. "When I did, I was either too young or not emotionally mature enough to understand or be very impacted by it. However, this past year has been a whirlwind, and I'm still not sure how it has affected me." And the third reason is her fear of expressing emotions. "Ask most people who know me, and they will tell you I lack all emotion, that I am cold-hearted. I am not, but it's hard for me to express emotion, although I want to prove to myself that I can. I am afraid I won't be able to do it, but I hope this class helps me."

Shannon's anxiety surprised me, for she wrote several impassioned essays on Thomas Hardy and D. H. Lawrence in an earlier course she took with me in the fall of 2006. She struck me then not as a person who seemed shy about expressing emotion but as a spirited and articulate young woman with strong opinions and an infectious laugh. My perception of her was obviously different from her self-perception. The reference to the "whirlwind" past year mystified me. It soon became apparent that it had something to do with her close-knit extended family, to which she refers in her opening essay. "My family is everything to me. They are my best friends. They are my advice. I do not know what I would do without them. I don't believe there is much more I can say other than that."

As it turns out, Shannon had much more to say, but before presenting her writings, I want to explore why someone might fear expressing emotions and becoming emotionally "jaded"—the same fear, incidentally, that we saw in Lia's writings. What makes emotions so dangerous that one wishes to hide them?

For an answer, we may turn to the work of Robert C. Solomon, a professor of continental philosophy at the University of Texas at Austin and one of the country's leading "emotion" theorists. The author of many groundbreaking books, Solomon died in 2007 at the age of sixty-five. In his last book, *True to Our Feelings* (2007), he suggests that we disregard emotions at our peril. "Nothing is more immediate to us than our own emotions, but nothing about us is more prone to self-deception, suppression, lack of recognition, and even straightforward denial than our emotions" (p. 28). He examines this paradox throughout the book, pointing out, in disagreement with Daniel Goleman (1995), the author of a best-selling book on the topic, that "emotional intelligence is not so much concerned with emotional control as it is about intelligence *in* emotions, that is, the essential conceptual and evaluative components of emotions, their insights, and not just their 'regulation'"(p. 164). In one of his most felicitous phrases, Solomon characterizes emotions as "engagements with the world, not mere self-enclosed feelings" (p. 204).

Solomon argues, in addition, that emotions are strategies: "They are instrumental in getting us what we want (and helping us to avoid what we do not want), and sometimes they themselves may be (or seem to be) what we ultimately want: true love" (p. 182). If Solomon is right that emotions are engagements with the world, then Shannon feared that our Love and Loss course would arouse her emotions and thus heighten her vulnerability. She feared, in other words, that she would attempt to escape from painful emotion by withdrawing into her self and disengaging from the world. Such an escape would preserve her invulnerability but also distance her from the many loves in her life.

Three of the four loves Shannon discussed in Assignment 1 were her relatives: her entire family, whom she listed as her "first and most important love"; her father, who is her "hero"; and her goddaughter, who is named after her. Three of her four losses also involved her family. "I do not like talking about my feelings, or my emotions. I do not like feeling vulnerable, but here I go." These losses included an uncle who died in 2007 from colon cancer; another uncle who committed suicide; and a grandmother who died in 2005 from Alzheimer's disease. Shannon ends Assignment 1 by revealing that she has never been more self-disclosing than in this essay. "I know a person can't see the time on a typed sheet of paper, but believe me when I say that this did not take me an hour or two. I typed and deleted this entire assignment four times."

Shannon's writings in Love and Loss are noteworthy because they show how she learned to express her feelings through words. This may not appear to be a remarkable discovery, but it was a singular achievement for her. She learned not only to express her feelings about the people who were dearest to her but also to use writing as an outlet for emotional release. Equally important, she learned she could express emotion and remain engaged with the world. Self-expression left her vulnerable, something she feared and wished to avoid, yet she never regretted any of her classroom self-disclosures. By the end of the semester she proved to herself that she could write powerful essays on love and loss. Two months after the course ended, a third uncle died, and she used the skills she developed in our course to write a heartfelt eulogy for him.

Shannon's writings are significant for another reason: they helped her classmates write about their own loves and losses. This was apparent from

Assignment 2, when I paired her with Lia. "When Shannon wrote her essay, she broke a personal barrier. For the first time in nine months, her bravery exceeded her fears and sadness. This emotionally jaded young woman poured more feeling into her story than I expected, and in the midst of her confessions, I related to her feelings about loss, love, and life. After our conversation in class on Monday, I learned to confront my feelings about my grandfather's death." Although it was purely through chance that I paired the two with each other—they sat next to each other when I gave Assignment 2—they proved to be exemplary biographers of each other's loves and losses, as we can see from the rest of Lia's essay:

> Shannon's Uncle Joe, her mother's second oldest brother, lived in Italy, and for this reason, she saw him rarely; regardless, she still spoke with him on the phone often, and the two relatives remained close. At age 10, Shannon traveled with her family to visit her uncle and stayed there for two months. These visits became a tradition, and her family visited him every three years.
>
> When Shannon and her family arrived, Uncle Joe greeted them with a warm smile. Shannon explains: "My uncle was a happy guy. He had a little store and was a country farmer. If I brought pictures of him, you would see what kind of man he was. He was always smiling, laughing, and sneaking snacks to me when my mom wouldn't allow it." Joe loved to sing, and during each visit, Shannon provided the dance entertainment to his amazing vocals. She describes the event: "We would sit outside the porch after dinner in the beautiful country, where I kid you not, every star in the universe would shine."
>
> During the summer of 2006, Shannon never knew she would see her uncle for the last time. At this visit, the 19-year-old woman discussed serious issues with him. Along with many other topics, he inquired about her future plans, love life, and school. Shortly after, Uncle Joe began suffering from severe stomach pains, and on Christmas Eve 2006, her mom's younger brother received a phone call that explained Uncle Joe was rushed to the hospital, but kept this a secret until Christmas Day. While waiting for positive news to arrive, Shannon's tight-knit family supported each other for the next few days. The doctors predicted her uncle had cancer, but needed lab tests to confirm the diagnosis. After a while, he began to sit upright and converse with people; however, his health failed to improve. With a now fragile and weak body, he said his goodbyes, and a priest absolved him of his sins. He told his son to marry his longtime love, which would make him the happiest man in the world. Uncle Joe's life clock ticked faster and faster as time went on, but as a brave man, he accepted his fate.
>
> On January 9th, 2007, his clock stopped ticking. Devastated, Shannon assisted her mom with phone calls to other family members. She kept her composure well, but when she called her Aunt Anne, she began to break. When her mom's brother went to buy plane tickets to Italy, Aunt Anne told her daughter about Joe's passing, which also saddened Shannon. Since her other uncle, Joe's youngest brother, suffered from a health condition, his doctor prevented him from flying; he would not make the funeral. Shannon explains, "He was hit the hardest. He fell into a relative's arms, looking for strength."

During that evening, Shannon's family ate dinner together before her parents, uncles, and aunts traveled to Italy for the funeral. She stayed back with her other shocked cousins and anguished uncle. After her parents left that night, she began to cry, and her cousin comforted her. "I completely broke. I thought I was going to faint—I lost all balance, I collapsed, and my cousin caught me. He walked me over to the couch and sat down. I couldn't make it that far and I sat on the floor. My cousin, who has never seen me like this, had no idea what to do, so he laid my head in his lap and just put his hand on my back and left it there for a half hour while I cried and cried." According to her parents, hundreds of people attended the funeral, which illustrated the love people felt for this extraordinary man.

Shannon's story reminded me that we often find it easier to numb ourselves from grief and anguish than to face and deal with the pain we feel inside. She tried to appear composed, but on the inside, felt like a wreck. When we learn to accept our unfavorable emotions, we will then start to heal.

Lia's essay offers us the factual details to understand Shannon's loss, but she does more than this, for in the last paragraph she explains why her classmate must "numb" herself to maintain her composure. Lia never implies that there is anything pathological about this self-numbing; rather, she sympathizes with her classmate's response to loss. (Two weeks later, in the "Shattered Assumptions" essay, Lia uses the same word to describe herself: "I preferred to feel numb instead of facing the unbearable pain.") Lia ends the essay with a crucial insight, one that reveals as much about herself as it does about her classmate. Throughout the essay, she combines her own words with Shannon's to suggest how both women collaborate in the storytelling.

"I knew this class was going to be emotional," Shannon admits in the opening sentence of her first diary, "it was right there in the description. I also knew that this was going to be a tough class for me since I am not used to writing or talking about my emotions." Shannon didn't anticipate that the first assignment would be so emotionally difficult. "I honestly did not think I was going to be able to write about four loves and four losses. Truth be told, I didn't even think I had four loves that I could write about."

Assignment 2 proved even more daunting for Shannon. Writing about the death of Lia's grandfather "Poppy," Shannon feared that her classmate might dislike the essay. "I thought Assignment 1 was hard, but I had no idea how much more difficult Assignment 2 was going to be. I had a hard time writing about my personal loves and losses. Imagine what I thought when I had to write about someone else's loss. I felt as though everything I wrote was not good enough." Shannon wanted Lia to know that she was doing her best to write about Poppy. Shannon ends the diary by saying that although the class is going well so far, "I'm sure it's only a matter of time before something inside of me clicks and I crawl back into my emotionally jaded shell."

Shannon didn't have to worry that her classmate would be displeased with the essay. Hearing Shannon's essay was a unique experience for Lia. "This week, when my partner read her paper about my experience with the death of my grandfather, I did not shed one tear; I did not even sob. For the first time since my grandfather's passing, I listened to her story with a pit of pride in my stomach instead of a merciless and excruciating pit of sadness." Lia added that she felt "brave that day—maybe even bold—because I cracked a slight smile after hearing my partner recite my story. Maybe I am starting to move on. Maybe I have realized my Poppy would want to see me smile after listening to his story."

Shannon uses her second diary entry to probe her fear of emotion, writing with a conversational style, as if she is speaking directly to the reader. "I've already told you that I'm not very emotionally forward. I never say I am completely devoid of emotions, however. What basically happens is I hold everything in because I don't like people seeing this side of me. Then there will be one day, usually once every six months, when I just simply lose it." These are the days when she sits in her room and cries for hours. "And I don't start crying because something terrible happened. Most of the time, I will do something like stubbing my toe, or spilling coffee on my white shirt. And most of the time, I mean always—it always happens that way. I hold everything in for such a long time, and one tiny thing will set me off. But I digress. I think I am more focused on my classmates' reactions so that I can take the focus off of my own."

Shannon discloses that she doesn't allow others to see her emotional side, yet she makes an exception with the reader—her teacher. By writing about her usual tendency to hold in emotions until they are explosively released, she seeks a way to control these unruly feelings. Just as writing about her classmate Lia enables her to "take the focus" off herself, reading a passage from my memoir about Barbara allows her to explain what it means to be "emotionally jaded." "I was reading *Dying to Teach*, and when I read a book I always keep a pen in my hand to underline my favorite lines or quotes. I didn't even make it past the introduction and I already had accumulated quite a few quotes to add to my list." She found the opening sentence of the second paragraph, "Life has a nasty habit of smashing assumptions," particularly compelling. She then continued reading and came to the excerpt from Dave Eggers's self-interview. "I will end after I quote him, as this is exactly what I think being emotionally jaded means. 'I don't hold on to anything anymore. Pain comes at me, and I take it, chew it for a few minutes, and spit it back. It's just not my thing anymore.'"

Shannon continues her responses to *Dying to Teach* in her third entry, disclosing that she suddenly found herself choked with emotion during an otherwise calm week in Love and Loss:

> I shed a tear this week. Okay—I shed more than one tear. I knew I was going to cry at one point during the course of the class. Okay, I lied again. I didn't know I was going to cry; it was only an assumption. I also thought that it would be during an actual class. I thought (I was almost 100% sure) that I would experience *emotional contagion* during one of the hour and

twenty minutes allotted to English 450. That's not how it happened. I was sitting at my desk and reading *Dying to Teach*.

I felt like this week was a lot less emotionally charged, as far as sad emotions go. Most of the essays that were read out loud were about my classmates' loves. I remember leaving class on Monday with a smile on my face. For the first time in a long time I really think that love is all you need.

The feeling which was leaving all smiles and giggles didn't fade quickly. That's why I wasn't expecting the tears so quickly. I was sitting and reading, and the next thing I knew, I felt the tears rolling down my face. Something had hit too close to home.

Toward the end of Chapter 1, you write about [Barbara's friend] Ellen Gootblatt and her final visit to your wife. "I was working in my office during Ellen's last visit on January 25, and when I heard her scream, I raced into our bedroom, where she and her boyfriend of several decades, Murray Koenigsbaum, were kneeling beside Barbara." I was stunned. My eyes went wide. One hand placed the book on my desk, the other hand went over my heart. I thought you were writing about the last moment of your wife's life.

After five minutes had passed, I picked up the book and began reading again. The next sentence explained the scream; Murray had proposed to Ellen. Again, I had to put the book down, and that's when I began to cry. I was relieved. I was also remembering the moment my mother found out that her brother had died. There was a scream. There was running. But nobody had proposed to anyone in my living room. My mother literally screamed her tears out and could not move. That is what I was reminded of when I read the sentence about the scream. A scene of tears and the inability to move was what I was expecting in the rest of the paragraph. I felt the same fear I felt when I heard my mother scream, but it was the relief I felt after reading the rest of the paragraph that sent me into tears.

Shannon's diary entry is fascinating because it represents a self-analysis, an effort to understand the present by probing its relationship to the past. Like a patient in analysis, she explores her feelings by working through various forms of resistance, as when she mentions twice in the opening paragraph that she "lied." I wouldn't call her opening statements lies so much as efforts to understand the complexity of her emotions. Each statement in the opening paragraph is followed by a qualification as she tries to convey the truth behind her tears. It is as if she is speaking to a psychoanalyst. She was, however, speaking to her English professor. She may have cast me into the role of the analyst, but I did not interpret her writings for her. Nor did I make judgments. Instead, I listened carefully and made supportive comments on her writings that allowed her to continue to examine her feelings. I do this with all my students. I was the person to whom Shannon was writing, but notice how she internalizes me in her construction of an inner dialogue between the self that aims for self-discovery and the other self that knows self-exposure can be painful and perhaps harmful. She implies in all three of her diary entries that emotions are so dangerous that she must "numb" herself.

Emotional numbness is not unlike "frozen emotion," a metaphor that describes the inability to grieve, as Ann Kaiser Stearns (1975) points out in *Living through Personal Crisis*. "Water, as it freezes and the molecules expand, has the power to burst steel pipes wide open. Likewise, frozen emotion assumes a power out of proportion to its original nature. In the middle of a very harsh winter it's wise to see to it that the water flows regularly through your home plumbing system." During the harsh seasons of grief, Stearns analogizes, one should "keep the channels open so that hurtful feelings are freely expressed. Frozen emotion, like a frozen pipe, has the potential for causing unexpected problems" (pp. 60–61).

Emotional numbness may not be as extreme as frozen emotion, but it represents a loss of physical or emotional sensation, and both Shannon and Lia use the word pejoratively to signify disengagement from themselves and the world. And yet there is a positive meaning to the word, as when a dentist uses an anesthetic like novocain to block the sensation of pain. The numbness lasts for a few hours, allowing the dentist to extract a tooth or fill a cavity that would otherwise be excruciatingly painful. Finding the words to describe a painful emotion also requires detachment—a degree of numbness. Writers may still feel pain during the act of writing—the detachment, or numbness, is not complete—but the act of writing leads to feelings of pleasure, control, and self-mastery.

However intriguing the metaphor of "frozen emotion" may be, there is the danger that it reveals, in Martin and Doka's (2000) words, a bias toward intuitive grievers. "For the male intuitive griever whose identity is determined solely by societal stereotypes, intense feelings of grief are more than a mere inconvenience; they represent a threat to the Self" (p. 58). Similarly, for the female instrumental griever whose identity is determined solely by societal stereotypes, the *lack* of intense feelings of grief is more than a mere inconvenience; it represents a threat to the Self. Martin and Doka use the term "dissonant" to describe a way of expressing grief that contradicts the griever's primary internal experience. The "perpetual suppression of feelings, where the griever's expression of grief is incongruent with his or her inner experiences, becomes a way to avoid the reality of the loss as well as a way to avoid feelings" (p. 59).

Ironically, the week that Shannon felt was the least emotionally charged for her proved to be the most wrenching. She found herself becoming emotional not from writing an essay or hearing a classmate's essay but from reading a chapter of my book. Reading about Ellen Gootblatt's scream of delight over a marriage proposal reminded her of hearing her mother's scream of horror upon learning of her brother's death. And so we see Shannon engaging in self-directed, controlled free association, without any prompting from her teacher.

Shannon's diary entry also reveals how a single word, in this case, "scream," can reawaken a traumatic memory. I would not have known about this memory had she not written about it in her diary entry. Writing about love and loss triggered a traumatic memory in her, but writing also enabled her to work through the pain, leading to greater self-knowledge and self-control. Even more than speaking, reading and writing are introspective processes that we can temporarily suspend when we find ourselves becoming emotionally overwhelmed. Shannon mentions putting down *Dying to Teach* for a few minutes to regain her composure before continuing her reading. I recall when Ellen Gootblatt was visiting Barbara for the last time how unnerved I was when I heard her scream, which I feared at the time was *conclamatio mortis*, the death shout that occurs in some cultures. Shannon also feared this, but what made her situation more terrifying was the memory of her mother's scream upon learning of a sibling's death. Shannon's tears of sorrow mixed with tears of relief, a response that no one who was emotionally jaded could understand.

Shannon's next essays and diaries focus on her reactions to her classmates' losses. "I don't want to use a cliché, but there is no other way to say this," she remarks at the beginning of her fifth diary entry. "On Monday, hearing Kamilluh read her essay on smashed assumptions sent chills down my spine. I felt every single goose bump on my body, to the point where I didn't think they would ever go away." Shannon doesn't use the term *emotional intelligence*, but she implies that what she has learned is nothing less than a profound understanding of herself and her classmates:

> This class has allowed me to open up in a way that I never have. I am not trying to say that I trust all of my classmates, or that my guard has completely gone done. All I know for certain is that writing about my personal experiences has given me a new way to express things that I never thought I would be able to express. I can read my essays, and people who under normal circumstances would never know these things about me now know. Even if something is read anonymously, I still feel as though my classmates are learning about me and my life.
>
> I'm finally getting in touch with my emotions, and I'm happy about that. However, on Monday, it was a different feeling. As I listened to Kamilluh reading one of the most powerful essays I've ever read, I was moved on a different level. I was so moved that it *scared me*. How could the words of a girl I barely know touch me to the point where I felt fear? At the same time, how could I say that I barely know Kamilluh, when I know something so personal about her?
>
> I left class on Monday right after Jeff dismissed us. I didn't stick around to chat with friends. I didn't take time putting my books back into my bag. I didn't do anything except walk out right away. The entire way back home, I couldn't get Kamilluh's voice and words out of my head. I couldn't stop thinking about my cousins, my cousins who are more like younger siblings to me. I simply couldn't stop thinking about this essay, and how it left me feeling.

Shannon's next two essays focused on the deaths of her grandmother and her uncle Joe. In Assignment 8, "Posttraumatic Growth," she observes that although her grandmother's death was devastating to her, it was her "final push into adulthood." In Assignment 9, "Writing to Life," she attempts to bring her revered uncle back to life. This was the loss that her classmate Lia had written about in Assignment 2, but now Shannon reveals new details about him, describing him as a larger than life figure, an avuncular man with a zest for life. "His big belly reminded me of Santa Claus, and I told him this. He would laugh at me and make a joke. He was always laughing. He was always making me laugh." She recalls the wonderful times they shared when she visited him in Italy, including the non-stop drinking, eating, and partying, and she then describes their final parting:

> It was the summer of 2006. This was the first time I saw my uncle cry. It was the last day of our vacation. We were at his house in the country, which is halfway up a mountain. The drive is atrocious. You are driving up a mountain in a continual spiral on a narrow street with no guardrail. The first time we went up there, the combination of stick shifting driving and my obscene fear of heights led to my father having to pull over (which on this road is really just putting the car in park) so that I could throw up. It's a beautiful house, but I wish I could just snap my fingers and make it appear. On the last day of my family's 2006 vacation, we were standing in the sunshine on the porch. I was saying goodbye to everyone, and then I came to my uncle, who wasn't crying yet. I hugged him, and I didn't want to let go. When I pulled back, he was crying. I told him not to cry, which didn't make any sense because I was crying as well. I told him that I was going to miss him. "Oh, stop. This isn't the last time I'm going to see you. Get rid of those tears." Once again, I told him that I was going to miss him and that I didn't want too much time to pass before I saw him again. Other than "I love you," those were his last spoken words to me.
>
> My uncle was a great man. He was easy going, but in a strict manner. I realize that sounds like a contradiction, but my uncle made it work. Because of the distance, we didn't get to see each other often, but the time we did spend together was cherished. I loved every moment, whether he was laughing, singing, or yelling. I will never forget the devastation I felt after he died, but I will never forget our memories either. Those memories overpower the hurt, and that is all I can ask for.

Shannon has come a long way from the young woman who feared she would soon crawl back into her emotionally jaded shell to the person who can recognize that "memories overpower the hurt." She embraces all of the emotions she experienced when she was with her dying uncle, both the joy and the sorrow, and we finally understand why the last year has been such a "whirlwind" to her, filled with bitter-sweet experiences about love and loss. She reaches these insights partly from her own writing, partly from her classmates' writings, and partly from her reading of *Dying to Teach*.

Like most of her classmates, Shannon used her last diaries to comment on her feelings about the end of the semester. She also reveals how she felt when she started crying in class as she read the essay about her uncle:

The fact that this class is so close to being over is making me more emotional than I have ever been throughout the class this semester. I talk about this class all of the time. I talk to my parents about the class. I tell my sister about the book. I tell my aunt about the essays that I write. I can't imagine not talking about English 450 anymore. I can't imagine not seeing my classmates twice a week—at least twice a week—anymore.

This class has helped me in ways that I never even imagined it would help me. Besides the fact that I have finally allowed myself to admit that I have emotions, I was opening up to a classroom full of people; these people barely knew me. I say that in past tense because we know each other now. As I read all of my essays in order, I see how much I have grown as a person. When I was writing those first assignments, I thought I was exposing myself on a level I had never reached before. I read my most recent essays and I see that that was not the case. Although I had slightly let my guard down, I hadn't reached my full potential. Now, I believe I am wide open for everyone to see. The best part is that I want it to be that way.

Last week was a tough week for me. I had a devastating conversation ending a relationship I did not want to end. Then I cried in class. ME. I CRIED. IN FRONT OF PEOPLE. After class, Jeff said to me, "The girl with no emotion. How ironic." It made me laugh, but I felt so vulnerable from crying that I ran home. The next morning, I had sunshine coming out of my ears. Maybe it was because I finally released everything that had been building up inside of me for so long. My roommate told me she thought I had lost my mind because I had painted my nails with a pink nail polish. I'm not a pink kind of gal, if you haven't gotten that vibe from me yet. I joked with her, telling her that God must have spoken to me in my dreams, because nobody was wiping the smile off of my face. She then told me that I had definitely lost my mind. And then I started thinking that I have four weeks until I graduate from college and I won't be in this class anymore. But I will continue writing, even if it doesn't come in assignment form and I don't have to read any of it aloud.

Shannon's last diary summarizes what Love and Loss meant to her, a summary made more difficult because she knows that in two weeks she will be graduating from college. "All of my thoughts are way too scattered to be put into words," she admits in the opening paragraph, "at least in a way that would make sense." Characteristically, she then finds the words:

At the beginning of the semester, I thought that I would use my last diary to reflect on the past 12 diary entries that I have written. Reading all of my past entries was more interesting than I thought it would be. In my first two entries I wrote about my "emotionally jaded" personality. I even wrote that I thought I was doing a pretty good job with my writing, but that it was probably only a matter of time that I would "crawl back into my emotionally jaded shell." As I continued reading my diaries, I realized that the complete opposite happened. My third entry revealed the first time I cried, which was while reading *Dying to Teach*. Jeff wrote in his commentary that it represented a "self-analysis, an effort to understand the present by probing its relationship to the past." The rest of his commentary was extremely interesting, and I asked Jeff to send it to me so that I could include it in my final diary—and here it is.

I continued to write on the ways that I was growing as a person, and how I was finally getting in touch with my emotions. Then I began to write on the bond that has developed between everyone in this class. I wrote on how we interacted in class, as well as how we interacted out of class. I spent some time praising classmates and their essays. I also used some diary entries to write about personal experiences. One entry was on something that had recently happened, and one was on something from the past. When I reread these entries, I couldn't believe how open I was. Before this class, I would have never written on some of these topics, and if I had written on them I would have never shared it. Now, as I reread my essays and entries, I'm proud of all that I have written, and I have this class, my classmates, and my professor to thank for it.

Two months after the semester ended, Shannon emailed me about the death of another maternal uncle in a construction accident. She had seen him only two days earlier at her cousin's moving-up day. She sent me a copy of her 1600 word eulogy, which describes his life when he came to the United States as a young man, not knowing a word of English. More joyous than sorrowful, the eulogy proceeds to "paint a picture of a bond that is not visible to the human eye," a "bond that can be felt only by the heart and soul." In loving words that combine thought and feeling, Shannon describes the nature of this invisible bond. "My uncle was killed in a freak accident. I still don't know why this happened, and I don't know if I will ever get past the trauma of experiencing such a shock. All I know is that I could not have gotten through this without my family." She ends the eulogy with a tribute to her relatives, who once again have helped her survive a grievous loss. "Through one of the most devastating experiences I have ever gone through, they were the ones putting smiles on my face and in my heart. We may have lost one hero, but we still have each other. We are each others' heroes, and that is something I wouldn't trade for the world."

Shannon felt a "flood of mixed emotions" rushing into her when she read the chapter containing her own writings several months after the course ended. "My leg started to shake, as it usually does when I start getting anxious. I didn't know what to expect. Which writings of mine did Jeff choose? Why was my foot tapping the floor at such a fast pace? Why was my printer running out of ink? Why wasn't it printing faster? I knew what Jeff thought about my writings, and I realized after the first few pages that reading Jeff's words was not my issue. It was reading my *own* words." She then explains why reading one's words may be different from writing or hearing them:

> Why would reading my own words be giving me such difficulty? I kept trying to verbalize my thoughts, but they weren't making sense. I had written those words. Hell, I had even read some of them aloud to a class full of people

I once knew as strangers. As I was reading some of my essays, I would come across certain sentences that would come out of nowhere and slap me in my face. I felt as though the few months that I did not even glance at my essays allowed the words to build up a raw kind of emotion, the kind of emotion that goes straight to your gut and can make you keel over.

I'm not sure what made reading my writing different from writing it or hearing it. Maybe it was the fact that I had not read the essays in a few months. Maybe it was the fact that my words were surrounded by someone else's as well. Maybe it was the fact that I recently went through a devastating loss, and some of my writing brought back painful memories.

There are plenty of times where I try to verbalize my thoughts. More often than not, however, my thoughts go too fast and get too scattered before I can verbalize them in a way that makes sense. So what do I do? I write. All of a sudden, everything becomes clear. My thought process slows down to a speed where my words can, for the most part, make sense. How does that answer my question? If my thoughts make more sense when they are on paper, wouldn't they make more sense when I read those words than when I say them out loud? I realized that reading my words was the verbal equivalent of hearing them. I realized that it was much harder to read your own words in a quiet room by yourself than reading them aloud or hearing them read aloud. I also realized that you need both experiences to fully grasp what you put on paper. Hearing the words gives you a much different feeling than does reading the words. Writing gives you a much different feeling than does speaking. When I put all of those different feelings together, I finally make sense.

Making sense of life and death is an ongoing struggle, one that perhaps ends only when our consciousness ends. As Shannon observes, rereading is part of the process of meaning making. Rereading is a way to revisit our earlier lives, allowing us to recall how we respond to loved ones' deaths, honor their memories, and forge continuing bonds with them. Reading, writing, rereading, and rewriting help us to slow down our cognitive and affective processes so that we can understand how we think and feel. Sometimes we may feel, like Shannon, that our sentences slap us in the face, evoking the kind of emotion that "goes straight to your gut and make you keel over." Notice how Shannon's metaphors of emotion emphasize their power to assault the body. And yet if emotions are capable of attacking the body and, at times, sickening us, she knows that they can be ignored, denied, or repressed only at our peril. This is what Shannon discovers in Love and Loss. In learning to treat the affective world with the respect it deserves, she grows in emotional intelligence—not just the regulation of emotion but the intelligence *in* emotions. She also learns that rereading our words about lost loved ones brings tears of sorrow and joy to our eyes, reminding us of the powerful ways in which emotions are engagements with the world. Knowledge such as this can last a lifetime.

"If I Could Not Write, I Would Not Survive"

Faith was blunt about her reasons for taking Love and Loss. "I've been told by my mother that all I have ever seemed interested in writing about is death. In all actuality I have spent my whole life dealing with death, so I am surprised by her criticism. I came looking for two things in this course, to learn how to improve my writing, and for the chance to write about a subject that I grew up knowing very well." Faith was initially ambivalent toward the course, "scared" about exploring her emotions. "I have spent many years overcoming the steps of bereavement, but I feel this class will be worth that chance. All I want is a chance to finally be heard without being told that I am wrong for speaking and writing about love and loss."

One can understand a parent's fear that a child seems to be obsessed with writing about death, but perhaps Faith's mother would be less anxious if she knew that other students felt the same need to write about dark topics. "No doubt some will think it morbid to consider death and dying in the context of first-year composition," Hurlbert and Blitz (2003) concede. "But for 10 years now, the two of us have been giving our composition students the assignment to write a book about what they are burning to tell the world, and in all these years, more than two-thirds of our students have elected to write about things that have caused them sorrow, about the deaths of loved ones, about the deaths of neighbors, even of hope itself" (p. 84). Marian MacCurdy (2007) agrees: "Our students will write about painful subjects whether we ask them to or not" (p. 47).

Many students write about suicide, including their own suicide attempts. Few people realize that suicide is, as Kay Redfield Jamison (1999) notes in *Night Falls Fast*, the third leading cause of death in young people in the United States and the second for college students. "The 1995 National College Health Risk Behavior Study, conducted by the Centers for Disease Control and Prevention, found that one in ten college students had seriously considered suicide during the year prior to the study; most had gone so far as to draw up a plan." The figures for high school students are more ominous: "One in five high school students said he or she had seriously considered suicide during the preceding year, and most of them had drawn up a suicide plan. Nearly one student in ten actually attempted suicide during the twelve-month period" (Jamison, pp. 21-22). Sharon Jayson (2008, August 18) reported in *USA Today* that American college students are becoming more suicidal. "A comprehensive study of suicidal thinking among college students found that more than half of the 26,000 surveyed had suicidal thoughts at some point during their lifetime." The study found that slightly less than half of those with suicidal thoughts told anyone. "Suicidal crises are a common occurrence on college campuses," observed the director of a major university counseling center. According to the American Foundation for Suicide Prevention, "over a lifetime, 20% of us will have a suicide in the family and 60% of us will know someone who dies by suicide."

Thinking about suicide does not imply that one is suicidal. "The thought of suicide," Nietzsche (1954) observes caustically, "is a great consolation: by means of it, one gets successfully through many a bad night" (p. 468). William J. Worden and William Proctor (2002) state in *PDA—Personal Death Awareness* that "Some experts believe that the ability to entertain suicidal thoughts is what keeps many people sane—and alive," an opinion the authors share (p. 163). And yet brooding constantly over suicide, believing that life is not worth living, and formulating a suicide plan are generally symptomatic of clinical depression and should always be taken seriously.

I believe that a course on death education should include instruction about suicide prevention. Over the years many of my undergraduate and graduate students have written personal essays or reader-response diaries about their own suicide attempts. Several of these writings appear in my books (Berman, 1994, 1999, 2001, 2004). These suicide narratives are survival stories. Students explore why they felt so hopeless that they were willing to end their lives—hopelessness is a leading predictor of suicide—and how they were able to overcome suicidal depression. (As clinicians point out, most depressed people are not suicidal, but most suicidal people are depressed.) I've never had a student romanticize or glorify a suicide attempt, nor have I had a student who regretted that a suicide attempt was not successful.

Faith's writings are significant because they educated her classmates and teacher about the darkest of subjects, suicide, and a related subject, cutting, a form of self-harm that is growing in frequency among college students as well. She wrote about these subjects not because she sought the attention or advice from her classmates and teacher but because she wished to be heard. She was indeed heard, and no one told her she was wrong for writing about love and loss. She never flinched when writing about the most challenging topics. "I never realized just how difficult it would be for me to figure out what my four loves were until I had to write them down," she admits at the beginning of her Assignment 1 essay. She lists her four loves as her current girlfriend, writing, the piano, and track and field. She became an English major because of her love for writing, a love that has sustained her through turbulent times. "My life has been filled with many difficulties, so writing became my salvation from everything in my life. I have hundreds of poems, half-started short stories and journals. I look forward to my English classes because it means I can see what other writers have done so I can do something even better. My mother does not agree with my passion for writing, but I think she is afraid that I will end up living out of a cardboard box."

"If I could not write, I would not survive," Faith states in an essay written near the end of the semester, and however overstated this assertion may appear, she never doubts that writing is an essential part of her psychological support system. Her words remind me of Alice Walker's (1996) similar observation: "It is, in the end, the saving of lives that we writers are about. Whether we are 'minority' or 'majority.' It is simply in our power to do this. . . . *The life we save is our own*" [italics in original] (p. 33). Like Alice Walker, Faith views writing as essential not only to her survival but also to her identity, as she reveals in her Assignment 1 essay. "It allows me to push aside any hurt or guilt that I may have and just create something that no one else can duplicate. My words are my own, and I know that even though I have spent many years in school being told I should not write about certain things, my words are something no one can take away from me." She feels the same way about playing the piano. "I remember one time I was playing [Beethoven's] 'Für Elise' at a friend's house, and her mother told me she had never heard a person play that piece with such emotion. I would slow down the first section of the piece until it had a sad echoing to it, mostly because it was a sad time in my life." Music and writing became Faith's only escape during this perilous time in her life. "I do not think I would have survived middle school and high school without a pen or my piano."

Survival, then, for Faith requires her to express dark emotions such as sorrow. Her writing and music have a melancholy echoing that conveys the many losses in her life, including the passing of a beloved aunt from AIDS; the premature deaths of many friends; the estrangement from her abusive father, whom she has not seen in several years; and the time when she mysteriously "lost herself" during adolescence. "I feel bad for those in my life during that time because I was not a pleasant person. I was even diagnosed with bipolar spectrum because the doctors could not pinpoint what was wrong with me. I was having severe mood swings, suicidal thoughts, and I was cutting my arms and legs. The only word I have found that really describes what I was feeling during this time period is 'numb.' I had lost interest in everything in my life: track, writing, eating, even my girlfriend." During this time Faith felt as if her body was shutting down as a result of years of physical and mental abuse. "I knew I did not want to die; something was preventing me from following through on my suicidal thoughts. Nevertheless, I was desperate to feel, which is what led to the cutting. I still have the scars on my shoulder from the last time I cut, which was about eight months ago. I still do not know what caused this period in my life; however, what I do know is that I did not recognize myself during this time, and that was scary enough."

To explore the time she nearly lost herself, when she was "numb," Faith characteristically turned to writing. Lia and Shannon also spoke about being numb, but Faith's numbness was different. Her essays record why she wanted to die, how she harmed herself, and how she was serendipitously saved from ending her life. I've never had a student write more insightfully or eloquently about suicide than Faith. Her essays show how writing can become a lifeline, an essential part of one's life support system. No matter how gloomy her essays were, they were always well written, containing an expressive power that moved everyone in the class. A fiercely competitive athlete, she began the course as a good writer and ended as an excellent one; she told a fellow student that she wanted to be the best writer in the class. However scary her adolescence was, she provides us with a remarkable self-analysis, one that begins with the opening assignment in Love and Loss. "I never had a writing assignment quite like this one. I never realized just how deep I was still feeling some of the issues I thought I put behind me. I also never realized how hard it was to come up with something I love. I would say that my life has not been the hardest life; but I can easily say it was not the easiest. I would agree that I have had more losses in my life than loves, but I am glad to say that I have loved."

Faith registered for Love and Loss before Patricia Hatch Wallace and I published *Cutting and the Pedagogy of Self-Disclosure*. Three of her classmates also wrote about cutting, but her essays were by far the most graphic and disturbing. Her writings conjure up the death-in-life existence of the clinically depressed, and they also show us how depression can be overcome. Her writings provide insight into the time when she almost lost herself, revealing her strength and courage as a survivor—and as a writer. Additionally, her writings demonstrate how students can teach and learn from each other in the self-disclosing classroom. She wrote far more about loss than about love, but rather than burdening her fellow students with sadness or grief, her writings proved to be life-affirming, even inspiring.

The early essay on "Shattered Assumptions" psychologically prepares us for "To My Left Arm." She opens the essay by stating she knows little about her father except that he lives in a nearby state. "I do not know his favorite color, or what his favorite food is, or even what he looks like. All I know is our story, because calling it a history implies existence, and he does not deserve the right to have an existence in my life." The earliest memory of her father occurred when he slapped her in the face. "It was over a Hershey Kiss. He told my sister and me that we could not have anymore, but my sister took another one and shared it with me. He thought I took it, and he hit me to punish me for disobeying him. According to him, though, he did not hit me because his hand wasn't in a fist. According to my father, slapping a three-year-old does not constitute hitting one." Faith recalls in detail the last day she saw him. "My mother had come out to the porch of her house with a rock in her hand, and was yelling at him, telling him to leave her property. I think he was dropping me off, or was coming to pick me up; all that information is obscure in my mind. All I remember is him looking me in the eyes and saying, 'I can't see you anymore because your mother is a bitch.'" She remembers her mother screaming at him to leave. "I remember watching him get into his car with my older sister (same father, different mother) in the back seat. I remember watching the dirt fly into the air as my father drove out of my life."

Because she could not take out her anger on an absent father, Faith became furious at her other parent. "I grew to be violent and angry toward my mother. I blamed her for my father leaving me behind. I was in therapy by the age of seven for my anger issues. I would lash out in my fits, hitting anything that was in my vicinity. To stop me from hurting myself, my mother would sit me between her legs and let me beat on her thighs. At a young age I learned to hate." She also learned to appreciate her mother's strength. "My father abused my mother, both physically and mentally. One day he ripped the phone out of our wall so my mother would not be able to call for help. I am thankful that my mother is a strong woman. Otherwise she might have stayed with him out of fear instead of leaving him as soon as he became out of control with his anger."

Faith concludes "Shattered Assumptions" by stating that she has not seen her father for 17 years; nevertheless, his name still "wreaks havoc" in her life. She continues to feel overwhelmed by her parents' constant court battles over child-support and by his lack of emotional support. And yet despite her bitterness and disappointment, she still finds herself inexplicably loving him and wanting him back in her life. "At one point in my life, he was my daddy, but as I grew older, he became the sperm-donor, the bastard, the mother-fucking asshole that looked me in the eyes and blamed my mother for his incompetence. He is the man who taught me how to hate and love at the same time. He is the man who helped create the darkness in my life that almost killed me." He's also the man who still makes her cry herself to sleep at night. "I may have grown up with many men in my life that helped shape me to be a better person, but I grew up without him, and that fact alone has been my biggest demon." She reveals in her next essay that the battleground in which she wages war with this demon is her body:

"To My Left Arm"
I know you think it is weird that I am writing to you, but I felt that I had to write the wrong I have done. I want to apologize to you for all the damage I have done to you over the last few years. I am sorry for all the bruising, cuts, scrapes and abuse that you have had to endure because of my lifestyle. But most of all, I want to apologize for all the pain that you have gone through from my own hands.

I never meant to begin cutting. I do not think anyone wants to cut him or herself, but something within me snapped, and I needed to get my pain out of my body. The first time I cut you, I was 13 years old. I was suicidal. I was angry. I hated the world for making me feel like I was not good enough.

I hated the fact that I was gay. I hated being afraid of my dark thoughts. In truth, I was angry with myself for my inability to feel connected to my world. My mom and I were constantly fighting over my brother, my schooling, my father, and my attitude. I could not express the pain I was feeling. How could I tell my mother that the only reason why I was alive was because my brother decided to hug me the night I was going to commit suicide?

I remember sitting against my door after my mom and I fought over going to her boyfriend's family's house for Thanksgiving. I did not want to go so she left me home alone. I sat there in disbelief that my mother chose me over her alcoholic boyfriend. My pocketknife was on the floor next to me. I am not sure how it got there, but I remember flipping it open and staring at the blade. I remember feeling desperate. I needed to feel anything besides the hopelessness that was settling in my stomach. I did not realize that I cut myself until I felt you throbbing in pain. I sat there crying as I cut you a few more times before putting my blade away. I cleaned you up and put on a long-sleeved shirt. I felt better, as if my pain was released; then I felt guilty for harming you. You had done nothing to me. You were loyal and strong and I damaged you. I wish I could say that was the last time I hurt you.

Many people found over the years that I was hurting you, but aside from sending me to counseling, no one stopped my assault against you. The last time I cut you was a year ago this March. My girlfriend and I were having problems; she could not handle my depression. I felt like my heart was going to explode from the pain I was harboring. A few months before I had carved hell into your forearm, a reminder of the pain that I was feeling. The scissors were right there and before I knew it, you were bleeding again. The cuts were deep, but you did not bleed as badly as you should have bled. I vowed after that day never to hurt you again.

The scars are there now, raised and constantly angry. Everyone asks me if you were in a fight with a rake. I laugh it off in embarrassment. I caused you that pain, and now you bear that constant reminder of the abuse you experienced. I will not lie to you when I say that the urge to hurt you has not returned. However, I cannot hurt you anymore. You do not deserve that pain. You come with me to therapy, and I am constantly rubbing you in hopes to soothe the pain of your past. I hope one day to gain your forgiveness for the wrongs that I have done.

I do not know why you have taken the brunt of my frustrations. Maybe it was because you would be there to remind me of the pain that I felt growing up. Looking back, it was the worst decision for me to make. Nevertheless, I know you would not want to dwell on the past. Instead, you would want me to make sure that my future was better, and that I was finally happy. I am sorry that it took hurting you to realize the truth. I am sorry it took hurting you to put me on the right path to forgiving myself. I am sorry.

Love,
Faith

In "Writing a Wrong," Faith personifies the innocent victim of her assault. She is remarkably self-analytical, revealing the many disappointments in her life and capturing the conflicting feelings of relief and guilt experienced from cutting. The act becomes a guilty pleasure that makes her feel human. Like other cutters, she longs for relief from intolerable psychological pain. Honesty compels her to admit that the temptation to cut herself is still there, but she is proud she has not cut herself in several months. She ends with an ardent plea for self-forgiveness.

"To My Left Arm" has a dialogical quality, evoking a conversation between self and other. The other remains silent, but the writer helps us to intuit its right to existence. Faith empathizes with both sides of the self, the "I" and the "you." Those familiar with the early twentieth-century Lithuanian-born Jewish philosopher Emmanuel Lévinas may sense that Faith honors the self's sacred duty to the other. The reader cares about both characters in the essay, the I and the you, the victimizer and the victim. We cannot avoid feeling saddened and disturbed by the speaker's anguish. We may even find ourselves in the position of the injured left arm, bruised and scarred by the essay's violence.

Nico was teaching the class when Faith read aloud her essay, and he was stunned by its power, as he records in his diary entry:

> Faith, a young woman of exceptional charm and candor, had asked if she could read her essay at the very end, since she had been absent and had not had a chance to read it aloud previously. I told her she was welcome to it, though I had no idea to what I was agreeing; had I known what was to unfold, I might well have asked her if she would mind saving it for Jeff's return. Her essay was as beautifully written as it was excruciating to take in. She wrote a letter of apology to her left arm, tenderly asking its forgiveness for all the years during which she hurt it. At first, the essay seemed funny, until I realized full force, *holy shit, she's writing about cutting!!!* The class was completely silent during the reading. Some students teared up. I was amazed that Faith was able to get through the reading without breaking down. It was as impressive a performance of composition as it was one of extreme strength, bravery, and self-control. When she was finished, no one spoke. It felt like all the air had been sucked out of the room. I didn't know what to say. I felt that I should say something, something meaningful, something that would sum up the class's feelings, Faith's bravery, her suffering, her ability to transcend that suffering through artistic creation. But I could think of no words that would express this. The silence lingered. I was ever so relieved when I thought of just the right thing to say: "A wonderful essay. Who has a favorite sentence?"

Faith's classmates could feel the anguish in the essay, and they appreciated the courage and strength it took to write it, as we can see from their diary entries. Her essay emboldened Lia to reveal that she is also a cutter:

> When Faith read about her cutting and almost suicide attempt, I felt relieved that I wasn't the only one in this class with these problems. I have befriended her throughout the course, and I have found that she has an

amazingly warm heart. If she went through with her suicide attempt, I would never have met her, and I am glad her brother hugged her that night. . . . I want Faith to know she is not alone; I want her to know that taking your life is never worth the consequences. Her essay was both powerful and evocative; out of all the essays she read so far, I feel this essay represents her most honest and heartfelt piece. I admire her bravery for revealing this self-disclosure. Although I am not sure if I will ever be able to disclose my feelings about my cutting, her essay made me consider writing about my struggles with self-mutilation and suicidal thoughts.

"To My Left Arm" was equally powerful to those who had not cut themselves. "Faith's essay to her left arm sent chills throughout my body," Scout admitted. "Her writing was strong and captivating. I held back tears as I heard her read about her experience with cutting. I could not believe the woman sitting next to me was the same person writing the letter to her left arm, apologizing for cutting her wrists. The letter was intense, and I will remember her writing because of the intensity with which she wrote." The essay also affected Chipo. "I was startled because usually I know if a story is sad or funny. But this story was creative and nerve-wracking. I loved how she wrote a story to her arm. But I just became silent. My classmates became extremely still when this essay was being read. When Faith finished reading, an awkward silence surrounded the room. Nico attempted to defuse this silence by commenting about a favorite sentence." Chipo added that he would have done his presentation on Faith's essay if he had read it earlier. "Even though I cannot relate to the experience, I would tell Faith that life is not always a sunny day but that it is what we do when there is a storm within our life that defines who we are."

If I have the opportunity to prescreen essays before they are read aloud, I sometimes wonder whether an essay is appropriate to read aloud. Occasionally I telephone students to make sure they feel comfortable reading aloud emotionally charged essays. For example, if a student is severely depressed, an essay on depression may be too upsetting to read aloud. There are other situations that might compel me to telephone students before they read their essays aloud. I've never come across a student essay that romanticizes suicide, but if I did, I would not allow the student to read it aloud for fear of the contagion effect. Fear of copy-cat suicides prevents schools from holding memorial services for students who take their own lives. There was nothing in Faith's essay, however, that caused me alarm. She never glorifies cutting, never implies that it is a constructive solution to her problems, never recommends it to her classmates, never intimates that she is in a life-threatening situation, one that would require me to notify the Counseling Center.

The following week Faith gave her class presentation on "To My Left Arm," which she chose as her most significant essay to date:

> The most memorable essay that I have written is "Writing a Wrong: To My Left Arm." It was the hardest for me to write, but it was the only topic I

could have written for this assignment. Nor do I believe that I could have written this essay for any other class than this one.

My essay was about the various times that I had cut my arm throughout the last eight years. I fashioned my essay as if I was writing a letter to my arm. I knew I would not be able to write it any other way. If I did not, I knew that the pain behind my story would be lost. It was also therapeutic to write an apology letter to my arm. It gave one of my limbs a life, allowing it to feel pain and anger towards me for the damage that I had caused. It made my history of cutting more real to those who never experienced someone who self-mutilated. Describing the scars as looking something like rake marks allowed the image of my actions to be seen. That is what made the letter hard to handle, being able to see how my actions caused me to damage myself. I had told my mother that I wrote a letter to my left arm apologizing for cutting it. She thought it was a great idea, and felt as if this moment was overdue. I agree with her and although it was hard, it was the most important assignment that I have done.

Reading a letter to my classmates was easy and hard at the same time. I was reading about mutilating myself, the most intimate and destructive part of my past. I thought I would feel ashamed for cutting. Cutting has been considered a social taboo, something that only the weak and the sick do to gain attention. My cutting was not about gaining attention. I did not want attention; I hid the cuts on my arm so no one would pay attention. I cut myself to feel something besides sadness. I've learned that replacing pain with pain is not an effective way to deal with pain. However, at that time it was my only solution. Reading my letter was hard because I was afraid that my classmates would judge me for hurting myself. As if what I had done was the most horrible act one could commit. I was afraid they would think that I was sick. I was afraid people would look at me differently.

I had read my letter after a funny essay had been spoken aloud, and I never heard such quiet before. My voice was the only sound in the room. There were no sounds of shuffling feet, classmates giggling under their breaths or sounds of paper rustling. I felt as if I had dropped a bomb in the middle of the class. No one was smiling, and I thought I saw some of the women with tears in their eyes. The most surprising thought I had was that I was not crying. I admit that I was shaking, and I found it hard to keep looking around the room as I continued to read. I'm certain that if Jeff had been there that day, I would not have made it through the letter. It is something about his eyes that would have made me start to cry. He is a very caring person and I know that I had to steel myself in order to handle this topic in front of 25 strangers.

When I finished reading, I felt as if one of my demons had finally been defeated. I could finally talk about hurting myself without feeling guilty. I realized that I did not have to apologize to anyone but myself. That feeling that I owed society a debt because I harmed myself was not there anymore, which was a relief because I do not believe that I wronged anyone with my cutting, except myself. That is something I wish I could get through to people who yell at me when they discover my scars. I understand that they care, and I understand that they get scared for my safety. However, my cutting is about me and the issues within me that I must control. It is about finding a way to deal with my inner demons in a healthy manner. It is a problem I see in society when issues of suicide arise. Many people take suicide personally, as if the person who committed suicide wronged them in some way. Although I agree it does seem selfish, I feel more for the person who committed suicide than for the people left behind. It meant that the person who committed suicide felt they had no way out. It meant that the world needed to wake up and pay attention to the problems that lead to that person's death. I wrote in my letter that my brother saved my life the night I was going to commit suicide. I will never be able to tell him that he saved my life because I don't want that burden to be put on his shoulders. I am thankful he hugged me, because he gave me my life back. But I felt it was important to mention my suicide attempt because it showed just how deep my problems were, and how dangerous depression can become.

The weakness of my essay was that I did not elaborate on certain events that lead to my cutting, nor did I speak about the other times in my life that resulted in my cutting. I did not mention many details about what led me to cut, just a few events that resulted in the most visible scars that I have. I have a scar on my forearm that has faded but is still visible, especially if I have a tan. I had just found out that my ex had cheated on me, and a few minutes before that I had found out that my uncle had died. I was already depressed because I knew that my uncle was dying, but after she told me that I could not handle the pain anymore. I grabbed my hunting knife and I ran it over my arm. It seemed to me the most natural act for me to commit. Afterwards I felt calm and more relaxed. Cutting was no different from a crack addict taking a hit because they could not handle his/her craving. I had also briefly mentioned the last time I had cut, which I said was about a year ago. I have an anxiety disorder that leads me to have intense mood swings. So if something in my life becomes stressful, my mood tends to make a dramatic swing. I was sick with mono at the time, which I later found out can cause depression, and my girlfriend had just finished yelling at me over the phone. As I said in my letter, I just reached for the scissors and left deep gashes in my left shoulder. Afterwards I panicked because my girlfriend said she would leave me if I ever cut. I tried hiding them but she found out and yelled at me again. It was ironic to me that I wanted to cut again after she yelled at me for cutting, but I forced myself not to cut. I ended up wearing rubber bands around my wrist for a few months after that incident. It was a controlled way for me to cause pain, but not cause myself bodily harm.

As I was reading, I was wondering about the questions my classmates were thinking. I wanted to ask them if they had any questions. I know it can be awkward when someone talks about a dark moment in his or her life and you want to know more about those moments. You feel as if it is not your business, but the curiosity was there. Only a few people approached me after I finished reading to congratulate me for getting through the essay, and to make sure that I was okay. Most of the class just quietly got up and left the room. Nico did a great job trying to break the awkward sentence in the room, and I was thankful he tried. I could see the struggle in his face and I felt sympathy that the day he was teaching was the day I was reading. He asked me if I read Jeff's book on cutting. I hadn't. It was easy to see that my essay affected him in the way that it affected many of my classmates. I saw that many people did not know how to react to what I had read to them. I was not surprised by the sentences they chose as their favorites, but I was surprised at the number of people who wanted to share their favorite sentences, even though the first few raised hands were hesitant. I laughed at the one grammatical error that I made ["chose me over her alcoholic boyfriend"] because it is an error I make often when I think faster than I write.

I was happy that I had the opportunity to write about this chapter in my life where I was not a strong person. I have been told my entire life that I was a strong individual who knows who she is and where she is going. For many years I wanted to scream that I did not feel strong and that I did not know what I wanted. Most of the time I did not understand why I was feeling the way I was feeling. It is hard to describe one's flaws, especially when they can be dark and violent. I feel that by being able to write and speak about cutting, I was able to show that I have become a stronger person for overcoming this darkness in my past. I also felt that it was an opportunity to break the ice on an issue that many people try to hide within themselves, and from the world around them. It is a hard subject to understand, and it is harder to live with the issue of cutting. Nevertheless, it is my reality and denying it can lead me back to the dark place that I was in a year ago. Yes, I will deal with it for the rest of my life, but I have grown stronger. I hope that my letter helped others understand the issues surrounding cutting, or at least puts another face to the issue.

Writing about the most terrifying issues in her life, Faith remains aware of the literary strategies she must use to tell her story. The word "fashioned" suggests her aesthetic self-consciousness. She knows that she must fashion or construct two different selves, younger and older subjectivities. She knows that because most of her classmates will not be able to understand the younger self who has mutilated her body, she must show rather than tell why she has cut herself and contemplated suicide. She also knows that reading her essay aloud may be viewed as an act of aggression, as if she "dropped a bomb in the middle of class." As in "To My Left Arm," she wounds her readers while simultaneously apologizing for wounding them. She must first make her readers suffer before she can reach an earned resolution of her pain. She writes with the pain of a victim, the strength of a survivor, the insight of a therapist, and the self-confidence of an experienced storyteller. She remains unusually sensitive to her audience, apologetic for distressing them.

Apologies notwithstanding, Faith does not require her audience to give her advice about how to live. She imposes no demands upon her classmates or teacher other than to listen carefully and empathize to the best of their ability. There is little we can tell her about herself that she does not already know. She does not want us to be her psychotherapist or her priest-confessor. Nor does she compare herself with Sylvia Plath or Anne Sexton, both of whom viewed themselves as martyred by their art. Quite the opposite. She tells us that writing is a form of release for her and a process of self-discovery. Writing about her scars, she reminds us, helped her to see the consequences of her actions. She also knows that writing is a recursive act: one can change one's life by changing one's writing.

What I find most compelling about Faith's class presentation on "To My Left Arm" is her ability to narrate to us her thoughts and feelings as she was reading aloud the essay while at the same time reporting on her classmates' responses to her reading. This is something I have trouble doing. I cannot read aloud an essay, either written by another person or myself, while remaining attentive to my students' responses to the reading. This is especially true when I read aloud an emotionally charged essay. The more I try to detach myself from my listeners, so that their tears do not affect my composure, the more I remain unaware of anyone's facial expression, including my own. Faith comments on a certain look in my eyes that might have prevented her from completing her reading. Again, this is something of which I am unaware. Notice how she remains both participant and observer throughout her class presentation. She is even able to criticize "To My Left Arm," believing that she had failed to elaborate on the events leading up to the cutting—a criticism that disappears if we consider her preceding essay on "Shattered Assumptions."

Faith wrote one more essay that she read aloud, on the penultimate class of the semester, in which she elaborates on the mysterious hug that had saved her life:

"Conversations with My 13-Year-Old Self"
I find myself pausing as I begin to write this essay. I knew it was going to be a hard topic to write, which is why I asked Jeff what he thought when I made my decision. I told him that this was going to be the hardest essay I have written. I surprised him when I said that, because he knew my essay about cutting was one of the more difficult topics I have chosen to write on. What could possibly beat my letter to my arm? It was one sentence in my letter which has led me to this moment. One sentence which has me repeating Pink's song, "Conversations with My 13-Year-Old Self," on my I-pod as I sit in plain view of every person entering and exiting the main library. It is this sentence that holds my life within its words, "How could I tell my mother that the only reason why I was alive was because my brother decided to hug me the night I was going to commit suicide?"

"I remember you," I said, looking into familiar eyes. They were blue, ice blue, that changed into slate blue, depending upon the day. She was dead silent. I remember that part too. I remember looking into my own eyes that were buried behind masks that fooled everyone but me. I remember looking myself in the eyes and saying, "I want to die."

Picture this, Bloomingburg, New York, the year is 2001, and a young girl who turned 14 that September sat in her living room with the shades pulled down. A bowl of popcorn in her lap and her cat at her side who sat in silence, even the television was silent. It was November, Thanksgiving, and she was alone because her mother chose her boyfriend over her daughter. Her arm was aching where she just cut herself; she watched the Buffy the Vampire Slayer Thanksgiving Marathon. Her cat Serena, a small, black and white runt, was purring next to her. Serena refused to leave her side, which at first was an annoyance, but became her refuge from her racing thoughts, as she ran her fingers through Serena's fur. Fury, hatred, resentment, and depression consumed her as she replayed the fight with her mother in her head.

They had been fighting for months, but that day was the breaking point. She did not want to have another family in her life; too many people had come and gone in her lifetime. It was the last time she was going to let another family disappoint her. Her mother wanted her to go to Thanksgiving dinner with her boyfriend's family, and the next day would be with their family. She knew that her mother and her boyfriend were not going to last. He was an alcoholic, and yet her mother insisted that she grow closer with his family. When she refused, her mother screamed at her for being a "selfish bitch," and told her that she could spend Thanksgiving alone. Her mother left as she cried, slumped against her bedroom door. She heard the front door slam and all the emotions boiled over her, leaving her numb and confused as she cut at her wrist.

She could not stop thinking about death. It had been a fact in her life, having lost many people she loved. She watched television shows that depicted violence and death, including the episode she was currently watching, "Hush." Any person who identifies as a BtVS fan would know that episode. The fear of not being heard as you were being murdered was enough to frighten anyone, and the episode earned the show its first Emmy nod for "best original writing." She watched in silence as a young man was murdered on the show, thinking about what it meant to die and not have anyone hear your cries. How her own mother did not hear her cries for help, and how her friends did not hear her as well. She was drowning, and for the first time since she was five, she decided that she would stop crying for help. It was obvious that no oné cared about what she thought or felt, and it was easy to forget about the people who left her behind. She survived the night; but it would be surviving the next few years that would truly test her will to live.

My life is far from the doom and gloom that seems to emanate from my body when I talk about the dark times in my life. I have loved and felt love, and there are many things that give me great joy. However, it has been writing that has always brought me my greatest comfort. If I could not write, I would not survive. A page does not yell at me for being vulgar, nor does it hit me in retaliation for abusing it with my pen. A keyboard can be replaced if I pound the keys too hard, and a click of the mouse produces blank canvases for me within seconds. I write my feelings, my thoughts, and my fantasies down because I know the page will not judge me. Writing has always been my greatest confidante, which is why I chose to look back into my old journals for this assignment. Looking back into my journals has brought back memories that I have long forgotten, and it has awoken emotions that I thought I had buried. My earliest thoughts of suicide began when I was 12 years old, which to many is shocking, but I am not surprised. The following are excerpts from my diaries and journals that I kept since I was 12:

"I still have dark feelings, angry and hateful feelings. I still wish to take those emotions out of my skin, just to feel something besides darkness. I still hurt. It has been eight years since the death of my Aunt and yet I still cry myself to sleep over losing her. I talk to her and my friend Roxy all the time. I miss my great-grandmother and my great-grandfather. I still blame my great-grandmother's side of the family for letting her die the way she did."
"No one sees the girl sobbing in the showers staring at the ceiling late at night. Now you don't see her . . . because you never got to know her. The girl who loves to write, sing, dance, have fun. The girl who enjoys quiet nights and crazy nights. Who is impulsive, but still maintains control. No, you didn't get to know me." "Just another night crying myself to sleep." "It's why I enjoy being alone . . . it's why I am content . . . it's why silence never scares me. Silence keeps me company; I never need silence when I am alone. I fear silence being with other people, because that is when I need silence the most."
"There are so many things swimming around in my head that I feel like I'm lost in a perpetual cycle of hate and destruction."

I may have had a life that was better than some; however, I also grew up with hatred and depression. My earliest memory is of my father, who hit me because he thought I ate the last Hershey Kiss. He was an abusive man, and my mother fought to take my brother and me far away from him before he did any damage. I was three years old. By the age of 15 I was a psychologist's dream, the proverbial golden child who excelled in school and maintained an image of happiness while struggling to contain her inner demons. I was my own worst nightmare. I felt as if my anger was going to consume my mind. I abused my body to the point of exhaustion. Nevertheless, I was able to convince everyone, parent and psychologist alike, that I was okay.

The night that I was going to commit suicide was another night of fighting with my mother. I was 15 years old, and I was gay. My mother blamed my friends, blamed the media, and blamed me for being a lesbian. For five months we had kicked and screamed at each other; our fights were heard throughout the neighborhood. That night was not a spectacular night, and it was not a spectacular fight. My mother blamed me for "lying" to her about my sexuality. *Yes, mom, it is my fault that between the ages of eight and fourteen I was unsure about my sexual identity. How dare I not tell you about my interest in women, both intellectually and physically? Especially after the time when a friend was sitting in our kitchen asking me why I did not have a boyfriend, and you asked me if I was gay. Yes, yes, I should have told you right then and there that I was a bull dagger, and that I dreamt about Xena and Gabrielle instead of Hercules and the other macho men of television.* My mother hated my girlfriend, and she told me that she could not stand the thought of another woman touching me. It did not matter to me that I thought it was natural for me to be with a woman. I lied to her and that was unacceptable. That night I gave up.

After she left our house, I grabbed a bottle of vodka from our kitchen cabinet, and the giant bottle of Tylenol, and brought them into my room. My brother was asleep in his room, or so I thought, and I went back into the kitchen. It was the act of walking back into the kitchen that troubles me, because I did not need anything. I thought it was just saying one last goodbye, but as I turned around, my brother was standing in the hallway. I had asked him what he wanted, but instead of answering, he grabbed me tightly around my neck and told me he loved me. I told him I loved him too, and he went back into his room. I walked back into my room, and my cat was on my bed. The bottle of vodka and pills were on my nightstand, and my knife was next to my pillow. I sat down next to these items and I started to cry. Serena lay across my lap as I sobbed, and in anger, I threw my knife across the room. After I calmed down, I put the vodka and pills away, checked on my brother, and went into my room. I wish I could say that some miraculous epiphany struck my mind about life; instead, I sank into my bed and went to sleep.

That was the farthest I have ever gone in attempting suicide. It does not mean I have not thought about it after that moment, nor can I say I have not reached a point in my life where I did not desire death. There have been many more times where it seemed as if death was my only solution. That is what happens to those with chronic depression. They die many emotional deaths in order to live. I hated my brother for hugging me that night for a long time. I blamed him for being selfish, and I blamed him for loving me when I could not love myself. I have come a long way from those moments. I still get depressed, but I have not harmed myself. I still think about death, but I no longer want to die. It has taken me a week to write this essay. I have been told, during this whole process, that I am a strong person to be writing about this experience. However, I do not feel it is how strong I am that defines me, but how weak I have been. Sometimes, it is those who are the strongest who do not survive.

I know I am not the only one in the world who has thought what I have thought, and done worse than I have done. There is a whole generation of ghosts that masquerade as people we see everyday. Their masks are planted tightly on their faces, with smiles and laughs constantly on their lips. We have grown up in a society where suicide is looked down upon. You are weak if you commit suicide; this is the message we are told when we are young. I do not condone suicide, but I cannot blame someone for committing suicide. For every action there is a reaction, a consequence of choices, which a person must accept. I don't dwell on what might have been, if my brother did not hug me, because that is a moot point. I'm alive, and aside from constant illness and physical injury, I am kicking. One day, I will die. I do not know how, or why, just a simple fact that I will eventually cease to be in existence with those around me. My scars remind me of the days where I thought I was going to die, and they remind me of the days I knew I was going to live. Jeff asked us to write as if we were going to die. However, if I had the chance to go back and talk to myself, I would say,

It gets worse before it gets better, and although you may not understand why, things happen for a reason. You grow up to love people and life with such

ferocity; you become willing to die, so others can live. You will lose those you love, and those who love you will eventually lose you. You are imperfect in every way, and that makes you beautiful. And please remember this, you apologize to no one. You are who you are meant to be, and don't let anyone ever take that away from you, my heartbroken, beautiful 15-year-old me. Oh, and don't bother looking for the knife. I emptied the entire room and, after four years, I have yet to find it.

One of the constants in Faith's essays and diaries, from the first to the last, is the importance of writing. We can see how writing offers her the unconditional understanding and support that she cannot receive elsewhere. She knows that her written words will never disappoint, deceive, or betray her. She knows that she can confide anything to the page without fearing its judgment or disapproval. "Writing has always been my greatest confidante." To be sure, there is the risk that others may read one's secret writings, but she does not worry about this possibility. Nor does she worry that she may be retraumatized by writing about or reading a traumatic experience. Nothing about writing scares her. Writing shores up her identity not only by reminding her of the dark past but also by pointing the way to a brighter present and future.

Faith never worries about the darker implications of writing, but I would be remiss if I did not point out potential dangers. Sometimes a writer's self-disclosure may lead to betrayal—readers taking advantage of the writer, whose dark secrets are now on paper, for everyone to read and exploit. Sometimes writers cannot find the right words to describe their thoughts or feelings: language is an imperfect tool, and there are many experiences that language cannot convey, such as mood disorders. As William Styron (1990) admits in *Darkness Visible*, "Depression is a disorder of mood, so mysteriously painful and elusive in the way it becomes known to the self—to the mediating intellect—as to verge close to being beyond description. It thus remains nearly incomprehensible to those who have not experienced it in its extreme mode" (p. 7). Writers may find themselves dissatisfied or even horrified by the words on the page, words that may appear years later as inadequate, clumsy, or misleading. "Words strain," T. S. Eliot (1952) writes in *Four Quartets*, "Crack and sometimes break, under the burden,/ Under the tension, slip, slide, perish,/ Decay with imprecision, will not stay in place,/ Will not stay still" (p. 121). Writing about one's demons may not lead to exorcism: sometimes words may unleash our demons, leading to deeper despair rather than catharsis or relief. Sometimes writing leads to self-wounding, as Paul Auster (1982) confides in his memoir *The Invention of Solitude*: "Instead of healing me as I thought it would, the act of writing has kept this wound open" (p. 32). Kathlyn Conway (2007) would agree, claiming that "for those who are ill or disabled, writing frustrates as much as it heals" (p. 3). Words may sometimes remind us of what we wish to forget—we may live to rue our words. Words may provoke criticism, envy, or hostility, and they may be misinterpreted, ridiculed, or ignored. Writers may believe that words are their own, but they cannot control how their words are used when others read and appropriate them. Negative reviews may not kill authors, but they sometimes undercut authors' self-confidence and willingness to continue writing. Sometimes the written page may appear judgmental and hypercritical. And sometimes writers may find themselves blocked: the inability to write about dark subjects may make the darkness unbearable. Faith was fortunate that she never worried about these possibilities.

It's ironic that Faith read aloud her essay on cutting during the one class I missed. "I'm certain that if Jeff had been there that day, I would not have made it through the letter. It is something about his eyes that would have made me start to cry." If Faith is right about this, my emotionality would have prevented her from completing her reading—an example of pedagogical contagion. Recall Kamilluh's statement that she almost "cringes" when I read aloud sad essays. Whether they react to my eyes or my voice, both Faith and Kamilluh call attention to the complex relationship between writer and reader, which in this case also involves the relationship between student and teacher. The relationship between writer and reader, student and teacher, is bidirectional, meaning that each has the ability to affect the other both positively and negatively. I suspect that many teachers remain unaware of how they influence their students' work.

To understand these relationships, we may turn briefly to the patient-analyst relationship. Freud coined the term *transference* to describe patients' projections onto the analyst of the feelings they have toward the significant people in their lives, including their parents. He used the term *countertransference* to describe analysts' similar projections onto their patients. One of the reasons analysts must first undertake a long training psychoanalysis is to understand and control their own projective tendencies, lest they burden patients with their own conflicts. Transference-countertransference dynamics appear in the classroom as well as in the analyst's office, albeit in less intense form. Faith's sensitivity to my anticipated tearful response suggests our transference-countertransference relationship. If my tears, a reflection of empathic unsettlement, had the effect of preventing Faith from reading her essay aloud, how would she have reacted if I had scowled in disapproval during her reading? How would she feel if a teacher made a "cutting" remark about her essay on self-injury? A teacher's conscious or unconscious expression of anxiety, fear, or condemnation, a symptom of negative countertransference, might have prevented her or her classmates from writing other self-disclosing essays filled with painful or shameful emotions.

Not all teachers or readers will be able or willing to follow writers such as Faith into such forbidding places, for there are risks. Even psychoanalysts experience these risks, as Judy Leopold Kantrowitz (1996) concedes in *The Patient's Impact on the Analyst*. "Although the asymmetry of the relationship means that the analyst by definition is in a 'safer' position than the patient, once the analyst permits this emotional openness, the analyst is engaging in an emotional risk. Without this emotional risk, no psychological change can take place. To be truly engaged is to allow oneself to be vulnerable to another person. Once engaged, the interaction that occurs between the patient and analyst provides an opportunity for the analyst, as well as the patient, to change" (p. 199).

Transference-countertransference dynamics are especially intense with suicidal patients. In a classic article called "Countertransference Hate in the Treatment of Suicidal Patients," psychoanalysts John Maltsberger and Dan Buie (1996) acknowledge that suicidal patients evoke feelings of malice and aversion in the analyst which, if not analyzed, may become a major obstacle in treatment. Similar feelings of malice and aversion may be awakened in readers and teachers who find suicide morally repugnant or who are threatened or infected by a personal essay about suicide. The same unruly countertransference dynamics may occur when one reads an essay about cutting. Few literature teachers are aware of the transference-countertransference dynamics that may arise from reading disturbing essays like Faith's, but they must know how to control these dynamics if they are to encourage students to write safely and openly about dark topics.

After Faith read her essay aloud, I asked each of her classmates to choose a favorite sentence. We went around the room, and by the time we finished, there were still many excellent sentences on which no one had commented. During our discussion someone suggested that Faith write an entire memoir about her experiences, a recommendation I hope she will take seriously. After class I told her that I would be happy to serve as her Honor's Thesis Director if she decided to write a memoir.

Faith's classmates felt strong sympathy for her and admiration for her writings, and they also demonstrated what the feminist philosopher Nel Noddings (1994) calls an "ethics of caring" in which the teacher embodies "pedagogical caring" (p. 70). So, too, does Carol Gilligan (1982) focus on an ethics of caring in her influential book *In a Different Voice*, in which she contends that education should focus not on abstract principles or ideals, as advocated by Lawrence Kohlberg, but on human relationships. We have seen an ethics of caring throughout Love and Loss. We don't often hear students claim that they learned to "care" from a particular teacher—this is not a question that appears on teaching evaluation forms—but learning to care for the other strikes me as one of education's most important goals. Although Noddings and Gilligan distinguish between male and female conceptions of ethics and morality, women being, in Noddings's view, more sensitive to "receptivity, relatedness, and responsiveness" (p. 2), Faith's male classmates and male teacher were also moved by her writings. Our responses to Faith's writings were not based simply on emotional contagion but on what Solomon (2007) calls the "'higher cognitive' sharing of emotion through imaginatively and quite self-consciously 'putting oneself in the other's place'" (p. 69). It is "in the presence of other people's suffering that we learn the appropriateness of compassion and the expectations surrounding it" (p. 71).

The praise that Faith's readers bestowed upon her writings became the verbal equivalent of a hug, one that she appreciated as a writer. It may be an exaggeration to compare the pedagogical hug with her brother's literal hug that saved her life;

nevertheless, writers need validation to keep on writing. We praised not only her ability to survive a bleak adolescence but also her courage and strength to write about her experience. Most of all, we praised the power of her writing. Her essays help us see both the darkness of her past and her increasingly hopeful present and future. Far from being exhibitionistic or self-flagellating, her writings are heartfelt, insightful, and memorable.

Faith's writings also demonstrate her ability to reflect upon an earlier period of life when she was explosively angry at the world. In her memoir *In Her Wake: A Child Psychiatrist Explores the Mystery of Her Mother's Suicide*, Nancy Rappaport (2009) makes the following observation: "As numerous studies show, impulsiveness and its cousins, aggression and explosiveness, are more closely linked to suicide than is the severity of the depression or psychosis. In other words, it is not the hopelessness that gets you—what suicide needs, ironically, is an adrenaline rush, a reckless abandonment of the survival instinct" (p. 253). "Conversations with My 13-Year-Old Self" reveals the toxic mixture of impulsiveness, aggression, and explosiveness that are linked to suicide. Serendipity, in the form of a brother's hug, proves to be life-saving for Faith, and writing about her experiences is also life-saving. Faith's writings allow her to construct a coherent narrative of her dark years, a narrative that reveals her capacity for reflection and posttraumatic growth.

The fear that Faith expressed during the first class of the semester—"I am scared about how deep this course might take me into my emotions"—never came true. She never lost emotional control, and she not only improved her writing but also fulfilled her desire "finally to be heard without being told that I am wrong for speaking and writing about love and loss." Her writings were darker than her classmates', filled with the many challenges she has encountered in her life. Some teachers might have deemed her writings too dangerous to read aloud. Significantly, the word *danger* in Chinese also means *opportunity*. Faith writes about dangerous, stigmatized subjects, including depression, cutting, and suicide, which all involve disenfranchised grief, but writing gives her the opportunity to understand her fears and master them. Her essays and diaries demonstrate that writing can be a counter-shame strategy, calling attention to shame and, in the process, overcoming it. Few of us will forget the story about how her brother's hug saved her life. Love cannot always keep a person alive, but it has the power to make a difference in a person's life, and when a person such as Faith writes about the meaning of a hug, love becomes even more powerful.

Nearly a year after the course ended, Faith remarked that she felt it was a "rare treat" to have her writings appear in the present book. She appreciated her classmates' supportive comments. "This is the first time I've really had a chance to see the responses my peers had, and their support meant a lot to me. Especially Cath's, who said that I had so much talent that I kept hidden. It meant a lot that they weren't just being nice, but truly honest and receptive to my work." Faith admitted that her struggle with depression and cutting is ongoing: "it is a process, just like writing, and it takes years to work through and overcome." The ability to share her writing with classmates was the "greatest opportunity" in her life:

> I thank the University at Albany for allowing Jeff to teach this course, for accepting the students that were in the class into the university, and for allowing me to pursue my writing in the way that I have always dreamed. This class was one of a kind and will stay with me forever. Not because of the contents we discussed, but because for the first time I felt free to express myself with just the pure intent of making my writing better. Who can say no to that?

CHAPTER 20—ANONYMOUS

"I Will Always Remember My Unborn Baby"

I didn't anticipate when I decided to teach a course on death education that three students would write essays or diaries about abortion. In making the difficult decision to end pregnancy, they rejected the right-to-life argument. Nevertheless, they found their experiences harrowing, not only because of the attendant guilt, anguish, anger, and loneliness they suffered but also because they could not stop thinking about their "unborn children"—the term they used despite their pro-choice views. The three students were still mourning their losses when they enrolled in Love and Loss. They also wrote follow-up essays and diaries in which they expressed their feelings toward their imagined offspring. The three students, Anonymous, Anonymous2, and Anonymous3, allowed me to read their writings aloud, but they did not want their identities disclosed to their classmates. We did not discuss the abortion essays in class, but many students offered comments in their diaries that I also read aloud anonymously.

The three abortion essays had a profound impact on everyone in the classroom. All three students reached important conclusions as a result of writing about their experiences and hearing their classmates' responses. Regardless of whether they identified themselves as pro-life or pro-choice, the other students learned a great deal about the reality and, in many cases, the trauma of abortion. The students increased their understanding of what is surely the country's most explosive social issue.

Curiously, most books on death education do not mention abortion as a topic for discussion—perhaps because death education is controversial enough without discussing this polarizing issue. Many commentators refer, without hyperbole, to the "abortion wars" raging in the United States. Needle and Walker (2008) point out in *Abortion Counseling* that "despite the development of modern methods of contraception in the United States, 1 in every 10 women of reproductive age in the United States each year become pregnant; about half of these pregnancies are unintentional. This means that approximately 3 million U.S. women a year are confronted with an unplanned pregnancy, with all the stress such a situation entails. Approximately half of these pregnancies are terminated by abortion" (pp. xiv–xv). The authors cite a researcher who estimates that 20% of American women have already had an abortion and that one out of three American women will have an abortion by age 45. Women who have abortions generally experience disenfranchised grief; they may grieve for years, particularly if they fantasize how their lives might have been different had they allowed the fetuses to develop.

Anonymous was the first of the three students. She noted in Assignment 1 that her first love was a "tie" between her parents and God. "God has held an important part in my life within the past four years. I restored faith in Him as a way to help me get through the difficult times I had in college with my family and to help me get through school. God has helped me become a better person and to accept the faults in my personality. Most importantly, God has allowed me to believe in a higher power that has made my relationships stronger." There was no indication in her early writings that she would write about having an abortion. She didn't list the event as one of her losses, nor did she imply that she was struggling to decide whether to disclose a secret to the class.

Anonymous stated on the first day of the semester that she wanted to learn more about death, but she didn't explain why. "I don't have any concerns about the course, although I am extremely emotional. However, I know that it will be difficult to read my work aloud because I have written a journal since I was nine years old, and I have never shared their contents with anyone." In her first diary entry she observed that she couldn't relate to death education because no one close to her had died—she hadn't even attended a funeral. In her second diary entry she returned to her fear of reading her essays aloud. "I don't know how I will get over reading my work out loud because it is something I have always struggled with. Writing has been a safe haven in my life since I was 10 years old, and I have never shared my deepest thoughts with anyone." She noted that even though she is an English major, she never lets her friends read her papers. "In a strange way, writing is my secret that I usually share with my teachers and no one else. It'll be interesting to see my progression as the semester continues because I hope that I can open up and feel comfortable sharing my work." The fear of public self-disclosure makes her later class revelations more remarkable. Anonymous wrote about her abortion for Assignment 8, on posttraumatic growth:

> In high school, most people would tell you that I was a lesbian. I had two serious girlfriends while I was in school, and I was not ashamed of it. I'm not ashamed now either. The reason why this is significant is because I never thought I would have a boyfriend. Of course I had boyfriends in elementary school and junior high school, but it was nothing serious. I never wanted to have sex with anyone of them. I went out with them because they were cute.
>
> When I came to college, my outlook on men changed. I was never a man hater or anything like that. But guys did disgust me because they were so much more aggressive than females. I still feel the same way now about some men. I always considered myself to be bisexual, even though I never had

any intention of having sex with a man. The attraction to males was always there, but sexual intimacy was never an option. These thoughts and feelings seem so ironic now because a lot has changed. I currently have a boyfriend, with whom I am intimate, and women are no longer an avid part of my life. However, the complications of having sex with a man have created severe repercussions for me.

I will not describe my first encounter with a man, but I will say that I did enjoy it. I didn't care that he didn't have breasts or that his touch was not as soft. What did concern me was the love that existed between us. We used condoms at first, but we eventually stopped. I was never worried about any of the consequences because I started to take birth control pills soon after our sexual relationship started. However, having unprotected sex is dangerous for many reasons. The most important reason to me was getting pregnant. I was never concerned with a sexually transmitted disease because I always trusted my boyfriend. Plus, I always told him that if he ever gave me anything, I would kill him. This is a threat that I will always stand true to.

During January of 2007, my worst nightmare came true. I was pregnant. The process by which I discovered this horrible news was surreal. I noticed that my period was a week late, and I was immediately panicking. I told my boyfriend, and he reassured me that I would eventually get it. I was terrified, but I trusted his comforting words. We were staying at my best friend's apartment in Albany at the time, and it was during the winter break. While there, I was extremely paranoid so I convinced him to drive me to CVS so I could buy a pregnancy test. He kept telling me that I wasn't pregnant because if I was, he would feel it. I thought it was ridiculous, although I know that some men experience sickness when their wives or girlfriends are pregnant.

We came back from CVS, and I quickly rushed to the bathroom so I could pee on this white stick. My boyfriend suggested that I pee in a cup and then place the test inside the cup to soak. I followed his advice. After waiting for five minutes, we looked at the test to see if there were two pink lines that would confirm my fear. There were two pink lines. However, one was more distinct than the other. My boyfriend interpreted the faded pink line as a malfunction with the test and then concluded that I wasn't pregnant. I disagreed. But it was better to psych myself out by assuming he was right.

When classes started, I went to work every day and I noticed that I was feeling sick. I would run to the bathroom every morning to throw up. I kept telling my boyfriend that I was pregnant, but he was in denial. I decided to take it upon myself and go to the health center. As I walked into the health center, I was a nervous wreck, but I was optimistic. I told the nurse that I wanted a pregnancy test because I missed my period. She administered the test and told me it would take a few minutes. As I waited for her to return with the results, my stomach was in knots. I knew in my heart that I was pregnant. When she came back, she told me to come with her. I followed her into the doctor's office. As I looked at this man sitting across from me, I already knew what he was going to say. "Ms. Blank, I'm sorry to say this, but your test results are positive and you're pregnant." I wanted to disappear. I vaguely remember anything he said to me after that. My eyes started to well up, and I wanted to leave. He told me that I should see the therapist in the health center to discuss my options. I immediately told him that wasn't necessary because I knew what I was going to do.

Unbeknownst to my boyfriend, when I was paranoid, I researched and found a Planned Parenthood here in Albany that I would go to in case I was pregnant. So when the doctor was talking to me, I tuned him out because I couldn't believe I was going to have an abortion. There was never a doubt in my mind that I was going to get rid of this unwanted child. As bad as it sounds, the child was truly unwanted, by me and my boyfriend. Our education and future careers were more important than having a child at 20 years old. When I left the doctor's office, I called my boyfriend hysterically crying to tell him the horrifying news. He took it very calmly and said, "Well, you know what *we* have to do, so let's do it." Who the fuck is *we*? *We* don't have to do anything. I'm the one who has this human being growing inside of me. Not you! Those were evil thoughts, but they were the truth. That's how I felt. From that moment onward, I was alone.

I made my first appointment at Planned Parenthood immediately. I thought this abortion process would be easy and I could forget about it as soon as possible. I was sadly mistaken. It took at least five appointments before I was scheduled for the procedure, a procedure that almost didn't take place. Let me start by saying that every appointment I went to, I was alone. When they took my blood, I was alone. When they tested me again to make sure I was pregnant, I was alone. When the nurse explained to me my abortion options, I was alone. When I opened my legs for a complete stranger as she placed a long penis-like structure inside of me to determine how far along I was, I was alone. My boyfriend never came with me on *any* of these visits.

Every morning, afternoon and night, I vomited. When I took showers I could see my stomach growing. I cried every single time I took a shower. I cried every day for months. I was crying because I was pregnant. I was crying because my boyfriend was not supporting me the way I thought he should. I was crying because I was going to have an abortion. As the appointments became more frequent, I grew attached to this creature inside of me. I loved him or her because they were a part of me. I wanted to see what he or she looked like. I wanted to play with them and tell them what I was feeling. Sometimes I would find myself talking to my stomach because only my baby knew how I was feeling and all the pain I was enduring.

The only people who knew about my pregnancy were my sister, my boyfriend, and my parents. Yes, I told my parents. I have an open relationship with them, and I didn't want to keep this depressing part of my life away from them. Subsequently, I was scared to tell my father because he doesn't believe in abortions. But my mother convinced me that telling him was the right thing to do. Surprisingly, he wasn't mad. He supported my decision and I love him for that. My mother wasn't happy about the pregnancy either, but she's more liberal than my father. She even told me that she would raise the baby for me if I decided to have it. But I would never want to burden my parents with my responsibility.

The day came for me to schedule the procedure, and I was both nervous and relieved. This had been a long dehumanizing process, and I was anticipating its end. To my surprise, the nurse scheduled my procedure to take place a month later. I started to cry hysterically and begged her to change the date to an earlier time. She insisted that there was no way I could have it done earlier. This was devastating to me because I was already a month and a half pregnant, which meant that if I didn't receive the procedure soon, I would be unable to have it at all. I didn't know what to do so I left and called my mother. When I told her the bad news she was furious. She told me I needed to speak up for myself and demand that I have the appointment sooner. At that point I was so weak and fragile that all I could do was cry. The idea of giving birth to a child was becoming a reality. I walked back to Planned Parenthood as my mother suggested, and she spoke to the manager in charge. My mother screamed at this woman continuously for not allowing me to have the procedure sooner. I was embarrassed for the woman but could care less about what she thought of the situation. After the woman got off the phone with my mother, she told me that I would be scheduled for the procedure next morning. Thank God I have a pushy mother.

I had my abortion at the end of January. Surprisingly, my boyfriend went with me. The nurses told me that I would need assistance getting home after the procedure took place, but I didn't think he would want to go. I was the first patient called into the office that morning. My boyfriend went into the examination room with me, and I took off all my clothes. My boyfriend stayed by my side. As I lay on the hard, cold medical bed, I was nervous and scared. I didn't want this procedure to prevent me from having children in the future. When the doctor came in, I was glad to know that he had performed hundreds of these procedures and he was well qualified. My boyfriend stood next to me and held my hand as the abortion took place. They numbed my lower body so I could not feel any pain, but I was awake throughout the whole procedure. I did feel lots of pressure, but I didn't see anything that was taking place. My boyfriend, however, watched the entire process.

After the abortion was over, I was traumatized. It was indeed the worst experience of my life. I will never forget about the baby I chose to abort, and I hope that God will forgive me for the choice I made. I was not equipped or ready to raise a child, and I don't regret my decision. This experience has made me look at my boyfriend in a different light; although we're still together, I'll always resent him for not being there for me as much as he should have. I understand that he was dealing with the pains of killing his child as well, but it was my body that was suffering. What hurts me the most about this situation is that I want to have children with my boyfriend, and I know that if I was to get pregnant by him in the future, I would have the child.

I have grown a lot as a person since this incident because it has taught me that I need to be more responsible. I will always remember my unborn baby and I mourn my child's death every couple of months. Throughout my pregnancy I wrote letters and poems to the baby which I destroyed because it hurt so badly. Now, I wish I had kept those letters and poems so I would have something to look back on. My boyfriend and I are still healing from what happened to us a year ago, and I don't think he'll ever understand how I truly feel about having an abortion.

Why does Anonymous write about her abortion? How does she want me, presumably her only reader, to respond? In narrating her experiences, she does not explore the complex legal, historical, religious, or philosophical implications of abortion. She is not writing a research paper, nor does she seek to persuade her reader that she was justified in having an abortion. She knows that she alone made the decision to end the pregnancy—and that she alone must live with the consequences. Why, then, does she write about this dark event? The answer, I believe, is that she wants to convey how she felt before, during, and after this experience. She attempts to describe the reality of the experience, especially the *emotional* reality of abortion. She takes an experiential approach to death education, focusing on cognitive and affective dynamics. Anonymous also seeks greater understanding—and self-understanding—of what has been the most traumatic event of her life. She doesn't invoke Nietzsche, but she would agree with his statement that whatever doesn't kill you, makes you stronger.

Anonymous's desire to "disappear" upon learning she is pregnant dramatizes the depth of her shame. As Leon Wurmser (1987) contends, shame, which derives from the Indo-European word meaning *hide*, is the most virulent emotion. Shame can be so intense that one wishes to hide or disappear. Anonymous's shame reveals the three meanings implicit in this emotion: "the *fear* of disgrace," the "*affect of contempt* directed against the self," and the "overall character trait preventing any such disgraceful exposure" [italics in original] (Wurmser, pp. 67–68).

The most powerful paragraphs for me are the eighth, when Anonymous repeats the sentence "I was alone" five times, and the ninth, when she repeats the words "I cried" or "I was crying" in five consecutive sentences. She shows rather than merely tells us the details of the procedure, and she makes no effort to spare us her pain and shame. Thus we learn about her horror over the news of her pregnancy, her shame in the presence of the physician, her anger toward her boyfriend, and her growing attachment to the new life inside her. She makes the reader suffer, as she herself suffered. She is harder on herself than most of her readers will be. A moral and responsible young woman, she finds herself doing something she feared was immoral and irresponsible. She doesn't regret her decision to end—she never uses the euphemism *terminate*—the fetus's life, but she makes no attempt to regard her unborn child as only a fetus. She concludes the essay on a hopeful note. She and her boyfriend are "still healing," but she remains convinced that he cannot understand how she feels about the experience.

I had not read Needle and Walker's (2008) *Abortion Counseling* when Anonymous turned in her essay, but I'm struck by the extent to which her essay supports their statement that women who have abortions go through the five stages of grief experienced by the terminally ill. "Initially the woman doesn't believe she is pregnant, nor can she think clearly about what to do about it. She then goes into the yearning period where she is willing to make bargains to try to make it all go away. The third stage is anger, and a woman who does not permit herself to grieve may get stuck there. A fourth stage, depression, may exacerbate an already existing condition of depression. The fifth and final stage is acceptance and doing whatever has to be done to meet her goals" (p. 113). Anonymous experiences denial at first, followed by yearning to make the problem disappear, then anger, depression, and finally acceptance. Significantly, she doesn't dwell on self-blame, which, according to Needle and Walker, occurs in women who tend to cope poorly with their abortions.

A few days before the assignment was due, Anonymous sent me an email. "Hi Jeff, I have a small request. I want to share Assignment 8 with the class. However, I would like to do it anonymously because the subject is too sensitive for me. I will be writing about how having an abortion has affected me. This will be the first time that I will be sharing this, much less writing about it. I want to know how I should go about it. Should I write the essay anonymously, make copies and give them to you? Or just give you a copy and have you read it out loud." Anonymous then thanked me for teaching Love and Loss. "You have touched my life more than you could ever know. See you tomorrow." I emailed her back immediately. "Thanks for the kind words about the course—I feel the same way! Why don't you write the essay—which you can give me tomorrow—and then I will read it aloud anonymously. I certainly see the connection between writing about one's abortion and death education. Will you be OK when you hear me read it aloud anonymously?" She assured me in the next email that she wanted me to read the essay aloud. "I already wrote the essay, and I've reread it a million times. I'll definitely be OK if you read it anonymously. I would like to give you a copy of it tomorrow if that's OK and you can give me your feedback. I don't know if I gave enough detail, and that's my biggest concern. I want the class to feel and understand how I felt—even though it will be anonymous. Thanks."

I quote our email correspondence for three reasons. First and most important, I wanted to make sure that Anonymous was psychologically ready for me to read the essay aloud. Neither she nor I could predict with certainty that she would not become unduly upset hearing me read it—there was the risk of retrauma. I was prepared to accept this risk if she was, but I wanted to be sure that this was something she wanted to do. Second, when she states that she has reread the essay a "million times," she reveals how crucial it is for her to express herself as clearly and specifically as possible. This is true of nearly all the students in my Expository Writing and Love and Loss courses. The more self-disclosing an essay is, the more a student wants it to be free of grammatical and stylistic errors. Finally, Anonymous's trust in her classmates and teacher was now strong enough for her to reveal the darkest secret in her life, one she never would have considered disclosing if she felt we would not value and protect her self-disclosure.

How did Anonymous's classmates feel about her essay? This is an important question, for I wanted to know whether abortion is an appropriate issue for students to write about in a course on love and loss. And so before I read aloud her essay, I gave out copies of the following in-class assignment:

Responses to Today's Anonymous Essay

I would like your responses to the anonymous essay that you are about to hear. This was a painful essay to write, and it may be painful to hear. Please write brief responses to the following questions. Don't sign your name. If you need more time, you may complete your responses at home and give them to me on Wednesday. I'll summarize your responses next week. Feel free to write your own essay or diary on this topic.

1. Was this an appropriate essay for me to read aloud? Please explain.
2. How is this essay related to love and loss?
3. What did you learn from the essay about the subject of abortion?
4. Would you define yourself as pro-choice or pro-life, and did your social and political attitude influence your feelings about the essay?
5. Did the essay change your pro-choice or pro-life views of abortion?
6. What would you like to tell your classmate who wrote this essay?

The anonymous in-class responses to the abortion essay confirmed the significance of the topic. Everyone felt it was appropriate for me to read the essay aloud, and the relevance of the essay to our course was easy to see. "Abortion is a topic that covers both love and loss," one person wrote. "Until you have an unwanted pregnancy, it is hard to explain your feelings about abortion." Another person wrote: "When a woman knows she is going to be a mother, maternal instinct is to automatically love the child. To choose to lose a child is devastating and can be traumatic." The students learned about the psychological pain of ending an unwanted pregnancy, including feelings of guilt, anger, loneliness, and depression. The essay affected everyone in the classroom, the four people who defined themselves as pro-life and the others who were either pro-choice (the overwhelming majority) or still undecided. Hearing the essay did not change anyone's attitude toward abortion, but the essay heightened everyone's understanding of the reality of abortion. Nearly everyone expressed empathy for the anonymous author, admiring her courage for writing about the experience and allowing me to read it aloud. Many said they were proud of her for writing about this ordeal:

I wish I could have been there for you. It could have happened to any of us—I'm just glad you're strong enough to overcome this event. I wish I could give you a hug and tell you how proud I am of you.

You are very brave and strong both in writing this and going through it. I'm glad you have such a loving and understanding family who was there for you when your boyfriend was not.

I cannot imagine what you went through before, during, and after your abortion. I often think about what would happen if I got pregnant at this age. What frightens me is that if I got pregnant, I would not have an abortion, even though it would probably be the best choice. I want to be a mother more than anything, and I think becoming pregnant would instill a feeling of motherhood in me that I could not push away. Even though I feel this way, I understand that this might not be the case with everyone. I am proud that you chose to share this experience with us.

Only one comment was negative. To the question whether the essay changed his or her pro-choice or pro-life views on abortion, one person responded, "Yes. I feel that this student was selfish and put herself first before her child. Because of her irresponsible actions, her child was destroyed." And yet the same person wanted to tell the author "that she is strong for doing what she did, and being able to write about her experience."

The anonymous essay affected many members of the class. Nowhere is education more intersubjective than in the empathic classroom, where everyone teaches and learns from the other. Hearing the essay reminded Cecilia of a friend's abortion not long ago. "After I heard the essay I called my best friend and apologized to her for not being there to hold her hand when she found out she was pregnant or to drive her to Planned Parenthood or to hold her as she sobbed about what she had done. To the anonymous writer of that heart wrenching and powerful essay: Your words struck a chord in all of us. We all left class on Monday night with a piece of your soul in all of us." Another classmate wrote about three friends who have had abortions. "All three of these people experienced a great deal of pain. I know my one friend who recently had an abortion can barely talk about it without crying." Lia experienced pain simply from hearing the abortion essay. "When she illustrated the actual abortion in graphic detail, my cheeks reddened with sadness and horror. The essay impacted me to the degree where I could not physically write down my comments in the handout until a day later. I commend the writer for her bravery and strength."

Several women wondered what they would do if they found themselves in the anonymous writer's situation. One woman did not need to wonder, however, because she had been in a similar situation a few years earlier, and her classmate's essay reawakened many turbulent emotions surrounding her own experience. Anonymous2 was the second woman to write about abortion, and she allowed me to read aloud her diary:

> Monday night's anonymous essay on abortion is a paper topic I have been expecting to come up in class. As you passed out the worksheet, I quickly skimmed over your questions and said to a classmate sitting next to me, "I knew this topic was going to come up eventually." She, however, seemed surprised.
>
> I think that the reason I expected it so much was because I too had debated whether I wanted to share my own situation with an abortion. On more than one occasion, I jotted down a thing or two but I was too ashamed to disclose it to the class. Having an abortion is a very private issue, and I did

not know if the class could handle it, and I certainly did not want to make them feel uncomfortable. I should have known better than to have underestimated my classmates. As you read along from the paper, I sat in my seat fidgeting like a child. Except for the beginning of the essay, about having lesbian experiences, I felt like I was reliving a part of my own life. It was a part of my life for which I have regretted and resented myself.

I was in a terrible relationship with a man I will call Fred. I had been trying to end the relationship for months because I could no longer take the physical abuse, and when I thought things could not get any worse, they did; I was pregnant. My body instantly felt different and I was scared to death. I did not know what to do or whom to turn to. I went straight to my mom. I know I probably should have told Fred first, but actually, I did not want to tell him at all. I knew he would want to keep the baby and he would make it much harder on me. There was no way I could keep this baby. If I did, Fred would have to be a part of my life forever, and I could not have that. Strangers who do not know my history with him would definitely read this diary entry and think I was being selfish for feeling this way, but the truth is, he was an asshole. My family disliked him, my friends disliked him, and even I did not like him. Don't get me wrong, at one time, I did love him, and I loved him a lot, but a person can take just so much of being bitten, kicked, and slapped around before they start to resent the person who is doing it to them. I knew right away I was going to have an abortion, and it broke my heart.

It was not the baby's fault that he/she was conceived; it was my fault. I should have been more careful. I thought about the future for the unborn baby, and [my] heart told me I needed to terminate; I always hated that word. The day before I had the appointment to have the procedure, I did what was right; I called Fred. We had been separated for almost three weeks, but I asked him to meet me. We met at the park and I told him. Just as I expected would happen, he cried and begged me to keep it. I was an emotional wreck. I only had my mom to support me. I did not dare tell anyone else what was going on; I was embarrassed. What would they think? Would they think I was a terrible person? The next day, I went for my abortion. I will never forget the experience. I hated myself for having to do it, but I did what needed to be done. It was the right thing for everyone. I do not agree that abortion should be used as a type of birth control. However, sometimes accidents happen. It took years before I was really "O.K." with my decision to abort. For years, I wondered how my life might be different if I kept the baby. Eventually, I came to realize, just as Kamilluh stated in her last essay, "things happen for a reason." Sometimes, it is a hard concept to accept, but it is the truth. I can tell that this is still a fresh wound for the anonymous author, and I wish that I could just tell her to hang in there because in time, this wound will heal; I promise.

Many of the details of Anonymous2's experience differ from Anonymous's, yet she clearly identifies with her. Hearing the first abortion essay, Anonymous2 feels like she is "reliving a part of her own life," a part of her past which still fills her with shame, but she is willing to write about it to reassure her classmate that she, too, will survive. I read aloud Anonymous2's diary entry to demonstrate how moved she was by her classmate's story. I thought it would be helpful for Anonymous to hear about a classmate's similar experience. Anonymous2 was speaking from experience when she states that "time heals all wounds," and despite my distaste for the cliche, I thought that her classmate would welcome such a comment by a person who went through the same ordeal. The next week, Anonymous turned in a diary entry in which she commented on her own essay, recording how she felt when writing it and then hearing me read it aloud:

> As you read my anonymous essay I was as calm as I could be. I knew that you were going to read it, so I prepared myself for it mentally. I knew that I wouldn't have any reaction to the words I had written prior because I was ready to share this part of my life with the class. It may seem strange but I'm glad that the class was able to hear about my situation. I know that I am not the only person who has experienced this, and I hope that my words have helped someone. This was the most honest essay I have written all semester. No woman knows what it is like to have an abortion until they are faced with it. I have always been pro-choice, and I would never change this political view. If I didn't have the opportunity to choose whether or not I wanted to have this child, I would have been forced to bring a child into this world that I didn't have the financial means to support.
>
> I looked around the classroom as you read my heartfelt and honest testimony, and what I saw was shocking. Most people did not have a judgmental look on their faces. In fact, they seemed to be rather understanding. I was relaxed by the expressions on my classmates' faces because I felt reassured. I'm sure that there are people who disagree with my decision. However, at least they can sympathize with what I chose to do. I will have to live with the decision to abort my child for the rest of my life. No one knows how grueling and heart wrenching the process was—except me. Until you are faced with a life changing decision such as having an abortion, you never know what you will do. I hope that I have enlightened people by subjecting my experience for a critique. On the other hand, if I have not done so, I am still grateful for the opportunity to be at peace with killing my unborn child.

Contrary to Anonymous's assertion, no one "critiqued" her personal essay. That is, no one sought to critique the essay in the usual meaning of the term: to assess the literary value of the text or to expose or "unmask"—a favorite word among some critics—its cultural, political, or psychological ideology, including its hidden self-contradictions or counternarratives. Such critique is valuable in other literature courses, where fictional characters and their authors are routinely analyzed and often over-analyzed, but it is dangerous in a personal writing course. I believe that Anonymous would have cringed if we attempted to "deconstruct"— another favorite word— her essay. Such critique is common in what Deborah Tannen (1998) calls an "Argument Culture," but it would discourage Anonymous's classmates from empathic listening. Students are willing to open up and expose their vulnerability in a personal writing course only if they know their feelings will not be "interrogated." That's why I avoid critique in courses such as Love and Loss. Ironically, the less one's classmates and teachers critique an essay, the more the writer is willing to engage in self-critique.

Anonymous's essay had a powerful impact on another classmate, Anonymous3, who asked me to read aloud anonymously the following essay, entitled "Suicide":

> Before reading this essay, I would like my classmates to know that my boyfriend and I have written this essay together. The essay is more from his point of few than mine. My boyfriend felt as if this essay would be a good way for us to get some of the pain off our chest, so I asked Professor Berman, and he said it was an excellent idea. It's about a life changing experience which occurred a few months ago.
>
> When most people think of suicide, the first thought that comes to their mind is the act of one killing him or herself. I would never consider committing suicide because I know the effect that it would have on my family and friends. However, at the same time, I feel as if I have already done so with my life. It feels awkward when someone asks me whether I would ever commit suicide and I tell him or her that I already have, because the emotion that comes with that admission breaks my heart and affects me mentally.
>
> To my unborn child, I would like you to know that I have so many emotions built up about you. I swear to you when I first found out that I was going to be a father, I almost cried because I was so full of happiness and joy. Even though you were no more than six weeks old, I had already begun to see visions of us spending time together, watching you take your first steps, saying your first words, taking holiday pictures as a family and so much more. I also began to think about you every minute, wondering whether you were going to be a boy or girl, and also what your physical features were going to look like.
>
> But the one thing that I prayed for every night was taken away from me. I never knew that my heart could open up so much and that I could have so much love for someone who has never taken a breath here on earth. When your mother first found out that she was pregnant, she was afraid to tell me because she had no clue of how I would react to being a parent. But what she quickly found out was that I was ready to take on the responsibilities like a man. Even though I felt as if I was ready, your mother, on the other hand, was not prepared to make this same commitment.
>
> She had begun to go through depression because she did not know whether or not she would be a good parent. She felt as if she would not have been able to play a positive role in your life because she would have had to drop out of college due to financial reasons and also because her father would disown her. Within her family you have a choice either to go to school as a student or you work a full time job. Believe me, my child, I begged and pleaded with your mother to have you, and when she decided not to keep you, it made me feel as if a part of me was murdered and also as if I had committed suicide because a part of me was gone. Afterwards, I had begun to notice that I was not the same person anymore. I know it was not easy for either one of us because I had visions of showing the world how brilliant

you were. I would have never been a father to turn my back on you, but it seemed as if no matter what I said, I didn't have any say in the decision of whether or not you were going to be born."

Although we never had the privilege to meet one another in the real world, I want you to know that when the doctor killed you by sticking that tube in your mother, he also killed a part of me. I think about you everyday and wish that I could have turned back the hands of time and tried harder to convince your mother to see that having an abortion is not the right thing to do. I don't want to make this seem as if your mother was only thinking about herself when making her decision. I understand that she wanted to get an education so that she doesn't have to depend on a man in her life for anything, and I can respect her for wanting to be a strong, independent woman.

I hope you can forgive her for making that decision. I know it might be very difficult for you to forgive her because it was truly difficult for me to forgive her, but I must admit that I still love her, and I am willing to do anything to help make sure that she will never make another decision like this again in her life without consulting me. After speaking with your mother, she has made it known that she deeply regrets her decision to abort you. She has let it be known that since having the abortion, she has had dreams and visions of your face and nightmares of hearing you shake your baby rattle. She also feels that the decision was an impulse made solely by her because she knew she would probably have to leave school and get a full-time job. Struggling to raise a baby is not exactly what she wanted for herself, and at the time she could not bear the disappointment of having a baby out of wedlock and disownment from her parents. Your mother still loves you nonetheless and has gone to God numerous times within the last two weeks for forgiveness. She would have liked to keep you, and still wishes she had. It's difficult to encompass all the reasons she originally had to terminate you, for they have no existing meaning anymore. The next time we decide to have a baby, even though it is a mere chance, I hope that you can live and experience a full life with your mother's eyes, your grandparents' intelligence, and our family's love.

I was startled when Anonymous3 asked me to read this essay aloud, but I readily agreed. The result is a poignant account of the father's distress. I was also startled when the father described the event as a suicide, but I can now see the appropriateness of the word. The death of his unborn child must have felt like the deliberate death of a part of himself, along with the death of his dream of fatherhood. I believe in a woman's reproductive rights, which means that it is her decision, and her decision alone, to have an abortion, and yet I also believe that the father's point of view should be considered. Many women in my classes have written about having an abortion, but this was the first time a man has written about opposing such a decision. Before reading the essay, I never imagined a father's sorrow over abortion. Though he disagrees with the mother's decision, he also understands and acknowledges her pain: this is what impresses me most about the essay.

I read Anonymous3's essay at the end of class, and I received the following email from Anonymous as soon as I returned home.

> "Hey Jeff, I was extremely touched and affected by the anonymous essay that you read in class today, and I just wanted to let you read my [enclosed] diary for next Wednesday that I just finished writing. Also, I wanted to know if I could have a copy of [today's] anonymous essay. I would like to keep it not as a keepsake from this class but as a way to have closure on this topic. I want to thank you for being my professor and for teaching this class because you have made me a better person.

I immediately emailed Anonymous3, who gave permission to give Anonymous a hard copy of the essay. The following week I read aloud Anonymous's response to the essay:

> Hearing the anonymous essay was more difficult than hearing my own essay. I don't understand why I didn't want to listen to the harsh realities that the essay exposed. I wrote an essay about this same topic a month ago, but hearing someone else go through the same torture was heartbreaking. I had flashbacks from my abortion when Jeff read the anonymous essay. I didn't know what to do with myself as I sat down and listened to what seemed to be a resemblance of my own confession.
>
> One of the reasons why I was so struck by the words was because it showed me another side to the effects an abortion can have on an individual's psyche. Her boyfriend told the story from his perspective, and I admire that courage. It showed me that while an abortion is a procedure that women endure, men also feel the pain. I asked my boyfriend to write an essay about how he felt about my abortion, and he keeps putting it off. I think it's because he doesn't want to revisit those horrible feelings. The difference with my boyfriend is that I don't think he ever let himself get attached to our unborn child because he felt that having an abortion was the only solution. He did tell me a few times that if I wanted to have the baby we would figure the situation out; but I didn't want to be blamed for ruining someone's life.
>
> I don't think people realize how intense and depressing it is to have an abortion for both the man and the woman. I'm glad that the anonymous person decided to not only write this essay but to share it with the class as well. This made me feel like I wasn't alone. After class I told one of our classmates that I was the anonymous writer of the first abortion essay. I wanted her to know because it was important for me to share this secret with someone. In addition, I have so much respect and admiration for this person that I wanted to hear how she felt about it. I wanted to tell her for awhile now, but I didn't know how to. I'm so glad that I told her because she was supportive and nonjudgmental. We never know what is going to happen in life or how we're going to deal with a situation until it arises. I *never* thought I would have an abortion. I always said I would never be that girl. But, I was. And I am *that* girl. I can never change that.
>
> I want the anonymous writer and her boyfriend to know that I understand how she feels. And I'm so sorry that she had to have an abortion. I'm sorry that

you can't take back what you did. But, it will be OK. God has forgiven you for making this decision. He understands why you had to do it and He will always love you. Don't question why this has happened to you because you will never be able to find the answers. Take everything in stride and know that this will make you a stronger person. Don't ever forget your unborn child. But don't live in regret because it will tear you up inside. As time passes you will heal, and when you least expect it you will find closure. Although I am in tears as I write this diary, please know that you can get through this. My boyfriend and I did.

After receiving this diary, I emailed Anonymous3 and received permission to give a hard copy of the essay to Anonymous. The following week a person commented on Anonymous3's essay. "When you read the paper written by the anonymous student and her boyfriend, it really broke my heart. Hearing this plea for his child's life was difficult. I hope together they both find closure in their decision and maintain a love that, despite this obstacle, can continue to grow." The essay also moved Anonymous2, who realized that she had never imagined how her own abortion had affected her former boyfriend:

> The anonymous essay which was read at the end of Wednesday's class made me think of something I have neglected to do. While I have already commented on my own personal experience with abortion, I have failed to look at it from the father's side, as well as the impact it may have caused the father. When I chose to abort, I thought only about the long term effect for myself and the baby, and I totally ignored the father's feelings. I know our situation was completely different from the anonymous couple; we were no longer together, and I was being abused. Yet, I can't help but feel bad for not giving him more say of the situation—I thought he was trying to convince me to keep the baby as a means of keeping me. I think that was his plan, but perhaps, he was actually suffering from the termination of "our" baby.

The Love and Loss weekly diaries reveal, often startlingly, the intertextuality of the course. Every week students respond to each other's writings, in both signed and unsigned essays and diaries, and they learn from their classmates' experiences. So, too, is the multiplicity of points of view dazzling. Students explore a variety of subject positions in their own writing, as we see in Anonymous's next essay in which she imagines her unborn child's point of view:

> Dear Mommy,
> I haven't known you for a long time because you didn't give me the chance to. I have tried to say that I'm angry with you for killing me without thinking about how great our life could have been together. I remember being in your stomach and going everywhere with you. I'm sorry that I made you vomit every morning, but as time went on you realized what foods I liked. I hated salad and every fruit or vegetable you tried to force me to eat. I know that you may like those foods, but I preferred McDonald's.

I noticed that while I was growing inside of you, you and daddy argued a lot. I remembered an argument the two of you had where I thought I was going to die. I couldn't hear exactly what was being said because there was so much yelling and cursing. But I do remember when daddy pushed you and you fell to the ground. I didn't get hurt because you made sure that you cushioned my fall. I was glad that you cared about me, even though you planned on getting rid of me from the start.

I was a growing fetus inside of you. I wanted to meet you and daddy one day because the two of you seemed so amazing. I was thinking about how successful you guys were going to be and what wonderful parents I would have; but none of that mattered to you. I can't reveal my gender to you, but I will say that I had daddy's ears and your nose. I realized that while you were pregnant with me you were depressed—more depressed than you've ever been. I liked when you would caress me and talk to me throughout the day. I felt comforted by your words and I knew I was loved. The times I hated the most were when you took showers. I think it was during these bleak moments that you noticed how big I was getting. What was I supposed to do—stay stagnant and limp? You sobbed uncontrollably as you held on to me and apologized for what you planned to do with me. I felt your pain. I felt your sorrow. I knew you were dying inside. I was in your body amongst the death.

The most horrifying moments of my existence were when you went to the doctor. Every time you walked into those green doors, I could taste the bitterness of death. I was terrified. I hoped that you would change your mind. I knew that deep down inside of you, you wanted to have me. Instead, you let daddy convince you that killing me was the only solution. You let your selfish reasons control your ideas of morality. I know how important school is to you. But what about me? Wasn't I important? In some ways I don't understand how you could have felt any remorse for what you did, because you chose an intangible dream over your own flesh and blood. Daddy never connected with me. You did. You were the one that fed me every day, kept me warm and made sure I was okay. I'll never understand your choice.

Remember when you received my vaginal sonogram? I'm sure you could never forget that day. I was excited that day, even though I could feel your apprehension and uncertainty. The doctor placed a phallic structure inside of your vagina. On top of that structure was a camera. The doctor took pictures of me with that camera. Although I was still growing, I wanted you to see me. But you turned your head as the pictures appeared on the screen. This was a gut wrenching blow. I knew in that moment that you didn't really want me. I've never felt so low. It hurts me because you don't even have an image of what your first child looks like. That makes me feel as if I don't count.

Obviously the worst day of my life was the last day of my life, January 31, 2007. I knew what was coming that day, I just didn't know how. I could feel the anxiety mount up inside of you. You were happy, yet scared. Daddy was there, so I know you felt comforted. When you took off all of your clothes, it was eerie. I wanted to stop you from making the biggest mistake of your life. But I couldn't prevent the inevitable from occurring. As you lied on the medical bed, my death became a reality. The numbing medication made me woozy. I knew I was going to die. The doctor suctioned my body out of you. It was fast and painful. As I flew into the machine that held my remains, I was dead.

I love you mommy. I know you made the right decision for you at the time. But I will never forgive you for taking my life. Only Lord knows what I could have been or the impact I would have had on your life. However, I do know that you'll always remember me. As what—I'm not sure. I want you to remember me as your first child—your *love child*.

Anonymous offers us new details through the baby's eyes. We see a violent argument between mother and father, the mother's growing attachment to her baby, the juxtaposition of birth and death. "I was in your body amongst the death" is my favorite sentence in the essay. The only grammatical mistake is the misuse of the past tense of "lie." A creative writer might have tried to create a younger voice, perhaps a murderous voice, as Toni Morrison (1987) does in *Beloved*, when she captures the slain child's haunting words. Nevertheless, Anonymous succeeds in describing a voice significantly different from her own, one that readers will not soon forget.

Over the years several students have written essays, diaries, or short stories to deceased loved ones or imagined the latter communicating with them from a world beyond our own. We saw an example of this when Chipo imagined his mother writing a letter to him on her deathday. Anonymous and Anonymous3 also wrote about communicating with the dead. I never realized the psychological and multicultural implications of these writings until I read a 1997 article published by Klass and Heath about a Japanese ritual known as *mizuko kuyo*. (The word *mizuko* means "child of the water" and *kuyo* refers to a Buddhist offering.) Klass and Heath note that the most common form of birth control in Japan is abortion, but this act is often traumatic for the parents, who are generally married and do not wish to have additional children, because of the Buddhist belief that the spirits of the dead may feel alone, neglected, and angry. Japanese parents seek to work through their grief by apologizing to their aborted children. "The problem of the aborted child is its radical isolation; it has no connection to anything living or dead. So the *mizuko* remains in limbo unless freed ritualistically to be reborn" (p. 10). In the ritual of *mizuko kuyo*, the parents offer statues that represent the spirits of the aborted children. The ritual "re-establishes the connection between the living and the dead and thus alleviate[s] the dead's bitterness, ill will, enmity, spite, or malice which grow from the anguish at being unconnected" (p. 4). Klass and Heath add that the Japanese feeling of regret over abortion becomes "linked to the need to apologize to the child and to bring the child into the web of family connections" (p. 7).

Writing a letter to or from an aborted child is like making a ritualistic offering to the dead: both actions seek to repair a broken connection. Robert Jay Lifton (1979) remarks in *The Broken Connection* that "death does indeed bring about biological and psychic annihilation. But life includes symbolic perceptions of connections that precede and outlast that annihilation" (p. 18). Even though Americans and Japanese have strikingly different religious and cultural belief systems, grief following abortion is common, as is the need to repair broken connections caused by the trauma of abortion. Writing a letter to or from an aborted child may play a role in helping parents work through the guilt, grief, and sorrow that might otherwise continue.

The weekend preceding the last class of the semester, I received the following email from Anonymous.

> Jeff, I just want you to know that I have not handed in Diary 13. The reason for this is because I was debating whether or not I should reveal myself to the class as the anonymous author of the first abortion essay. However, after today's class, I've decided to dedicate my last diary to this confession. I would like to read the diary out loud myself during Monday's class. This is very important to me and I just want to share this one last thing with the class. I hope you understand. I will email you a copy of the diary before Monday's class. Thank you for being you. Ayla."

> "That's fine with me, Ayla," I responded. "If you change your mind, that's also fine! Thank you for the trust you have placed in all of us. Jeff." She read the diary aloud on the final day of the semester:

> I contemplated writing this diary and sharing it with the class for a long time. First I would like to say that being a part of this class was one of the most amazing experiences I've had in college. I never thought that I would be so close to complete strangers. The bond we have can never be replaced. I plan on keeping all the essays that I've written as memories. The reason why I decided to share this diary with the class is because I want you all to know that I am the anonymous writer of the first abortion essay.

> I thought it was very important to put a face to the story. I listened to all of you reveal the most intimate stories about your lives and while I did so as well, none of you knew it was me. So, yes, I am the girl who had the abortion during her junior year of college. If it wasn't for this class I would never be able to come to terms with my decision. I'm glad that I had the opportunity to share a piece of me with all of you. You are all more important than you can ever imagine. I know that you will not judge me for what I did and I'm grateful for that.

> We have been through a lot this semester, and I hope that we can all grow as individuals because of it. I will cherish those moments for the rest of my life and I hope you all do the same. While we are all sad this class had to come to an end, we must all open a new chapter in our lives that will be more fulfilling than this one. I love you all.

Ayla's decision to reveal her identity surprised me, if only because she had stated in her first diary that she is a private person: "Writing is my secret that I usually share with my teachers and no one else." She now entrusted her secret with everyone. I was not surprised, however, by the love she expressed for everyone in the class. It is appropriate to feel love for those who offer, as we did, unconditional support. She offered her classmates and teacher pedagogical love, which they reciprocated in turn. A few weeks earlier Lucy expressed in a diary entry the same kind of love. "Each week, I have found myself falling into a deeper love with this class. I love how one minute we are smiling and laughing, and the next we can switch over to a serious tone, to absorb an essay, or a part of an essay that is somber. I love hearing how people felt when writing a paper or when hearing a paper by another classmate read aloud. And I love that for the hour and twenty minutes we are together, I have a judgment-free outlet for my thoughts. I love it."

What shall we say, finally, about the abortion essays? The three students wrote safely about the most traumatic event in their lives. Writing about trauma did not retraumatize them. Their essays spoke to everyone in the classroom, regardless of whether one was pro-life, pro-choice, or undecided. These writings did not change anyone's position on the most vexing social issue in the country, but they deepened everyone's *emotional* and *experiential* understanding. The student writings become more remarkable when one considers how often discussions of abortion lead not to greater understanding but to fierce arguments and narrowed sympathy. There were no explosive outbursts in the classroom, no name-calling, no retreat into hardened ideological positions, which often occur when people talk or write about this controversy. No one felt angered, humiliated, or shamed by another member of the class. No one regretted a written or spoken comment. The abortion essays were not only confessional but transformative. Collectively, they reaffirmed one's "Write to Life."

Instead of infection and disconnection, the students felt a strong connection with each other. This attachment bond is striking, especially during a discussion of the country's most divisive social issue. There is also a connection between the living and the dead. Just as we saw how writing strengthened Chipo's attachment to his relatives, so can we see how Ayla's writing repaired a broken connection with her unborn child while, simultaneously, allowing her to distance herself from the guilt, grief, and depression surrounding traumatic loss.

Ayla states unambiguously in her last diary that Love and Loss has helped her to come to terms with her abortion. The three processes that are involved in the movement from loss to recovery, as proposed by Robert S. Weiss (1993)—cognitive acceptance, emotional acceptance, and identity change (p. 280)—are implicit in her writings. Such recovery may be ongoing and dependent upon the nonjudgmental acceptance of others, an acceptance that she found among her classmates. This nonjudgmental acceptance is based on empathic listening. Benard and Slade (2009) present compelling evidence that empathic listening is the "key strategy for educational change, one which is too often ignored" (p. 366). The ability to listen empathically is also an indispensable quality for death educators (Durlak, 1994, p. 257).

In reflecting upon how our Love and Loss course responded to the three students' writings about abortion, I recall a passage in Richard Powers's (2006) novel *The Echo Maker* in which a neurologist observes about a young man severely injured in an automobile accident, "it's not what you think you feel that wins out, it's what you feel you think" (p. 131). The context of the remark is not limited to Capgras syndrome, a rare brain injury in which individuals can remember the details of their lives but not their emotional significance. Rather, there is often a disconnect between feeling and thought that calls into question the belief that the self is, in Powers's words, "whole, willful, embodied, continuous, and aware" (p. 381). This disconnect is strikingly apparent in abortion narratives, in which what students *think* is often contradicted by what they *feel*. In Capgras syndrome, flattened emotional response defeats cognitive recognition; in abortion narratives, traumatic memories often defeat cognitive processing. Writing essays about abortion in an empathic classroom helps to narrow the gap between thought and feeling, leading to greater self-understanding and self-forgiveness.

"I was very skeptical at first to read your chapter because I had not read my abortion essay in awhile," Ayla emailed me nearly a year after Love and Loss ended. "But after reading it, I was fine. I did not feel any sadness. More importantly, I did not regret any of my decisions to write this essay or to reveal myself to the class. This was about healing and finding closure. What better way to do this than to tell my darkest secret to a room full of people who became my closest allies." She was intrigued with my references to *Abortion Counseling*:

> I think it is important for people to realize that they're not alone when dealing with abortion issues, and by some of my classmates' responses, I see that I have at least opened some of their hearts. I was surprised to read that one of my classmates thought I was selfish, but at the same time, I understand where they're coming from. It was a selfish decision in retrospect; however, at the time that was my only option. The quotations from *The Echo Maker* explain it eloquently: what you think is often contradicted by what you feel. You may think you have all the answers to a question, until someone actually proposes the question; then you realize you never knew the answer from the start.

The abortion essays produced many surprises, including one that I did not reveal during the semester: Anonymous3 was one of the *males* in the class! He had told me after hearing Anonymous's essay that he wanted to write about his girlfriend's recent abortion, but he felt self-conscious doing so because there were only five men in the class of twenty-five students. "If you read my essay aloud, the other men will feel uncomfortable, since there are so few of us." It was his decision to disguise his gender. He gave me permission to reveal his gender when I distributed copies of the complete manuscript to members of the class several months after the semester ended. I assumed that Ayla would be surprised upon learning that Anonymous3 was a male classmate, but as it turned out, I was the one surprised, as she observes in her email:

The writer of the Anonymous3 essay revealed himself to me shortly after I revealed that I was the writer of the first anonymous essay. I had another class with this student, and even though our Love and Loss course was over, the other class we had together was not. I saw him the next morning in another English class, and as he walked by me to say hi, he dropped a black and yellow folder on my desk. As I opened the folder, I saw his anonymous essay. I quickly read it and closed the folder. When class was over I gave him his folder back and not a word was said. I was shocked that he was the anonymous writer, but at the same time, there was nothing to be said. We had a mutual respect and understanding for each other and that was clear. The powerful connection that we developed by being in this class will never be forgotten. Not only do we have your book as a reminder, but we have our memories. I would not change any aspect of this course.

Reading *Dying To Teach*

It's strange to write a memoir about one's deceased wife (Freudian slip: I wrote deceased "life"), assign it to students in a course on Love and Loss, and then report on their essays. Is it pedagogically appropriate to require students to read such a book? Can they read an intensely personal memoir—one that the author's adult daughters still cannot complete—without being infected by its sorrow? Can students write honestly and openly without feeling pressured into telling a professor what they think he wants to hear? Can a professor's summary of his students' responses be credible? How does such personal self-disclosure change the student-teacher relationship? These are daunting—some would say *impossible*—challenges for students and teacher alike.

Dying to Teach is, in part, a study of how the undergraduates in my spring, 2004 Expository Writing course responded to my wife's illness and death. Toward the end of her life, I read to them my "Eulogy for Barbara," and I kept them informed about her rapidly declining health. Immediately after her death, I began writing about our life together after her diagnosis. I sought to show how illness transformed our lives, individually and collectively, and how each of us confronted the physical and psychological challenges of terminal cancer. I also tried to show how each of us struggled to remain close to each other even as death drew us apart.

In presenting my Love and Loss students' responses to *Dying to Teach*, I realize that readers will soon grow weary and wary of praise, no matter how sincere it is. To minimize this difficulty, I have omitted all references to my "courage," "strength," or "heroism." I don't regard myself as particularly courageous, strong, or heroic. It may appear counterintuitive, but it's easier to present students' criticism of their teachers than their praise of them—no one doubts the truthfulness of the former, while many may doubt the truthfulness of the latter.

I debated over whether to assign *Dying to Teach* to my students, whether to require my students to write on it, and whether to devote an entire chapter to evaluating their comments on it. I knew that this chapter would be the most difficult to write, for it compelled me to re-read the book—and myself—through my students' eyes.

The assignment on "Reading *Dying to Teach*," came near the end of the semester, late enough for students to read the entire book. I asked them to discuss the following questions:

> How would the course have been different if you had not read the book? Were you surprised by anything I wrote? Have you discussed the book with relatives or friends and, if so, how did they respond? What were your favorite sections of the book? The most boring sections? Were there sections that were too painful or difficult to read? Does the way I present myself in the book—the "narrator" as a "character"—seem similar to or different from the way I appear in class? Speculate on what you will remember about the book—if anything—10 or 20 years from now.

Not all the students commented on every question, but everyone who responded to the first one felt the course would have been different, and less powerful, without reading *Dying to Teach*. Ayla speaks for her classmates when she observes: "The course would have been extremely different without the book because we wouldn't know anything about you." She felt that it is easier for students to share heartfelt stories about their lives when they know that their professors have experienced similar events. "I feel as if I have been let into a major part of your life that will always be dear to your heart. I appreciate your words and descriptions of your wife because I have shared gut wrenching moments in my life as well."

Many students were surprised that I disclosed the moments when I became angry at Barbara and made hurtful statements to her that I instantly regretted. I included these examples of anger because I did not want to imply I was a perfect caregiver. Gloria was glad that I didn't "sugarcoat" Barbara's death. Cassie was surprised when I described how upset I became when one of our dogs—who could sense Barbara was dying—chewed a hole in our couch. "There's a particular part of the book that made me cry. Jeff writes, 'I became so angry at Sabrina when I saw the damage to the furniture that I turned around to Barbara and screamed, 'When you die, I'm getting rid of these dogs' (p. 79). Wow. These words cut deep." My anger and frustration shocked Cassie, but the more she thought about my situation, the more she understood my fear of losing Barbara. Another surprise for Cassie was when Barbara raised the question of suicide. "After I read this section, I called my roommate into my room and read it aloud to her. She started to cry and asked if she could borrow the book when I was finished. I think I called her down because I wanted to say the words out loud to see another person's reaction. These words were horrifying to me because it must have been so hard for Jeff to truly know whether or not Barbara wanted him to give 'all the medication.' It also shows the reader the confusion and lack of communication that Jeff was faced with during this time." Kasia was glad that I didn't portray myself as perfect. "He didn't omit the times when he said hurtful things to Barbara or the times that he lost hope."

My anger also startled Chipo. "When Berman says to Barbara, 'You're torturing me' (p. 78), I was surprised he admitted to saying harsh words to his spouse. But that statement reveals that he makes mistakes like any human being. I think this statement leaves him vulnerable to harsh criticism from readers of this memoir. It also shows how dealing with a sick loved one is not easy." Significantly, reading this passage allowed Chipo to reflect upon his own life:

> When my grandfather became ill from a severe health condition, the drugs he was prescribed would sometimes make him hallucinate. Although I set up home care for him, arranging a nurse to come visit once and a home aide three times a week, I laughed several times when he would explain he saw little people out the window and within the apartment. I would first try to rationalize with him how that was not possible. I would say, "have you ever seen people that size before?" But to no avail; he would insist that what he saw was true and instead of being helpful, I laughed about it. I think that was my way of trying to hide from the fact that my grandfather needed more attention not just from my family but from me as well.

Perhaps what most surprised my students, including those who had taken other courses with me, is my lack of religious faith. They could not imagine how I coped with Barbara's death without believing that we would be reunited in the next world. "I know you do not believe in heaven," Lia wrote, "but I believe otherwise—at least in some sort of afterlife. I believe that everyone's heaven is different, and based on what he or she feels heaven looks like. I hope that my theory is true because if it is, I am happy to know that there will be a day when you and Barbara unite again." Lucy recalled an exchange we had a year earlier:

> In the other class that I took with Jeff last summer, we each had to write a 10 page paper about one of the books that we read during the four weeks of class. In the paper, we had to agree with two statements that Jeff had written in his book *Surviving Literary Suicide* or made in class. We also had to disagree with two of these statements. When I sat down to write my paper, I wondered with what I could possibly disagree and be able to dispute with a strong case. There was one remark Jeff had made at the start of the four weeks that had always been in the back of my mind: "Every love inevitably ends in loss," a belief to which he referred in the Introduction to *Dying to Teach* (p. 2). When he said that, I had no argument. I couldn't help but agree. Some of my classmates tried to disagree with him on the spot, but found it to be impossible—Jeff tends to think through what he is going to say thoroughly before he says it.
>
> I thought more about the statement and realized Jeff was wrong. I wrote, "Love is never lost, and true love never ends. It is merely deferred until a later date. It is my belief that there is a reunion awaiting all of us. Although we may feel a sense of loss at the time, it is never gone forever; that love will always come back to us." As a bonus to writing a paper in which we had to disagree with our professor, Jeff also made each person read

both of his or her disagreements aloud. When I read this disagreement out loud, my voice was shaky, and I had no idea how he was going to react. He smiled and said, "In this case, I hope you are right."

One student made a statement that disturbed me. "Jeff introduced me [in *Dying to Teach*] to a woman and to a family I would love to be a part of, even though I am very much in love with my own family. If Barbara never had cancer, I fear I would not have the chance to know her." The student then wondered whether Barbara's cancer was a blessing in disguise. "I do not mean to say that I can be happy she was forced to leave the earth too soon. However, I cannot help but recognize the impact she and Jeff have on so many students. I guess it is a tribute to the true nature of Barbara; she impacts even the lives of people whom she never knew, even after her death. Her legacy remains within Jeff and her family, and I feel I got to know her just by getting to know Jeff." I admire the forthrightness of this statement, and I can understand why some readers might feel this way; nevertheless, at no time have I or anyone in my family regarded Barbara's cancer as a blessing in disguise. I am reminded of an even more astonishing remark from an undergraduate following a talk I gave in Taiwan in June, 2008 on "Mourning and the Pedagogy of Self-Disclosure." A young man asked me, in faltering English, which situation I preferred: writing a book about my dead wife or not writing a book because Barbara was still alive? I looked incredulously at him, assuming that the meaning of his question was somehow lost in translation, but he then repeated the question in Chinese to one of his English professors, who translated it in the same way. I didn't want to appear discourteous, but I couldn't prevent myself from blurting out, "Do you know what the expression, 'no-brainer means?' Why would anyone prefer a book over a living person?"

Many students found Barbara's letters to be the most moving sections of *Dying to Teach*. Nicholette's favorite section was Barbara's letter to her father.

> I was amazed how detailed the letter was, and I think she was an excellent writer. Jeff wrote that he thinks she wrote this detailed and long letter so that her grandchildren will be able to learn who she is, which really touched my heart. I think that Barbara was significantly strong minded to be able to write such a powerful letter knowing that this is what her grandchildren are going to use as a substantial guide to Barbara Berman. Of course, family members will keep her alive, but her writing, I think, is what her grand-children will always remember.

Bianca also singled out Barbara's letter to her father. "I especially enjoyed the letter to her dad, reminiscing about the time they used to spend in Coney Island together. Certain things reminded me of time spent with my own parents as a child, and I still love to reminisce about the good ol' days, as I like to call them." Other students mentioned Barbara's letter to Arielle, written on her thirtieth birthday, when she was pregnant with her first child, our first grandchild. Lucy wondered about the kind of letter her own parents might write in a similar situation.

> When I cried while reading this letter to Arielle from her mother, I was thinking of my own mother. I was thinking of what she would say to me, of what she has said to me. I noticed the love radiating through Barbara's letter, the love that soon she would not be there to give. I felt scared, scared that this could happen to anyone, that it could happen to one or both of my own parents.

Isabella's most memorable sections were my daughters' eulogies. "Through these, everything Jeff reveals about Barbara is reaffirmed." Ayla liked best the photographs in the book. "I know that it may sound weird that I don't have a specific passage to reference; however, I think that the photos you chose served as the most significant details. The pictures that you chose told me a story of your life. They also showed how both you and your wife aged throughout the years."

The darker moments of *Dying to Teach* moved other students, such as Kasia. "The best part of the book for me happened also to be the hardest for me to read through without crying. This was the section where Professor Berman is describing Barbara's last days. It doesn't seem real to think that you can know that the person you love most is going to die within the week, and you don't completely lose your mind. It was wrenching to read that a husband so devoted to his wife couldn't do anything else but count down the days till her death. I do not know what could be worse. That part of the book was difficult for me to get through because it was written honestly and vividly." Maggie quotes the following sentences—"Living with death allows us to acknowledge the continuing presence of absent people, the way in which they remain alive to us. They have left us, but we have not left them"—and then comments: "When I reached the top of page 6, I began crying. The quote seemed to come right from my own heart. I didn't want to move on after my grandpa died, and no one could understand that. I wanted desperately for everything to be the way it was: to be happy, picking beans with him in his garden. It was during this sentence that I fell in love with the book." Gloria's favorite sentence occurs on page 97, when I write: "I hope that when I am lying on my deathbed, I will have learned everything that she was dying to teach." From this sentence she concludes, "Berman appreciates the fact that Barbara tried so hard, despite her physical condition, to teach her family how to survive without her. It really sums up the woman she was, amazing. I think this may be where he got the idea for the title of the book as well."

Chipo's favorite part of *Dying to Teach* was the section called "The Language of Condolence" because it relates to his own life. "I like this section because when I received condolence cards when I lost my mother in December 2001, I wondered what friends were trying to say. I still have those cards because they were a source of support that helped me cope during the death of my mother. I also enjoy [the section on] gratitude because it reveals how someone appreciates what another person gives them. Berman writes, 'gratitude arises in response to a gift freely given by another'" (p. 217).

No one felt that reading *Dying to Teach* was "boring," but Cassie felt herself losing interest during the "scholarly" sections. "In many of the chapters Jeff quotes from various authors and poets. He uses their words to make a point or explain various phenomena. I found it difficult to connect these passages with Jeff's words because I have never read many of the books he talked about. These unfamiliar names and plotlines scrambled on the pages, and I found myself looking for one word: Barbara. I wanted to know everything about her, and these other people's opinions did not matter to me." Some of my friends and colleagues felt the same way when they read the manuscript, believing that the many scholarly references interrupted the narration of Barbara's story. I remember saying at the time that I was writing the book for a university press audience and that I was trying to situate Barbara's story in the context of other narratives on dying and death, but the scholarly apparatus makes the story less interesting for some readers.

All of the students found *Dying to Teach* painful to read. The most difficult section for Chipo occurred when I discussed Barbara's violent hallucinations shortly before she lapsed into a coma. "I thought 'Teaching and Writing as Rescue' was a painful section to read, when Professor Berman wrote about 'injecting her every eight hours with an antipsychotic so that she would not telephone the police screaming she was being murdered, as she did on one occasion' (p. 129). I think it was very revealing, and now I better understand why his daughters have not read the book." The most heartrending moment of the book for Lucy was my eulogy. "I felt his pain, and I wanted to take it away. I did not feel burdened with his loss, and I did not feel depressed with what he shared; I felt empathy." The saddest part of the memoir for Saverio was when Barbara asked me to give her a fatal dose of morphine. "I understand, like you say, that she may not have been in her right mind when she said this. What if she wasn't? After reading that line, I was contemplating those words, 'Could you give me all of my medication?' I cannot imagine how those words haunted you; I imagine they still might today."

There was unanimous agreement that I presented myself in *Dying to Teach* the same way I do in class. Kasia speaks for many of her classmates when she states that while reading the book she could hear me speaking the words because she now knows what my voice sounds like. Chipo also believed that I come across the same way in the book and in the classroom: "as someone who cares and is not afraid to show emotions and admit to mistakes he has made."

What will students remember about *Dying to Teach* in 10 or 20 years? Bianca will remember how Barbara's story reminded her of her grandmother's death. "My grandma is the only person close to me who has died, and because her death was only a year ago, everything still reminds me of her. I will also remember how Jeff and his daughters were able to cope with Barbara's death, and how their eulogies were so detailed and touching that I couldn't help but shed tears." Nicholette will remember how our family has dealt with Barbara's death. "From this book I will remember how Jeff, his daughters, and his family were able to cope with Barbara's passing. I will also remember how strong minded Barbara was during the last few months of her precious life." Kamilluh will remember that writing memorializes loss. "I see a man who is missing his wife in ways I cannot explain, and using his writing to keep her alive. His memory will fade in some ways, as mine will when I get older, and so as a writer the best way to remember is by putting the memories onto paper. That is something I will probably do with my cousin as well."

Cath

Three students wrote diaries or essays *Dying to Teach* that I will never forget. Their writings reveal as much about themselves as about Barbara. The most striking of the three came during the third week of the semester, when Cath devoted her entire diary entry to a description of her feelings about the book's front cover, which contains a haunting photo of Barbara:

> I find it difficult to read Jeff's book. I enjoy every page I read. This seems to be impossible, but both those sentences are true. There are many reasons why this book is hard for me to read. One of these reasons is the book itself. I am afraid of hurting the book. Why am I afraid of hurting a stack of paper and ink? Because of the face on the front. I'm afraid of breaking it. I hate that when I read the odd pages I get the urge to bend the cover of the book. Doing this crushes Barbara. Her young innocent face is being bent so that it is easier for me to hold the book. I hate that. Her face, which knew nothing of the cancer that would one day take her life, is staring out in black and white—I feel guilty letting the pages bend.
>
> That is the easy reason to explain. The second is the important one. Most important reasons are hard to understand. It's easy for me to read about almost anything. The idea of death doesn't completely scare me (although the idea of someone else I love dying—that terrifies me). But I can accept reading stories of death and heartache. This story is different. It's different because the story is real to me. I cannot put a distance [to it] as I can to fictional characters. I cannot pretend real people are fictional to make it easier. I can't do any of this because I've seen Jeff. I can see him and his love for Barbara. I see her pictures in his office. I can hear him speak about her. I can hear in his voice the love he has for Barbara. It will always be a "has" and never a "had." I can hear that, and I can see it.
>
> Since I know all this about Jeff, I cannot prevent myself from caring. It makes me sad to read about happy times—but I find myself smiling. I have conflicting feelings in the space of a paragraph. Sometimes within one sentence I feel many different emotions. Sometimes I feel nothing. I go numb because it's easier. I do the easier reaction because I don't know what else to do. I have no idea how I would react to the same situation. I'm not sure I could make it through. I fear it would take a power I do not possess.
>
> I get sad when I look at the pictures. I get sad because I always think of how a picture is a memory of an event that will never happen again. You can

try to do the same activity, but it will never be the same as the original. Pictures also make me incredibly happy. Pictures are memories, and that alone is enough to put a smile on my face. I can see Barbara's eyes and smile in the picture of Arielle.

I have a collection of Jeff's books now. This one was the one I looked forward to reading more than any other. I'm pleased.

One last point. Barbara mentioned looking into her dog Pandora's eyes. A student of Jeff's talked about how eyes are the window to the soul. I agree. I have a strange fear of my own. Sometimes I can't look certain people in the eyes. When I am in an uncomfortable relationship, or scared, I cannot make eye contact, even with people I love. I get overwhelmed and scared, and I have to divert my eyes.

I reflected on Cath's words the entire day. She captures one aspect of Barbara's character, her brooding, melancholy nature. Cath knows that the photo on the cover of the book is only an image, a representation, yet she believes the careless reader can somehow hurt Barbara. I don't believe that Cath regards the photo as a fetish object, at least not in the Freudian meaning of the term, which signifies a woman's lack of penis, her biological "castration." But she does seem to endow the photo with magical powers, as if it is a religious icon or a *secular* fetish, which is, as Solomon suggests (2002), "any object of excessive attention and devotion," such as "glorification of the death experience" (p. 116). Cath and I glorify not Barbara's death but her life; we aren't, in Solomon's terms, converting death to the meaning of life but celebrating a beautiful life prematurely cut short by death.

There is something uncanny about Cath's language, something that is familiar to me but difficult to express. As soon as *Dying to Teach* was published, I found myself repeatedly caressing the image of Barbara on the cover and silently speaking to her, as if by doing so I could somehow feel her skin and communicate to her. This is not something I thought about until I read Cath's diary. Barbara comes alive to Cath through the photos in my book and on my office wall, through my written words in *Dying to Teach*, and through my spoken words in the classroom. Cath writes about an ethics of caring that extends to Barbara and to me, and perhaps to everyone who has lost a loved one.

Reflecting upon Cath's diary, I realized that my attachment to the photo of Barbara on the cover of *Dying to Teach* is an example of what Vamik Volkan (1981) calls a "linking object"—an object belonging to the deceased—in my case, a pictorial representation of Barbara—that allows a mourner to maintain a relationship with the deceased. In Volkan's view, a linking object allows a mourner to cope with the separation anxiety surrounding death and thus represents a triumph over loss. Volkan believed, initially, that linking objects are a sign of a mourner's pathological grief, but he later recognized that linking objects can be a source of inspiration and creativity.

Susan Sontag (1978) refers to photography as an "elegiac art, a twilight art," and her comments help me to understand my obsession with this haunting image of Barbara. "Most subjects photographed are, just by virtue of being photographed, touched with pathos," Sontag observes. "A beautiful subject can be the object of rueful feelings, because it has aged or decayed or no longer exists. All photographs are *memento mori*. To take a photograph is to participate in another person's (or thing's) mortality, vulnerability, mutability. Precisely by slicing out this moment and freezing it, all photographs testify to time's relentless melt" (p. 5). I agree with Sontag's observation though not with her statement that photography is a "predatory act": "to photograph people is to violate them, by seeing them as they never see themselves, by having knowledge of them they can never have" (p. 14). According to this view, any attempt to know another person is predatory. Nevertheless, I agree with Sontag's belief about the "talismanic uses of photographs [to] express a feeling both sentimental and implicitly magical: they are attempts to contact or lay claim to another reality" (p. 16).

I read Cath's diary entry aloud, and I then told the class how deeply her words affected me. Her diary entry remains the most eerie reaction to the book that anyone has expressed to me. The photo on the front cover of *Dying to Teach* assumes a living reality for both Cath and me that transcends representation. I had taken the photo of Barbara in 1967, shortly after our college graduation, and I enlarged it and then hung it on my university office wall when we arrived in Albany in 1973. I've always found the photo spellbinding, particularly Barbara's eyes, which look mysterious and shadowy, ethereal and otherworldly.

Shannon

If Cath's response to *Dying to Teach* represents one extreme, Shannon's response represents the opposite extreme, opposite in its mood, tone, and imagery:

> I finished *Dying to Teach* yesterday. I took my time reading this memoir. I wanted to put as much time into reading this as Jeff put into writing each word. Now I want to put just as much time into writing my own words. When I finished reading the last page, I did not react the way I had expected to react. I thought I was going to be able to sit down at my computer and write my initial essay in less than 30 minutes. I didn't sit at my computer. I didn't write. I didn't even make a single note.
>
> I rolled up my sweatpants. I put on my yellow gloves. I snatched my bleach and a sponge from the laundry room. I pulled my hair up and out of my face. That's right—I started to bleach the shower. Actually, I bleached the whole bathroom. Then I moved onto the kitchen. I swept and washed the floors. I did my laundry and I washed all of the dishes. After my apartment was made sparkling clean by yours truly, I made myself a delicious meal. I love to cook, and I always take my time when preparing a meal. This time, however, I spent extra time cutting the chicken and the vegetables. After dinner, I made a batch of chocolate chip cookies. I asked myself why I was doing all of this. Why was I cleaning and cooking when I should have been doing homework? I guess I wanted to reassure myself that I could get by on my own.

In *Dying to Teach*, Jeff does what he asks of his students in every assignment. With every word, he shows us rather than tells us. However, it was not his words that I most appreciated; it was the inclusion of his family photos. With every word I read, I had the real image of Barbara in my mind. It was not one that I composed while reading descriptions, the way I do with characters when I read fictional literature. I know that if I had not seen photos of Barbara, my created image would have been just as beautiful. Barbara's beauty lingered in every word on every page. But there are no words that can describe the beauty of a woman such as Barbara. My created image surely would not have done her justice.

As I was reading *Dying to Teach*, I found myself growing attached to a woman I was never given the privilege to meet. I found myself seeing similarities between the two of us, which only strengthened my attachment. Barbara was a woman with many talents. She knew how to make a beautiful wedding dress for her daughter, and she also knew how to fix the toilet. Jeff touched on her perfectionist personality many times throughout the book. I welcome you to my world. When people see me walking around in my four inch high heels and fabulous outfits, they assume that I'm a pretty girl, and that's as far as it goes. They don't think that I can take those stilettos off just as easily as I put them on and change the oil in my car. The story about the almost imperceptible mistake which the mason made makes me laugh every time I think about it. I would have been one of the people who noticed the mistake. Recently, my father cobblestoned our entire driveway, and he used four different colored bricks to make a pattern. I came home from my work one day over the summer and stood on our raised lawn while staring at the driveway. My father asked me if I liked how the driveway was coming out. To his surprise, I told him that I did not. My reasoning was that one of the red-toned bricks in the circle pattern was not the same red as the others. "You have got to be kidding me, right?" I told him I was not, and I also told him that if he didn't fix it, I would not park in the driveway. "You are so annoying, Shannon. You are so annoying because you are absolutely right." He wouldn't have noticed had I not said anything, but I did, and he fixed that entire portion of the driveway.

Barbara's "curious night rituals" also fascinated me, because I have one of my own. Ever since I received my first iPod, I began falling asleep with it. Music soothes me, and it helped me fall asleep. After a while, however, it became a necessity. Now, I can't fall asleep without my iPod. That is not the weird part, though. It has become so necessary for me to fall asleep with my iPod that on those occasions that I don't have it, I have to plug my ears with my own fingers so I can simulate the feeling of headphones in my ears, otherwise, I will not be able to fall asleep. My ex-boyfriend thought this was hilarious, and there were times when he would hold my hands behind my back so that I couldn't plug my ears. It's hard to pick a favorite part of this memoir, but if I had to choose, it would be the details that Jeff included, the kind of details that I have just listed. I felt, and still feel, as if I had known Barbara. I knew how this story was going to read, but I didn't want it to end. I cried when it did.

> I have discussed both this class and this book with relatives and friends, but nobody had a stronger reaction than my mother. Maybe it's because she herself is the mother of two daughters, or because she also knows what it feels like to love someone more than life itself. I will never be entirely sure. The day after I had my mid-semester conference with Jeff, I was sitting with my mother drinking coffee. My coffee was cold because I wouldn't shut up. I told my mother everything that Jeff had told me during our conference. Then I told her about *Dying to Teach*. I told her the story, including details that Jeff included in the book as well as the ones he has added throughout classes. My mother listened carefully, while she was shaking her head in saddened disbelief. I suddenly realized that I had the book with me in my bag. "Mom, you have to see this book. Jeff told us that the picture on the cover was his favorite picture of Barbara and his favorite picture of all time." When I handed my mother the book, *she* began to cry. She was in awe of Barbara's beauty. She looked through the rest of the pictures and continued crying silently. She kept repeating these words: "What a beautiful woman," I guess a picture really is worth 1,000 words. I happen to be lucky enough to know what those 1,000 words are.

My face breaks into a smile whenever I reread Shannon's words. I identify with many of her rituals, including her manic energy when cleaning, something I myself do when I take a "break" from writing. (Her obsessive cleanliness parallels my obsessive neatness.) She praises my ability to show instead of tell, but the student surpasses the teacher in her ability to make us see the many sides of her colorful personality. I couldn't write as vividly as Shannon does when I was an undergraduate—and I still can't. This is not false modesty, merely an expression of my pleasure over the exuberance of her writing. Cath and Shannon are both attached to Barbara but in dramatically different ways. Cath's relationship to Barbara is intimate, intense, protective; Shannon's relationship is playful, upbeat, mirthful. Both depict different sides of Barbara's complex personality. And both reveal aspects of their own personality as well.

Daphne

Reading about Barbara reminded other students about their own deceased relatives. This was true for Daphne, whose grandmother had died two years earlier:

> Before the first day of class, I went to the bookstore to purchase Jeffrey Berman's memoir, *Dying to Teach*. I was unaware, at first, that this required text was not only essential reading for the class, but for my understanding of death as well. I was shocked by the first few words on the back cover, which include the description of why Berman was writing his book. The words *pancreatic cancer* struck a chord in me. I immediately called my mother, who suggested that I consider taking a different course instead of Love and Loss, which to her appeared incredibly depressing. It is true I had my doubts about Love and Loss as well. However, on the first day of class I watched as a

handful of students were pleading with Berman to allow them into the class, and so I decided that there must be something worth staying for.

Then I listened to Berman talk about his wife. He talked about her with sweetness and he told us about his career and his teaching philosophies. It was then I discovered how influential this class would be for me. We were asked to write down why we had decided to take this class. I of course first thought of my grandmother's battle with pancreatic cancer. I signed up for Love and Loss because I had loved, and therefore I had lost and I wanted—no, needed to grow. Just as Berman had grown from writing about his loss, I felt a need to write, to expose my thoughts to paper. A feeling which I am sure we as a class are all aware of now. This need to express our loss is much like a swaying pendulum knocking at each side of our brain. You can only ignore it for so long. It was through this class that I began to write, and the gloomy pendulum began to slow down.

When Berman writes that their last trip was to Maine, I nearly dropped the book from my hands. My grandmother and I had decided to take one last family vacation to Maine the summer before she died. It was July 2005, and on the last night there we had stopped at a local, pirate inspired, seafood restaurant. My grandmother, like Barbara, had ordered the lobster though she was not fortunate enough to have enjoyed it. Instead, her chemotherapy treatments had changed her appetite and her taste buds, so my grandmother could not enjoy the lobster the way she had in the past.

I discovered that the end of Barbara's life was near as I read over Berman's words. He described that he would share a bed with Barbara "even toward the end, when she was making awful gurgling noises—the 'death rattle'" (p. 72). At these words I cannot say that I did much at all. I was overwhelmed with emotion, which I was not aware had even existed. The remembrance of that awful sound was frightening. I can remember moments when this death rattle first began when I would listen closely to make sure my grandmother wasn't choking. I sat next to her bed in hospice, staring out of the stained glass window. I tried constantly to prop her head appropriately so that she could breathe better. I felt as if I was a mother, watching her baby in a crib. I just watched as my grandmother's chest rose, and for every gurgle of the death rattle my heart stopped for fear that this would be my grandmother's last breath.

Jeff's words also startled me because I wanted so badly to lie next to my grandmother while she was in her Hospice bed. I believe that at some moments I wanted to go through with it with her, so that she wouldn't be so alone. For much of my childhood and adolescence I spent the weekends at my grandmother's house. We would often fall asleep together on the couch rubbing each other's feet; we were content from the accompaniment of each other. Imagine a summer afternoon lying on the grass with the sun gently touching your skin and a glass of fresh lemonade. The contented feeling of a summer day was with me always as I lay next to my grandmother, but I couldn't fit next to her in her hospice bed, and I feared what the nurses would think about me. But, as tears fill my eyes now, I regret that the most, not lying next to her for one last time. It wasn't enough to hold her hand, because she couldn't hold my own hand back. I think that if I had gotten the chance to lie next to her and rub her back, maybe I could have helped, maybe she wouldn't have struggled for so long, and maybe she wouldn't have had that death rattle that seems to sound like a baby struggling for air.

Dying to Teach was very difficult for me to read. There were constant similarities that the feelings of sadness and pain were too close to bear. I must admit that I had to skip over spots that my eyes would tear up at. I hope that one day I can go back and read it all the way through, which is precisely why I intended to add Berman's book to my shelf, but for now the growth from my loss is a slow moving train. Eventually when the wheels begin to turn faster, I hope to pick up Berman's memoir again. Still, I have learned much more about the way others face death, and it has given me the chance to accept my loss and continue to understand the loss of my grandmother, and the losses I will continue to endure.

Reading *Dying to Teach* was an epiphany for Daphne when she came across my description of Barbara's death rattle. "We slept next to each other throughout our married life, even toward the end, when she was making awful gurgling noises—the 'death rattle.' I was so physically and emotionally exhausted that I fell asleep in a minute or two, despite the noise that ordinarily would have kept me awake. Each morning as soon as I awoke I would look at her, checking to see if she was still breathing" (p. 72). My description reminded Daphne of her grandmother's death rattle, and the memory was so traumatic that she had never written or spoken about it before, as she confided to me in an email shortly after the semester ended:

When my eyes followed over that portion of the book, they flooded with emotion. It was the weirdest thing. I was on a plane ride to Florida for vacation, a relatively pleasant experience. But when I read your words, everything around me started to blur. I cried for nearly a half hour. It was a night flight, so everyone around me was sleeping, but I will never forget that moment. It was like Proust and the madeleine. The idea of the death rattle brought me back, to the images, sights, sounds, and smells of my grandmother in the hospice bed. And no, I had never admitted that to anyone, that all I wanted to do was to lie next to her in bed. I hadn't even admitted it to myself.

Daphne's statement recalls John Kotre's (1995) observation about traumatic memories: "Emotion has a paradoxical effect on memory, partly because there are so many different emotions. Much of the time it acts like a flashbulb, lighting up the autobiographical memory system so that it records a good many details. But there are occasions when emotion is so overwhelming, and everything happens so fast, that memory goes into a daze." One of the examples Kotre cites is losing a loved one. "Events may become a blur because the emotions they arouse are painful or sad. We remember the day a loved one died but not much of the days that followed. There was just too much happening during that time, and besides, we were just not ourselves" (p. 99). Reading *Dying to Teach*, Daphne finds herself transported back in time, and she recalls in heartbreaking detail her grandmother's final days, including the reversal of roles she experienced when she felt like she was mothering her grandmother, "watching her baby in a crib." Daphne was the only student who implied in her essay that parts of the book were too painful for her to read—too painful to read now, but not, perhaps, too painful to read in the future. She was overwhelmed with emotion when she read about Barbara's death rattle, but notice how she finds the words to describe her feelings. Her language is filled with insight verbs: "discovered" (a word she uses twice), "understand" (which she also uses twice, along with the noun "understanding"), "know," and "learned." These insight words convey her emotional and cognitive growth.

Without exception, all of my students felt it was pedagogically appropriate to read and comment on their professor's book. No one felt pressured by the assignment—in part, because I told them at the beginning of the semester that they were not required to write on any assignment that was too personal or threatening. Because I did not grade any of their writings on content or degree of self-disclosure, they felt free to express their thoughts and feelings about the book. Most of them took the assignment "personally," that is, they related *Dying to Teach* to their own experiences, past, present, and future. As far as I know, the students in *Dying to Teach* did not believe they were "being cast as instruments of their professor's emotional recovery," as Robin Paletti (2008) claimed in a review of *Dying to Teach* (p. 894). None of the 16 Expository Writing students whose letters appear in the Appendix to the book made this criticism, nor did any of the 25 Love and Loss students make this criticism. Paletti's belief that the "classroom ought respectfully be regarded as a venue for academic pursuits, rather than therapeutic ones" (p. 894) implies that the two goals are mutually exclusive rather than, in my view, complementary. Smeyers, Smith, and Standish (2007) support my belief that educational goals are consistent with therapeutic ones: "Is it in no sense the business of education to help us lead more fulfilling lives, cope with our emotions, understand ourselves a little better, empathize with very different people and cultures? Our sense of what education can be stands to be enriched, not diminished, by a sufficiently nuanced appreciation of its connections with therapy" (p. 18).

It has long been known that counterphobic motivation is often present in mental health professionals, who help themselves when they help others. So, too, is counterphobic motivation present in artists, teachers, and the clergy. Many writers have acknowledged a therapeutic impulse behind their stories. Virginia Woolf (1976) admits that until she was in her forties, she was haunted by her mother's death, which occurred more than a quarter of a century earlier. Writing *To the Lighthouse* enabled the novelist to come to terms with maternal loss: "I suppose that I did for myself what psycho-analysts do for their patients. I expressed some very long felt and deeply felt emotion. And in expressing it I explained it and then laid it to rest" (p. 81). Reading a novel like *To the*

Lighthouse allows teachers and students alike to explore the theme of maternal loss and, in the process, understand how they have dealt with loss in their own lives.

Counterphobic motivation also appears in Randy Pausch's (2008) best-selling book, *The Last Lecture*, published in 2008, shortly before his death. A computer science professor at Carnegie Mellon University, Pausch was asked to give a lecture on the question, "What wisdom would we impart to the world if we knew it was our last chance?" Diagnosed with terminal cancer in 2006, he decided to lecture on the importance of overcoming obstacles to pursue one's dream. Called by his doctor a poster boy for the healthy balance between optimism and pessimism, Pausch knew that his audience might be unable to reconcile his healthy appearance with his impending death, and so he addresses this question at the beginning of his lecture. "'If I don't seem as depressed or morose as I should be, sorry to disappoint you,' I said, and after people laughed, I added: 'I assure you I am not in denial'" (p. 17). He then gave his lecture in which the classroom became a venue for *both* academic and therapeutic pursuits.

Many students concluded that they find it easier to accept death now that they have read *Dying to Teach*. This was especially true for Daphne. Reading her essay, I began to wonder why I had clutched Barbara's lifeless hand in bed during her final days, when she lay comatose while I fell asleep. Oddly, I had never asked myself this question. Before her diagnosis, we never held hands while falling asleep, though we often walked hand in hand. Was the hand-holding a romantic gesture, a recognition that we loved each other till death do us part? Was it, to use Daphne's words, a way for me to "go through with it"—her dying, that is, "so that she wouldn't be so alone." Was holding Barbara's hand a way for *me* to avoid feeling alone? All of these reasons help to explain why I held her hand. What I find striking about Daphne's essay is that it demonstrates the power of continuing bonds, the paradox of remaining attached while letting go. Daphne's essay also demonstrates the intersubjectivity of teaching. Just as *Dying to Teach* enabled her to disclose for the first time crucial details about her grandmother's death, her essay helped me to understand why I needed to hold onto Barbara for dear life.

Syllabus for English 450:
Writing about Love and Loss

In this course we will focus on how writers use language to convey love and loss and the ways in which they seek consolation and hope through religion, nature, art, deeds, or memory. We will explore different kinds of love—love of God, family or friends, romantic partner, or self; we will also explore different kinds of loss—loss of religious faith, family or friends, romantic partner, or self-respect. The only required text in the course is my new book about my wife, Barbara, who died on April 5, 2004: *Dying to Teach*, published by SUNY Press, and available in the university bookstore. I hope that my story of love and loss will help you write your own stories.

Please note that this will be an emotionally charged course, and there may be times when some of us cry in class. How can one not cry when confronting the loss of a loved one? Tears indicate that we are responding emotionally as well as intellectually to loss; tears are usually a more accurate reflection of how we feel than are words. I'll try not to make Love and Loss morbid or depressing—indeed, I believe there will be more smiles than tears in the course. The only requirement for the course is empathy: the ability to listen respectfully and nonjudgmentally to your classmates' experiences. The class will not be a "support group," but we will support each other's writing. Our aim is to write about the most important people in our lives while at the same time improving the quality of our writing. Throughout the course we will test James Pennebaker's thesis in his influential book, *Opening Up*, that writing about stressful events produces dramatic improvements in our health, including slower heart rates, stronger immune responses to infection, and a general sense of well-being.

Writing Requirements: The minimum writing requirement for the course is 40 acceptable pages, typed, double spaced. (Please use Times New Roman 12 font). By "acceptable" I mean that in order for a particular piece of writing to count toward the required 40 pages, it must be generally well written and free from serious grammatical problems. Everything must be typed, preferably on a word processor so that you can easily make revisions. Plan on submitting an essay every week. I will usually give you specific assignments on which to write, but there will still be considerable freedom in the way you handle each assignment. You will have advance notice for each assignment. If you find a writing topic too personal or painful, you can write on another topic of your choice. (Please indicate to me in an email if you are not writing on an assigned topic.)

We will run the class as a workshop. For each class, four or five students will be asked to bring in sufficient copies of their assignment for everyone. We will discuss each student's work every three-to-four weeks. You'll know in advance when it is your turn to bring in copies.

When it is your turn to make 27 copies (including copies for Nico Suarez, my teaching assistant, and me), please photocopy, collate, and staple the pages together—otherwise there will be a blizzard of papers when they are distributed. There are several photocopy machines in the library as well as in nearby stores such as Shipmates in Stuyvesant Plaza. There's also a photocopy service in the Campus Center. To save space and therefore money, single space the material you reproduce for the class. One single spaced page equals two double spaced pages. If you are turning in an essay only to me, not to the entire class, then double space it.

Please note that it is important for you to provide copies of your writings to your classmates on time. For each time you do not have copies available to the rest of us, you will be required to write an additional five pages, above the 40.

You may exercise the "anonymity option" when it is your turn to bring in copies of an essay for the class. If you feel that your essay is too personal or painful to sign with your name, you may bring in a single copy for me, with the word "anonymous" written at the top of the first page. Please indicate whether you allow me to read the anonymous essay aloud, without any discussion, or whether you do not want me to read the essay aloud anonymously. I will tell you in advance whether you can exercise the anonymity option. I hope that you will use this option sparingly, since if everyone used it all the time, we would have nothing to talk about in class.

Please keep a folder of all your work. When I return your writings to you, along with my comments, place them in a folder. At the end of the semester, I will ask you to submit your folders to me, so that I can look over your writings again to see how you have progressed as a writer. I will not record how many pages you have written; that's why it is imperative for you to keep all your writings. To complete the course on time, you will need to show me all 40 pages on April 30 so that I can return them to you on our last class, May 5.

In addition to the 40 pages, I would like you to write a weekly diary entry exploring your feelings about the course. Include in the diary your "tear-to-smile" ratio. Plan on submitting a one-page diary entry every Wednesday. I won't grade the diaries, but they are a requirement of the course, like attendance.

I will not grade the essays on content—the topics on which you will be writing do not have right or wrong answers. Nor will I be grade your essays on the degree of self-disclosure. Rather, I will grade only on the quality of your writing. Each week I will focus on a different aspect of grammar and style. Well written essays will have few grammatical errors, especially comma splices, dangling or misplaced modifiers, punctuation errors, colloquialisms, and wordiness. I will go over in class how to avoid these problems.

There will be two oral class presentations. Each student will be expected to give two brief (three-to-five minutes) class presentations. The oral presentations should focus on a memorable essay you or a classmate wrote for the class.

Attendance is important. You are allowed three unexcused absences. If you miss more than three classes without a good reason (such as a documented medical problem or a death in the family), then you will not pass the course. Please try to come to every class, especially when it is your turn to have an essay discussed. If you can't make a class, please call or email me.

Office: HU 348
Office Phone: 442-4084
Home Phone: 355-4760 (Please call before 9 p.m.)
Email address: Jberman@albany.edu
Office Hours: Monday and Wednesday, 4:15-5:15 and by appointment

WRITING ASSIGNMENTS

Assignment 1
Writing about Four Loves and Four Losses in Your Life
Due: Monday, January 28

For Assignment 1, please write an essay about four loves and four losses in your life. Begin with the loves, and rank each in order of importance, one being the most important and four being the least important. (If you have several relatives, they can collectively count as one love.) Then rank the four losses in order of importance. Devote a paragraph or two to each of the loves and losses, explaining how each has affected you. Toward the end of your essay, discuss whether there have been more loves or losses in your life. Also discuss whether it was easier writing about the loves or the losses. Have you ever had another writing assignment like this one in high school or college? Your essay should be double-spaced, about three pages long, which is the maximum page credit you can receive from this assignment.

Assignment 1 is due next Monday, January 28. Please bring three copies of your essay, one for me and the others for the next two writing assignments.

Assignment 2
Writing about One of Your Classmate's
Loves or Losses
Due: Wednesday, January 30

During the second half of Monday's class, I will pair you with a classmate, and each of you will share your Assignment 1 essays with the other. Each will then interview the other about the four loves and four losses and then write an essay focusing on *one* of the loves or losses. The interview will allow you to learn more information about your classmate's life. The two of you should agree which of the loves or losses you will write about; if there is disagreement, defer to the person about whose life you are writing. This essay will be due on Wednesday, January 30. Please bring 27 copies of this essay to class; we will spend the next two or three weeks reading the essays aloud. The Assignment 2 essay should be about one or two pages long, *single-spaced*. (Essays that you photocopy for the class should be single-spaced so you can save money; essays turned in to me alone should be double-spaced. I will count one single-spaced page as two double-spaced pages for the 40 page writing requirement.) The maximum page credit you can receive from writing assignment 2 is four pages (double-spaced).

Important: Since you will be writing about a classmate's life, it is especially important for you to be sensitive, empathic, and accurate. Please telephone your classmate after you have written a first draft of the Assignment 2 essay and read it aloud to make sure that he or she feels comfortable with your essay. This is necessary because I don't want anyone to be hurt by this or any other writing assignment in our course.

Assignment 3
Writing about How an Experience of
Love or Loss Has Changed a Classmate
Due: Monday, February 11

Assignment 3 is a continuation of Assignment 2. I will pair you with another classmate, whom you will interview in class. You will then write an essay describing how love or loss has changed your classmate's life. Be as specific as possible. If you are writing about love, try to *show* us the importance of this love, so that we feel joy, happiness, warmth, gratitude. If you are writing about loss, try to *show* us the importance of this loss, so that we feel sadness, hurt, anger, or shock. You need to make only two copies of this essay, one for your classmate and the other for me. The essay can be as long as you wish.

Assignment 4
Shattered Assumptions
Due: Wednesday, February 20

I begin *Dying to Teach* by discussing how my wife's diagnosis of terminal illness shattered our assumptive world. Write an essay about an experience of love or loss that has shattered your own assumptive world. Be as specific as possible in discussing these shattered assumptions. What new assumptions do you now have as a result of this experience of love or loss? I would like a third of you to bring in copies for everyone in the class.

Assignment 5
Writing a Wrong
Due: Monday, February 25

"The act of writing about something painful can help right a wrong that has been done to you," observes Louise DeSalvo in her book *Writing as a Way of Healing* (p. 10). Writing can also right a wrong that we have done to another person. For Assignment 5, write an essay or letter in which you try to right a wrong that has been done to you or that you have done to another person. I'll ask a third of you to bring in enough copies for everyone in the class.

Assignment 6
Holding Two Opposed Ideas without Becoming Paralyzed
Due: Monday, March 3

"The test of a first-rate intelligence," F. Scott Fitzgerald (1945) writes in his autobiographical book *The Crack-Up*, "is the ability to hold two opposed ideas in the mind at the same time and still retain the ability to function" (p. 69). Write an essay about love or loss in which you acknowledge two opposed ideas or feelings, such as the coexistence of love and hate, attraction and repulsion, desire and fear, or blame and forgiveness. Do these opposed ideas or feelings make it harder or easier for you to accept love or loss? If you haven't brought in copies of Assignments 4 or 5 for your classmates, please bring in copies of this assignment.

Assignment 7
Class Presentation
A Memorable Essay Written by You or a Classmate
Due: Monday, March 10

For your class presentation, I would like you to discuss a memorable essay written by you or a classmate in this course. Assignment 7 should be written and thus will count toward the required 40 pages, but it will also serve as your oral presentation. If you are speaking about your own essay, you need to make only one copy of it; if you are speaking about a classmate's essay, please make two copies, one for your classmate and the other for me.

If you are writing about your own essay, begin by summarizing it in one paragraph: what is the essay about, and for which assignment was it written? Was it hard or easy to write? Can you recall the tear-to-smile ratio of the essay? How did you feel when you were reading the essay aloud? How would you judge the strengths and weaknesses of the essay? How did your classmates and teacher react to it? Were you pleased or displeased with their responses? Have you spoken about the essay to any relatives or friends; if so, what were their reactions?

If you are writing about a classmate's essay, begin by summarizing it and then discuss how it affected you. Did the essay surprise you? What were its strengths and weaknesses? Have you continued to think about it? Has it influenced your own thinking and writing?

Plan on a three-to-five minute presentation. It's a good idea to rehearse the oral presentation before class so that you can time it. Try to speak in a strong voice, establish eye contact with your classmates, and avoid verbal tics. We'll hear the class presentations on March 10 and 12.

Assignment 8
Posttraumatic Growth
Due: Monday, March 17

Tedeschi, Park, and Calhoun note in *Posttraumatic Growth* that people have the ability to re-create their lives following a devastating loss and grow in new and unexpected ways. As I suggest in *Empathic Teaching*, growth includes changes in perception of self, interpersonal relationships, and meaning of life. Write an essay in which you discuss how an experience of loss has led to posttraumatic growth.

Assignment 9
Write to Life
Due: Monday, March 31

For Assignment 9, I would like you to try to bring a person back to life, verbally, as I attempted to do in my memoir about Barbara. You can do this in several different ways: the deceased can write a letter to you, or you can imagine a conversation with him or her. Alternatively, you can describe an experience when you were with him or her. Try to show rather than tell. Describe how this person looked, spoke, acted, and felt. Describe what made this person different from everyone else you have known. Describe how you attempt to keep this person alive. This will be perhaps the most challenging assignment of the semester.

Assignment 10
Reading *Dying to Teach*
Due: Monday, April 7

For Assignment 10, I would like you to discuss what you have learned from reading *Dying to Teach*. How would the course have been different if you had not read the book? Were you surprised by anything I wrote? Have you discussed the book with relatives or friends and, if so, how did they respond? What were your favorite sections of the book? The most boring sections? Were there sections that were too painful or difficult to read? Does the way I present myself in the book—the "narrator" as a "character"—seem similar to or different from the way I appear in class? Speculate on what you will remember about the book—if anything—10 or 20 years from now.

Assignment 11
What if Love Doesn't Work Out?
Due: Monday, April 14

Most of us want to fall in love—and remain in love—but the reality is that love often fails. Fifty percent of first marriages and 60 percent of second marriages end in divorce. Many of you have written wrenching essays about the breakups of your parents' marriages. Even if you remain in love you may lose your spouse or partner to death, as I have.

Write an essay in which you imagine how you might react to the situation of falling out of love with another person—or having a loved one die. If you wish to research this question, you might ask your relatives or friends how they feel about not having a spouse or partner.

Assignment 12
Write as if You Were Dying
Due: Wednesday, April 23

"Write as if you were dying," Annie Dillard exclaims in her book *The Writing Life*. "At the same time, assume you write for an audience consisting solely of terminal patients. That is, after all, the case. What would you begin writing if you knew you would die soon? What could you say to a dying person that would not enrage by its triviality?" (p. 68).

This is a startling command, one that probably none of us has imagined. See if you can accept Annie Dillard's challenge. What would you write if you knew you were dying soon? Or what would you write to a dying person?

Assignment 13
Learning from a Classmate
Due: Monday, April 28

Please describe how hearing a classmate's essay or diary on love or loss has changed your understanding of one of your *own* experiences of love or loss. Remember that although we can't change the past, we can change our understanding of the past—and in doing so, we can change our present and future. This essay will count toward the 40 pages, but it will also be the basis for your second class presentation during the final week of classes.

English 450
Death Education In The Writing Classroom
Permission To Use My Writings For Research
June 2008

I hereby give Jeffrey Berman permission to use one or more of my essays or diaries from English 450: Writing about Love and Loss, which I completed in the spring of 2008, and for which I have received a final grade. Professor Berman intends to write a book called *Death Education in the Writing Classroom* that will be based on that course. The book will explore how students wrote about deceased relatives and friends, and the impact of their writings on their classmates as revealed in the diaries. I have freely given him permission to use my writings. I understand that I can call Jeffrey Berman at (518) 355-4760 or email him at jberman@albany.edu for further information about the study.

I understand that if I have any questions concerning my rights as a research participant that have not been answered by the investigator, or if I wish to report any concerns about the study, I may contact the University at Albany Office of Research Compliance at (518) 437-4569 or at orc@uamail.albany.edu. I further understand that my name will not appear in my writings. I have disguised my writings to my own satisfaction and do not wish further disguises to be made. The University at Albany Institutional Review Board has approved this research project. If I find myself becoming anxious as a result of this study, I understand that I can contact the University Health Center at (518) 442-5454; the Psychological Services Center at (518) 442-4900; or the 24 hour Crisis Hotline, Capital District Psychiatric Center at (518) 447-9650. If I am not in Albany, I may call the toll free number: (800) 365-9139.

One copy of this document will be kept together with the research records of this study. Also, I will be given a copy to keep.

The potential benefit of this study is that it will help teachers to encourage their own students to write about death education. Readers will learn the many academic and psychological benefits of death education. All of the students who took "Writing about Love and Loss" concluded that it was helpful to them in increasing their understanding of love and loss. They also found that writing is an effective form of mourning loss. Many of the writing assignments were emotionally charged, but no one reported becoming at risk as a result of the course.

Before submitting his book for publication, Jeffrey Berman will send me a copy of the chapters containing my writings. If, after reading the chapters, I feel uncomfortable with the way in which he has used my writings, I reserve the right to withdraw permission. If I do withdraw permission, I will notify him in writing within three months of receiving the draft copy.

I understand that my participation in this research is completely voluntary, that I may discontinue participation at any time without penalty or loss of benefits to which I may otherwise have been entitled.

After Jeffrey Berman's book is published, my writings will be destroyed. No reports about any writings will contain my name.

All information obtained in this study is strictly confidential unless disclosure is required by law. In addition, the Institutional Review Board and the University at Albany officials responsible for monitoring this study may inspect Jeffrey Berman's research data.

I have read, or been informed of, the information about this study. I hereby consent to participate in the study.

Name _____   Date _____

Signature_____

Local Address _____

Local Phone _____

Cell Phone _____

Email Address _____

Permanent Address _____

Permanent Phone _____

Do I want my real name cited in the Acknowledgments Page of the book?
Yes _____   No _____

Three different pseudonyms (false names) by which you can call me in the book:

_____, _____, _____

References

Association for Death Education and Counseling (ADEC). (2004). *Code of Ethics.* Retrieved September 25, 2007 from http://www.Adec.org/about/ethics.cfm.

Attig, T. (1996). *How we grieve: Relearning the world.* New York: Oxford University Press.

Auster, P. (1982). *The invention of solitude.* New York: Sun.

Balk, D. E. (Editor-in-Chief). (2007). *Handbook of Thanatology.* New York: Routledge.

Belenky, M. F., Clinchy, B. M., Goldberger, N. R., & Tarule, J. M. (1986). *Women's ways of knowing.* New York: Basic Books.

Benard, B. & Slade, S. (2009). Listening to students: Moving from research to youth development practice and social connectedness. In R. Gilman, E. S. Huebner, & M. J. Furlong (Eds.), *Handbook of positive psychology in schools* (pp. 353-370). New York: Routledge.

Berman, J. (1994). *Diaries to an English professor: Pain and growth in the classroom.* Amherst: University of Massachusetts Press.

Berman, J. (1999). *Surviving literary suicide.* Amherst: University of Massachusetts Press.

Berman, J. (2001). *Risky writing: Self-disclosure and self-transformation in the classroom.* Amherst: University of Massachusetts Press.

Berman, J. (2004). *Empathic teaching: Education for life.* Amherst: University of Massachusetts Press.

Berman, J. (2007). *Dying to teach: A memoir of love, loss, and learning.* Albany: State University of New York Press.

Berman, J. (2009). *Death in the classroom: Writing about love and loss.* Albany: State University of New York Press.

Berman, J. (2010). *Companionship in grief: Love and loss in the memoirs of C.S. Lewis, John Bayley, Donald Hall, Joan Didion, and Calvin Trillin.* Amherst: University of Massachusetts Press.

Berman, J. & Wallace, P. H. (2007). *Cutting and the pedagogy of self-disclosure.* Amherst: University of Massachusetts Press.

Bettelheim, B. (1977). *The uses of enchantment.* New York: Vintage.

Bishop, W. (1997). *Teaching lives.* Logan: Utah State University Press.

Boss, P. (1999). *Ambiguous loss: Learning to live with unresolved grief.* Cambridge: Harvard University Press.

Brabant, S. & Kalich, D. (2008). Who enrolls in college death education courses? A longitudinal study. *Omega, 58* (1), 1–18.

Bracher, M. (1999). *The writing cure: Psychoanalysis, composition, and the aims of education.* Carbondale: Southern Illinois University Press.

Calhoun, L. & Tedeschi, R. G. (2001). Posttraumatic growth: lessons of loss. In R. A. Neimeyer (Ed.), *Meaning reconstruction & the experience of loss* (pp. 157–172). Washington, DC: American Psychological Association.

Camus, A. (1955). *The myth of Sisyphus and other essays* (J. O'Brien, Trans.). New York: Vintage.

Conway, K. (2007). *Illness and the limits of expression.* Ann Arbor: University of Michigan Press.

Cousins, N. (1979). *Anatomy of an illness as perceived by the patient.* New York: Norton.

Critchley, S. (2009). *The book of dead philosophers.* New York: Vintage.

Csikszentmihalyi, M. (1990). *Flow: The psychology of optimal experience.* New York: HarperCollins.

Damasio, A. (1994). *Descartes' error: Emotion, reason, and the human brain* (Rev. Ed., 2005). New York: Penguin.

Delbanco, N. (2005). *Anywhere out of the world: Essays on travel, writing, death.* New York: Columbia University Press.

Derlega, V., Metts, M., Petronio, S., & Margulis, S. (1993). *Self-disclosure.* Newbury Park, CA: Sage.

DeSalvo, L. (1999). *Writing as a way of healing: How telling our stories transforms our lives.* San Francisco: HarperSanFrancisco.

Dick, P. (1974). *Flow my tears, the policeman said.* New York: Daw Books.

Dillard, A. (1980). *The writing life.* New York: Harper & Row.

Doka, K. J. (1989). *Disenfranchised grief: recognizing hidden sorrow.* New York: Lexington Books.

Doka, K. J. (2002). *Disenfranchised grief: New directions, challenges, and strategies for practice.* Champaign, IL: Research Press.

Dunne, J. G. (1989). *Harp.* New York: Simon and Schuster.

Durkheim, E. (1952). *Suicide: A study in sociology* (J. A. Spaulding & G. Simpson, Trans., G. Simpson, Ed.). New York: Free Press. (Original work published in 1897)

Durlak, J. A. (1994). Changing death attitudes through education. In R. A. Neimeyer (Ed.), *Death anxiety handbook: Research, instrumentation, and application* (pp. 243–262). Washington, DC: Taylor and Francis.

Eliot, T. S. (1952). *The complete poems and plays: 1909-1950.* New York: Harcourt, Brace and World.

Farber, B. A. (2006). *Self-disclosure in psychotherapy.* New York: Guilford.

Feifel, H. (Ed.). (1959). *The meaning of death.* New York: Blakiston.

Fitzgerald, F. S. (1945). *The crack-up.* New York: New Directions.

Forster, E.M. (1910/1985). *Howards end.* New York: Buccaneer Books.

Foucault, M. (1995). *Discipline and punish: The birth of the prison* (A. Sheridan, Trans.). New York: Vintage.

Frantz, T. T., Farrell, M. M., & Trolley, B. C. (2001). Positive outcomes of losing a loved one. In R. A. Neimeyer (Ed.), *Meaning reconstruction & the experience of loss* (pp. 191–212). Washington, DC: American Psychological Association.

Freud, S. (1917/1957). Mourning and melancholia. In J. Strachey (Ed. & Trans.), *The standard edition of the complete psychological works of Sigmund Freud* (Vol. 14, pp. 237–258). London: The Hogarth Press. (Original work published in 1917)

Freud, S. (1914/1957). On narcissism. In J. Strachey (Ed. & Trans.), *The standard edition of the complete psychological works of Sigmund Freud* (Vol. 14, pp. 67–102). London: The Hogarth Press. (Original work published in 1914)

Gilligan, C. (1982). *In a different voice: Psychological theory and women's development.* Cambridge: Harvard University Press.

Goldman, L. (2002). The assumptive world of children. In J. Kauffman (Ed.), *Loss of the assumptive world: A theory of traumatic loss* (pp. 193–204). New York: Brunner-Routledge.

Goldstein, G. & Benassi, V. A. (1994). The relation between teacher self-disclosure and student classroom participation. *Teaching of Psychology, 21,* 212–216.

Goleman, D. (1995). *Emotional intelligence.* New York: Bantam Books.

Gorer, G. (1965). *Death, grief, and mourning in contemporary Britain.* New York: Doubleday.

Hall, D. (1978). *Goatfoot milktongue twinbird: Interviews, essays, and notes on poetry, 1970–76.* Ann Arbor: University of Michigan Press.

Hall, D. (2005). *The best day the worst day.* Boston: Houghton Mifflin.

Hall, D. (2008). *Unpacking the boxes.* Boston: Houghton Mifflin.

Haney, M. R. (2004). Ethical dilemmas associated with self-disclosure in student writing. *Teaching of Psychology, 31,* 167–171.

Hatfield, E., Cacioppo, J., & Rapson, R. (1994). *Emotional contagion.* Cambridge: Cambridge University Press.

Heilman, S. (Ed.). (2005). *Death, bereavement, and mourning.* New Brunswick, NJ: Transaction.

Helping the grieving student: A guide for teachers. Portland, OR: The Dougy Center.

Herzog, J. (2001). *Father hunger: Explorations with adults and children.* Hillsdale, NJ: Analytic Press.

Hood, C. L. (2003). Lying in writing or the vicissitudes of testimony. *Composition Forum, 14,* 133–150.

Hurlbert, C. M. & Blitz, M. (2003). Equaling sorrow: A meditation on composition, death, and life. *Composition Studies*, 31, 83–97.

Jamison, K. R. (1999). *Night falls fast: Understanding suicide.* New York: Alfred A. Knopf.

Janoff-Bulman, R. (1992). *Shattered assumptions: Towards a new psychology of trauma.* New York: Free Press.

Jayson, S. (2008, August 18). More than 50% of college students felt suicidal. *USA Today.*

Jourard, S. M. (1964). *The transparent self: Self-disclosure and well-being.* Princeton, NJ: Van Nostrand.

Jourard, S. M. (1971). *Self-disclosure: An experimental analysis of the transparent self.* New York: Wiley-Interscience.

Joyce, J. (1961). *Ulysses.* New York: Modern Library. (Original work published in 1934)

Kafka, F. (1977). *Letters to friends, family, and editors.* R. Winston & C. Winston, (Trans.). New York: Schocken.

Kantrowitz, J. L. (1996). *The patient's impact on the analyst.* Hillsdale, NJ: The Analytic Press.

Kastenbaum, R. (1992). *The psychology of death* (2nd ed.). New York: Springer.

Kesey, K. (1962/1973). *One flew over the cuckoo's nest.* New York: Viking Critical Edition. (Original work published in 1962)

Klass, D. & Heath, A. O. (1996-97). Grief and abortion: *Mizuko kuyo*, the Japanese ritual resolution. *Omega, 34*, 1–14.

Klass, D., Silverman, P. R., & Nickman, S. L. (Eds.). (1996). *Continuing bonds: New understandings of grief.* Washington, DC: Taylor and Francis.

Kotre, J. (1995). *White gloves: How we create ourselves through memory.* New York: Free Press.

LaCapra, D. (2001). *Writing history, writing trauma.* Baltimore: Johns Hopkins University Press.

Larson, T. (2007). *The memoir and the memoirist: Reading and writing personal narrative.* Athens, OH: Swallow Press/Ohio University Press.

Laub, D. (1992). An event without a witness: Truth, testimony, and survival. In S. Felman & D. Laub, *Testimony: Crises of witnessing in literature, psychoanalysis, and history.* New York: Routledge.

Lawrence, D. H. (1981). *The letters of D. H. Lawrence* (Vol. 2). G. J. Zytaruk & J. T. Boulton (Eds.). Cambridge: Cambridge University Press.

Leaman, O. (1995). *Death and loss: Compassionate approaches in the classroom.* London: Cassell.

Lifton, R. J. (1979). *The broken connection: On death and the continuity of life.* New York: Simon and Schuster.

MacCurdy, M. M. (2007). *The mind's eye: Image and memory in writing about trauma.* Amherst: University of Massachusetts Press.

Macrorie, K. (1974). *A vulnerable teacher.* Rochelle Park, NJ: Hayden.

Maltsberger, J. & Buie, D. (1996). Countertransference hate in the treatment of suicidal patients. In J. Maltsberger & M. Goldblatt (Eds.), *Essential papers on suicide* (pp. 270–289). New York: New York University Press.

Martin, T. & Doka, K. J. (2000). *Men don't cry . . . women do: Transcending gender stereotypes of grief.* Philadelphia: Brunner/Mazel.

McCabe, M. (2003). *The paradox of loss: Toward a relational theory of grief.* Westport, CT: Praeger.

McCarthy, P. & Schmeck, R. R. (1982). Effects of teacher self-disclosure on student learning and perceptions of teacher. *College Student Journal, 16*, 45–49.

Mental health: A college issue (June 2009). *NEA Higher Education ADVOCATE.*

Miller, J. H. & Rotatori, A. F. (1986). *Death education and the educator.* Springfield, IL: Charles C. Thomas.

Moffat, M. J. (Ed.). (1992). *In the midst of winter: Selections from the literature of mourning.* New York: Vintage.

Moller, D. W. (1996). *Confronting death: Values, institutions, and human mortality.* New York: Oxford University Press.

Montaigne, M. (1946). To philosophize is to learn how to die. In E. J. Trechmann (Trans.), *The essays of Montaigne* (Vol. 1). New York: Oxford University Press.

Morris. V. (2001). *Talking about death won't kill you.* New York: Workman Publishing.

Morrison, T. (1987). *Beloved.* New York: Knopf.

Murphy, J. (1988). Forgiveness and resentment. In J. Murphy & J. Hampton (Eds.), *Forgiveness and mercy* (pp. 14–34). Cambridge: Cambridge University Press.

Murray, D. M. (2001). *My twice-lived life.* New York: Ballantine.

Nadeau, J. W. (1998). *Families making sense of death.* Thousand Oaks, CA: Sage.

Needle, R. B. & Walker, L. E. A. (2008). *Abortion counseling: A clinician's guide to psychology, legislation, politics, and competency.* New York: Springer.

Neimeyer, R. A. (Ed.). (2001). *Meaning reconstruction & the experience of loss.* Washington, DC: American Psychological Association.

Neimeyer, R. A. (2001). Reauthoring life narratives: Grief therapy as meaning reconstruction. *Israel Journal of Psychiatry and Related Sciences, 38,* 171–183.

Neimeyer, R. A., Laurie, A., Mehta, T., Hardison, H., & Currier, J. A. (2008). Lessons of loss: Meaning-making in bereaved college students. *New Directions for Student Services, 121,* 27–39.

Nietzsche, F. (1954). *The philosophy of Nietzsche,* W. Kaufmann (Trans.). New York: Modern Library.

Noddings, N. (1984). *Caring: A feminine approach to ethics & moral education.* Berkeley: University of California Press.

Noppe, I. C. (2007). Historical and contemporary perspectives on death education. In D. E. Balk (Ed.), *Handbook of thanatology* (pp. 329–335). New York: Routledge.

Nussbaum, M. (2001). *Upheavals of thought: The intelligence of emotions.* Cambridge: Cambridge University Press.

Paletti, R. (2008). Review of *Dying to teach. Death Studies, 32,* 891–895.

Parkes, C. M. (1975). "What becomes of redundant world models?" A contribution to the study of adaptation to change. *British Journal of Medical Psychology, 48,* 131–137.

Pausch, R. (2008). *The last lecture* (with Zaslow, J.). New York: Hyperion.

Pennebaker, J. (1997). *Opening up: The healing power of expressing emotions.* New York: Guilford Press. (Original work published in 1990)

Pennebaker, J. (Ed.). (1995). *Emotion, disclosure, & health.* Washington, DC: American Psychological Association.

Powers, R. (2006). *The echo maker.* New York: Farrar, Straus and Giroux.

Quindlen, A. (1994). *One true thing.* New York: Dell.

Rappaport, N. (2009). *In her wake: A child psychiatrist explores the mystery of her mother's suicide.* New York: Basic Books.

Robak, R. W. & Weitzman, S. P. (1995). Grieving the loss of romantic relationships in young adults: An empirical study of disenfranchised grief. *Omega, 30,* 269–281.

Roth, P. (1991). *Patrimony.* New York: Simon and Schuster.

Seligman, M. E. P. (2002). *Authentic happiness: Using the new positive psychology to realize your potential for lasting fulfillment.* New York: Free Press.

Silin, J. (1995). *Sex, death, and the education of children.* New York: Teachers College Press.

Silverman, P. R. & Nickman, S. L. (1996). Concluding thoughts. In D. Klass, P. R. Silverman, & S. L. Nickman (Eds.), *Continuing bonds: New understandings of grief* (pp. 349–355). Washington, DC: Taylor & Francis.

Smeyers, P., Smith, R., & Standish, P. (2007). *The therapy of education: Philosophy, happiness and personal growth.* New York: Palgrave Macmillan.

Solomon, R. C. (2002). *Spirituality for the skeptic: The thoughtful love of life.* New York: Oxford University Press.

Solomon, R. C. (2007). *True to our feelings: What our emotions are really telling us.* New York: Oxford University Press.

Solomon, R. C. & Flores, F. (2001). *Building trust in business, politics, relationships, and life.* Oxford: Oxford University Press.

Sontag, S. (1978). *On photography.* New York: Farrar, Straus and Giroux.

Spiro, H. (1996). Facing death. In H. Spiro, M. M. Curnen, & L. P. Wandel (Eds.), *Facing death: Where culture, religion, and medicine meet* (pp. xv–xx). New Haven: Yale University Press.

Stearns, A. K. (1985). *Living through personal crisis*. New York: Ballantine.

Styron, W. (1990). *Darkness visible: A memoir of madness*. New York: Random House.

Sue, D. & Sue, D. (1999). *Counseling the culturally different: Theory and practice* (3rd ed.). New York: Wiley.

Swartzlander, S., Pace, D., & Stamler, V. (1993, February 17). The ethics of requiring students to write about their personal lives. *Chronicle of Higher Education*, 39.

Tannen, D. (1998). *The argument culture: Moving from debate to dialogue*. New York: Random House.

Tedeschi, R., Park, C., & Calhoun, L. (Eds.). (1998). *Posttraumatic growth: Positive changes in the aftermath of crisis*. Mahwah, NJ: Lawrence Erlbaum.

Tyson-Rawson, K. (1996). Relationship and heritage: Manifestations of ongoing attachment following father death. In D. Klass, P. R. Silverman, & S. L. Nickman (Eds.), *Continuing bonds: New understandings of grief* (pp. 125–145). Washington, DC: Taylor & Francis.

Vance, E. (2007, May 11). A professor's own grief informs a course on mourning in literature. *The Chronicle of Higher Education*, p. A22.

Volkan, V. (1981). *Linking objects and linking phenomena*. New York: International Universities Press.

Wald, P. (2008). *Contagious: Cultures, carriers, and the outbreak narrative*. Durham: Duke University Press.

Walker, A. (1996). Saving the life that is your own: The importance of models in the artist's life. In M. Eagleton (Ed.), *Feminist literary theory: A reader* (2nd ed., pp. 30–33). London: Blackwell.

Weiss, R. S. (1993). Loss and Recovery. In M. S. Stroebe, W. Stroebe, & R. O. Hansson (Eds.), *Handbook of bereavement: Theory, research, and intervention* (pp. 271–284). Cambridge: Cambridge University Press.

White, M. & Epston, D. (1990). *Narrative means to therapeutic ends*. New York: Norton.

Whitehead, A. N. (1954). *Dialogues of Alfred North Whitehead* (as recorded by L. Price). Boston: Little, Brown.

Whitlock, J., Eckenrode, J., & Silverman, D. (2006). Self-injurious behaviors in a college population. *Pediatrics, 117,* 1939–1948.

Woolf, V. (1976). *Moments of being: Unpublished autobiographical writings*, J. Schulkind (Ed.). New York and London: Harcourt Brace Jovanovich.

Worden, J. W. (2002). *Grief counseling and grief therapy: A handbook for the mental health practitioner* (3rd ed.). New York: Springer.

Worden, J. W. & Proctor, W. (1976). *PDA—Personal death awareness*. Englewood Cliffs, NJ: Prentice-Hall.

Wurmser, L. (1987). Shame: The veiled companion of narcissism. In D. Nathanson (Ed.), *The many faces of shame* (pp. 64–92). New York: Guilford Press.

Yalom, I. D. (2008). *Staring at the sun: Overcoming the terror of death*. San Francisco: Jossey-Bass.

Zinner, E. S. (2002). Incorporating disenfranchised grief in the death education classroom. In K. J. Doka (Ed.), *Disenfranchised grief: New directions, challenges, and strategies for practice* (pp. 389–404). Champaign, IL: Research Press.

Student Writers

Addison	Jacob
Ayla	Javarro
Beth	Kamilluh
Bianca	Kasia
Cassie	Lia
Cath	Lucy
Cecilia	Maggie
Chipo	Nicholette
Daphne	Saverio
Faith	Scotty
Gloria	Scout
Isabella	Shannon

Index

STUDENTS

Addison, 26, 43, 45-48, 55, 95-98, 99, 118-120
Ayla, 26, 30, 36, 44, 70, 183-203, 206, 209
Beth, 57, 70, 99, 103, 111
Bianca, 25, 41, 99, 208, 210
Cassie, 123, 206, 210
Cath, 20, 26, 43, 60, 81, 109, 118, 181, 211-213
Cecilia, 20, 55, 117, 191
Chipo, 12-13, 20, 31, 45-46, 70, 88, 98, 111, 115-133, 147, 201, 207, 209-210
Daphne, 25, 42, 43, 69-70, 147, 215-219
Faith, 13, 77, 100, 111, 163-182
Gloria, 31, 43, 55, 70, 109, 117, 206, 209
Isabella, 33-39, 41, 81-84, 111-112, 209
Jacob, 58, 61-64, 103, 111

Javarro, 20, 57, 105-107, 111
Kamilluh, 19-20, 58-61, 85-87, 104, 158, 179
Kasia, 50-56, 60, 81-84, 123, 206, 209, 210
Lia, 13, 71, 101, 111, 118, 135-149, 153-155, 157, 166, 169-170, 207
Lucy, 20, 30, 41-43, 50-52, 55, 57, 63, 103, 207, 208, 210
Maggie, 25, 29-30, 42, 111, 209
Nicholette, 26, 34-39, 41, 43, 57, 111, 208, 210-211
Saverio, 26, 87-88, 103-104, 109, 210
Scotty, 20, 71, 147
Scout, 20, 31, 44, 88-89, 93-95, 123-124
Shannon, 13, 20, 26, 71, 117-118, 151-162, 166, 213-215

DATE DUE

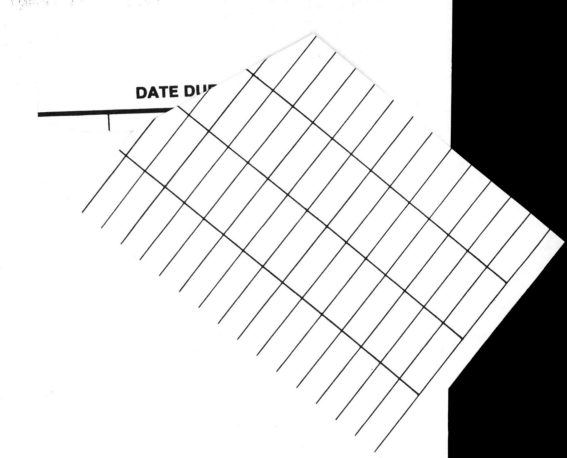